Adobe® Photoshop® 5.5

Classroom in a Book®

Adobe

www.adobe.com/adobepress

Contents

Creating Animated Images for the Web

Lesson 15

ImageReady Web Techniques

Lesson 16

Getting Started

Adobe® Photoshop® 5.5 delivers powerful, industry-standard image-editing tools for professional designers who want to produce sophisticated graphics for the Web and for print. Included with Photoshop 5.5 is ImageReady™ 2.0, and its powerful set of Web tools for optimizing and previewing images, batch processing images with droplets in the Actions palette, and creating GIF animations. Photoshop and ImageReady combined offer a comprehensive environment for designing graphics for the Web.

About Classroom in a Book

Adobe Photoshop 5.5 Classroom in a Book® is part of the official training series for Adobe graphics and publishing software developed by experts at Adobe Systems. The lessons are designed to let you learn at your own pace. If you're new to Adobe Photoshop or ImageReady, you'll learn the fundamental concepts and features you'll need to master the programs. If you've been using Adobe Photoshop or ImageReady for a while, you'll find Classroom in a Book teaches many advanced features, including tips and techniques for using the latest version of these applications and for preparing images for the Web.

The lessons in this special Web edition include new information on designing Web graphics. Both Photoshop and ImageReady let you compress images, editing interactively to select the best balance of file size and image quality. ImageReady also provides a fast and simple way to create animated GIF images. You can create and edit images directly in ImageReady, or work with images created in Adobe Photoshop, moving seamlessly between the two applications.

Although each lesson provides step-by-step instructions for creating a specific project, there's room for exploration and experimentation. You can follow the book from start to finish or do only the lessons that correspond to your interests and needs. Many of the lessons include special "For the Web" tips, techniques, and explanations. Each lesson concludes with a review section summarizing what you've covered.

Prerequisites

Before beginning to use *Adobe Photoshop 5.5 Classroom in a Book,* you should have a working knowledge of your computer and its operating system. Make sure you know how to use the mouse and standard menus and commands and also how to open, save, and close files. If you need to review these techniques, see the printed or online documentation included with your system.

Installing Adobe Photoshop and Adobe ImageReady

Before you begin using *Adobe Photoshop 5.5 Classroom in a Book*, make sure that your system is set up correctly and that you've installed the required software and hardware. You must purchase the Adobe Photoshop 5.5 software separately. For system requirements and complete instructions on installing the software, see the *InstallReadMe* file on the application CD.

Photoshop and ImageReady use the same installer. You must install the applications from the Adobe Photoshop 5.5 Application CD onto your hard disk; you cannot run the program from the CD. Follow the on-screen instructions.

Make sure your serial number is accessible before installing the application; you can find the serial number on the registration card or CD sleeve.

Starting Adobe Photoshop and Adobe ImageReady

You start Photoshop and ImageReady just as you would any software application.

To start Adobe Photoshop or ImageReady in Windows®:

1 Choose Start > Programs > Adobe > Photoshop 5.5 > Adobe Photoshop 5.5 or ImageReady 2.0.

In Photoshop, if you have deleted the preferences file, the Adobe Color Management Assistant appears.

2 Click Cancel to close the assistant without adjusting the monitor.

For instructions on how to calibrate a monitor, see Lesson 12, "Setting Up Your Monitor for Color Management," in this book.

To start Adobe Photoshop or Adobe ImageReady in Mac OS:

1 Open the Adobe Photoshop folder, and double-click the Adobe Photoshop or Adobe ImageReady program icon. (If you installed the program in a folder other than Adobe Photoshop, open that folder.)

In Photoshop, if you have deleted the preferences, the Adobe Color Management Assistant appears.

2 Click Cancel to close the assistant without adjusting the monitor. For instructions on how to calibrate a monitor, see Lesson 12, "Setting Up Your Monitor for Color Management," in this book.

The Adobe Photoshop or Adobe ImageReady application window appears. You can now open a document or create a new one and start working.

Copying the Classroom in a Book files

The Classroom in a Book CD includes all the files needed to complete the lessons in this book. These files are stored in individual lesson folders (named Lesson01, Lesson02, etc.), which are, in turn, stored in a single folder called Lessons. In order to use these files, you must copy the Lessons folder to your hard drive prior to beginning the lessons. To save room, you can copy individual lesson folders to your hard drive as you need them.

To install the Classroom in a Book files:

1 Insert the Classroom in a Book CD into your computer's CD-ROM drive.

2 Open the CD-ROM drive icon.

• Double-click My Computer, then double-click the PS55_CIB icon (Windows).

• Double-click the PS55_CIB icon on the desktop (Mac OS).

3 Drag the Lessons folder from the PS55_CIB window to the desktop.

To copy individual lesson folders, open the Lessons folder and drag the desired lesson folder from the Lessons window to the desktop.

4 Close the PS55_CIB window and remove the Classroom in a Book CD.

Note: As you work through each lesson, you will overwrite the Start files. To restore the original files, recopy the corresponding Lesson folder from the Classroom in a Book CD to the Lessons folder on your hard drive.

Restoring default preferences

The preferences files store palette and command settings and color calibration information. Each time you quit Photoshop or ImageReady, the position of the palettes and certain command settings are recorded in the respective preferences file. When you use the Photoshop color management assistant, monitor calibration and color space information is stored in the Photoshop preferences files as well.

To ensure that the tools and palettes function as described in this book, restore the default preferences for Adobe Photoshop or Adobe ImageReady before you begin each lesson. These preferences can be restored by deleting the preferences file or simply moving it from its default location.

Important: If you have adjusted your color display and color space settings, be sure to move the preferences file, rather than deleting it, so that you can restore your settings when you are done with the lessons in this book.

To restore default Photoshop preferences:

1 Exit Adobe Photoshop.

2 Locate and open the Adobe Photoshop Settings folder (which is in the Photoshop application folder).

3 Remove the Adobe Photoshop 5.5 Prefs file from the Adobe Photoshop Settings folder.

• To delete the Prefs file, drag it to the Recycle Bin (Windows) or the Trash (Mac OS).

• To temporarily remove the Prefs file (so that you can later restore your current settings), drag it to the desktop.

Note: The first time you remove your preferences file, be sure to drag it onto the desktop (or some other location), instead of deleting it. This will enable you to restore your settings when you are done with these lessons. For subsequent chapters, you can simply delete the preferences file. When you are ready to restore your settings, exit Photoshop and drag the preferences file from the desktop back into the Adobe Photoshop Settings folder (which is in the Photoshop application folder). In the warning dialog box that appears, confirm that you want to replace the existing version of the file.

To restore default ImageReady preferences:

Do one of the following:

• In Windows, hold down Ctrl+Alt+Shift *immediately* after launching the application. (If you get to the application splash screen, you were not quick enough.) Click Yes in the warning dialog box that appears.

• In Mac OS, delete the Adobe ImageReady 2.0 Prefs file from the System Folder/Preferences folder, or (if you want to be able to restore your settings later) move the file to the desktop.

Note: *Because of the way that ImageReady default preferences are restored for Windows, there is no way to restore your own settings later.*

Using the reference guides

Three printed documents are included with Photoshop 5.5.

Adobe Photoshop 5.5 User Guide Supplement Contains an overview of the functionality that Photoshop and ImageReady share, and gives detailed information on the features new to Photoshop 5.5 and the advanced Web features available in ImageReady 2.0.

This cross-platform user guide provides instructions for using Photoshop and ImageReady on both the Windows and Mac OS platforms. The text notes any differences in procedures and commands between platforms.

Complete documentation of all ImageReady features and all Photoshop features is also available in the online Help systems of the respective applications.

This user guide assumes you have a working knowledge of your computer and its operating conventions, including how to use a mouse and standard menus and commands. It also assumes you know how to open, save, and close files. For help with any of these techniques, please see your Windows or Mac OS documentation.

Adobe Photoshop 5.5 with Adobe ImageReady 2.0 Quick Reference Card Contains basic information about the Adobe Photoshop and ImageReady tools and palettes, and shortcuts for using them.

Adobe Photoshop 5.0 User Guide Contains complete information about using Photoshop 5.0. This user guide covers all features that are not new to Photoshop 5.5. This same information is also available in Photoshop 5.5 online Help.

Using the tours, tutorials, and movies

Several tutorials and movies introducing you to Photoshop and ImageReady are included with Photoshop 5.5.

Chapter 1 of the *Adobe Photoshop 5.5 User Guide Supplement* is an instructional Quick Tour that provides an overview of features new to Photoshop 5.5—this tour focuses primarily on the Photoshop and ImageReady Web features. The graphics and document files used in the tour are included on the CD so you can follow along.

Four Photoshop 5.0 tutorials in PDF format are included. These are excerpted from the *Adobe Photoshop 5.0 Classroom in a Book*, which is sold separately. These step-by-step instructions help you learn how to create typical documents. All files used in the tutorials are included on the CD. (These tutorials cover features that have not changed between Photoshop 5.0 and Photoshop 5.5.)

Three Photoshop 5.0 movies are also included. The Photoshop 5.0 Quick Tour movie gives a basic overview of Adobe Photoshop features. The New Features movie introduces and demonstrates new features in Adobe Photoshop 5.0, including reeditable type, layer effects, the History palette, and new transformation commands. The Layers movie teaches you how to use layers.

Other learning resources

Other learning resources are available but are not included with your application.

Official Adobe Print Publishing Guide Provides in-depth information on successful print production, including topics such as color management, commercial printing, constructing a publication, imaging and proofing, and project management guidelines. For information on purchasing the *Official Adobe Print Publishing Guide*, visit the Adobe Web site at www.adobe.com.

Official Adobe Electronic Publishing Guide Tackles the fundamental issues essential to ensuring quality online publications in HTML and PDF. Using simple, expertly illustrated explanations, design and publishing professionals tell you how to design electronic publications for maximum speed, legibility, and effectiveness. For information on purchasing the *Official Adobe Electronic Publishing Guide*, visit the Adobe Web site at www.adobe.com.

The Adobe Training and Certification program Are designed to help Adobe customers improve and promote their product proficiency skills. The Adobe Certified Expert (ACE) program is designed to recognize the high-level skills of expert users. Adobe Certified Training Providers (ACTP) use only Adobe Certified Experts to teach Adobe software classes. Available in either ACTP classrooms or on site, the ACE program is the best way to master Adobe products. For Adobe Certified Training Programs information, visit the Partnering wit Adobe Web site at partners.adobe.com.

The Adobe Web site Can be viewed by choosing File > Adobe Online if you have a connection to the World Wide Web.

Web Tour

A Web Tour of Adobe Photoshop 5.5

This interactive tour of Adobe ImageReady, excerpted from the Adobe Photoshop 5.5 User Guide Supplement gives an overview of key features of the program. More detailed instructions on how to use the features in this tour are given in individual lessons throughout this book.

This Tour provides an overview of the key features of Adobe ImageReady and also describes some of the integrated Web preparation features of the Adobe Photoshop application. The Tour points out ways to use the two applications to maximize the quality of images, reduce file size, and prepare color for online display in a Web site. You'll also learn ways to create special effects in Adobe ImageReady, such as initiating effects when a pointer is rolled over or clicked on part of an image, and creating interactive animations.

Depending on your needs, you can use either Adobe Photoshop or Adobe ImageReady to prepare images for the Web. For example, if you are working on a single image and want to quickly optimize it for use on the Web, you can use the Save for Web command in Adobe Photoshop. To perform more complex Web preparation functions, such as optimizing multiple images in a single Web page, or creating special rollover and animation effects, you can use the advanced features in Adobe ImageReady.

Getting started

To show you many of the features of ImageReady, including how to create and optimize an online display, you will create a Web page that showcases the products of a fictitious artist called Vincent Michael.

First you will prepare elements of the Web page image using Photoshop 5.5. Then you will perform more complex Web preparation functions and special effects using ImageReady.

You will start by opening two files—a logo and a photograph of a sculpture—in Adobe Photoshop.

1 Start Adobe Photoshop.

2 Choose File > Open, locate the file 001.psd in the Tour1>T1_Start, and click Open.

3 Choose File > Open, locate the file 002.psd in the Tour1>T1_Start_start folder, and click Open.

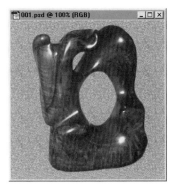 

The first step in this Tour highlights one of the most powerful features of both Photoshop and ImageReady—the ability to compress images by *optimizing*.

About optimizing images

When you prepare images for use on the Web, you optimize them by compressing the images to decrease their download times. You can optimize images in either Photoshop or ImageReady depending on your needs.

You can optimize images interactively, trying different image quality settings and evaluating the resulting image quality versus the compressed file size. You can see the trade-off in image quality as you decrease the file size, so you can choose the appropriate settings for your needs.

 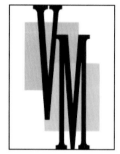

Compare the original image at size 125K and the optimized image at size 8.5K.

You can optimize files in four common file formats: GIF, JPEG, PNG-8, and PNG-24. The two most widely used formats are JPEG and GIF. Photographs generally yield the best results when saved as JPEGs, and illustrations with areas of solid color are best saved as GIFs.

Note: *Images that contain transparent areas or animations must be saved in the GIF format, since the JPEG format does not support these features.*

To see the difference between optimization file formats, you will compare the original image with the JPEG and GIF formats.

Optimizing a photograph as a JPEG

In this first step you will optimize the sculpture photograph in JPEG format and compare the image quality to the original image.

1 Click anywhere within the window of file 001.psd (the sculpture image) to make it active.

2 Choose File > Save for Web. The Save for Web dialog box appears, displaying the sculpture image in the center window.

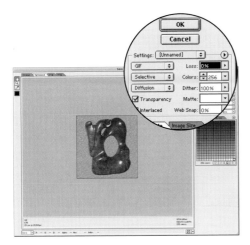

3 Choose JPEG Medium from the Settings menu at the upper right of the dialog box.

The Settings pop-up menu resets all of the optimization settings to preset values. Notice that when you select JPEG Medium, you automatically change the file format, quality, and blur settings. (As you will see in a moment, if you selected one of the GIF formats from the Settings pop-up menu, you would see a different set of options and values.)

4 If the Optimized view is not already showing, click the Optimized tab at the top of the dialog box to view a compressed version of the image. At the bottom left you can see the format, the compressed image size, and an estimated download time.

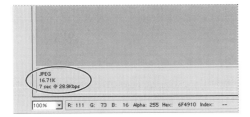

If you want to compare the quality of the original image to the optimized image, click the 2-Up tab.

Later in the Tour you will explore the functions of the 2-Up and 4-Up tabs (present in both the Photoshop and ImageReady applications) in greater detail.

5 In the dialog box, click the 2-Up tab. This format displays the original image in a window side-by-side with the optimized image.

You can see that the optimized image size is substantially smaller than the original image size. You can compare the two images to see if the quality of the compressed image is acceptable for your needs.

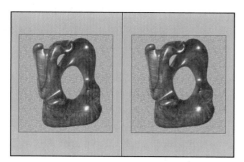

Viewing original image next to the optimized image

Since you will be using the original image in the final Web page, you should now close the sculpture image without saving the optimization settings.

6 Click Cancel to exit the Save for Web dialog box.

7 Choose File > Close, and click No if prompted to save the image.

Optimizing a graphic as a GIF

Photographs such as the sculpture are typically best optimized in the JPEG file format. But graphic images, such as the logo of the furniture maker, are typically best optimized in the GIF format.

Compare how this graphic image looks when saved in the GIF versus the JPEG file format.

1 Click anywhere within the window of file 002.psd (the logo image) to make it active.

2 Choose File > Save for Web.

3 In the Save for Web dialog, choose GIF 128 Dithered from the Settings pop-up menu to change the optimization settings to preset values. *Dithering* simulates a larger number of colors and is helpful to avoid color banding when images have large numbers of colors or smooth gradients.

4 In the dialog box, click the Optimize tab. The information at the bottom of the window shows a compressed file size and an estimated download time.

5 In the Optimize palette, select GIF32 No Dither in the Settings pop-up menu. This setting uses fewer colors in the GIF palette and turns dithering off. You can see how this setting creates a smaller compressed file size.

6 Now you can see how the image would appear when optimized with a JPEG setting. In the Optimize palette, select JPEG Low from the Settings pop-up menu, and then click the 2-Up tab.

You can see that the compressed file size is smaller, but the image quality is not as representative of the original image.

Original image   *JPEG file format*   *GIF file format*

Since you will use the original logo image in the final Web page, you should close the image without saving the optimization settings.

7 Click Cancel to exit the Save for Web dialog box.

8 Choose File > Close.

Using the Jump To command to move between applications

Adobe Photoshop and Adobe ImageReady are designed to work together, and you can move easily between the two programs with a single command. The Jump To command makes it easy to work interchangeably on an image by editing in one program, making additional changes in the other, and then moving back to the first program. The changes you make to the file in one program can be updated in the other program immediately after using the Jump To command.

1 In Photoshop, choose File > Open, locate 003.psd (the main Web page file) in the Tour1_Start folder, and click OK.

2 Do one of the following:

• Click the Jump To button on the bottom of the toolbox.

• Choose File > Jump To > ImageReady.

The ImageReady application opens, with the Web page image active.

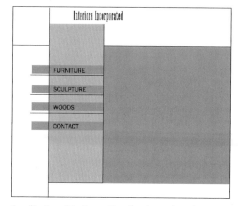

Art displayed in ImageReady after using the Jump To command

Placing and scaling images

Now you'll place the sculpture and logo images in the main Web page.

You can move images from one file to another in ImageReady using the Place command, or by dragging the image from one file to another. In the example, you will drag the sculpture and logo images into the Web page file.

1 In ImageReady, choose File > Open, locate the 001.psd file (the sculpture image), and click Open.

2 Select the move tool (⊹), and then drag the sculpture image to the 003.psd Web page window and into the large green square on the right.

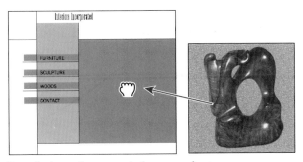

Drag the image from one window to another to copy the image.

When you release the mouse button, the image is copied into the file. Since the image is already sized correctly for the area in which it is being placed, there is no need to scale the image.

3 Choose File > Save to save the changes.

4 Close the 001.psd file.

5 Choose File > Open, locate the 002.psd file (the logo image), and click Open.

6 Select the move tool (⊹), and click on the logo image to select it.

7 Drag the logo to the 003.psd Web page window, near the blank square at the upper left of the Web page.

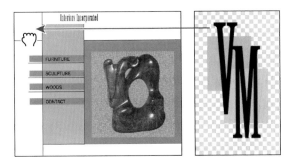

Now you must scale the image so that it is the right size to fit into the target area, and then move it into position.

8 Choose Edit > Transform > Scale. A scale box appears around the logo image.

You'll scale the logo while holding down the Shift key, which constrains the scaling to the original proportions.

9 Hold down the Shift key, and drag one of the corners of the scale box toward the center to reduce the image size. Stop when the logo is appropriately sized, and click Enter or Return to complete the transformation.

10 After the image has been scaled, you can position it by dragging.

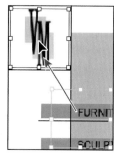

Drag the scale box to reduce the size of the image,
and then drag the logo into position with the move tool.

11 Select the file 002.psd, and choose File > Close.

Entering and formatting type

Now you can add text to the Web page. In Adobe ImageReady, you use the type tool to add horizontal or vertical type to an image. If you need to change type characteristics, you can also specify the font, style, color, tracking, leading, kerning, and alignment.

Keep in mind that you can easily move between Adobe Photoshop and Adobe ImageReady, using the File > Jump To command to manipulate text and apply effects to it. Any new text layers created in Photoshop appear in the Layers palette in ImageReady, and the text is as editable in ImageReady as it is in Photoshop.

For the Web site that you are creating, you will add the name of the fictitious furniture maker, Vincent Michael.

1 Select the type tool (T). The pointer changes to an I-beam.

2 If the type palette is not showing, choose Window > Show Type.

3 In the Type palette, select a font and a type size. (In our example, we used Frutiger* Roman and a type size of 48.)

4 If the Layers palette is not showing, choose Window > Show Layers. In the Layers palette, click on the Button text layer to select it.

5 In the toolbox, click the Default Foreground/Background Color icon ( ) to select black as the foreground color.

6 Click in the white area above the sculpture image, at the upper right of the Web page.

7 Type the text **Vincent Michael**.

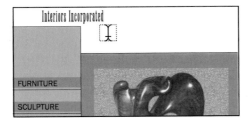 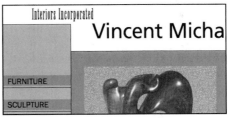

Entering text with the text tool

8 Now drag the text into better alignment using the move tool. Select the move tool ( ) in the toolbox. Position the move tool over the text, and drag the text so that it appears just above the horizontal line above the sculpture.

If the type is too large or too small, select an appropriate size.

9 Choose File > Save to save your changes.

Applying a layer effect

Notice that in the Layers palette, when you click in the document with the type tool you create a separate type layer.

A major advantage of layers is that when you apply an effect to a layer, the effect is applied to *all* of the elements of the selected layer—even if the elements are not all selected in the main window. For example, you can apply a drop shadow to all of the text on a layer simply by selecting the layer on which the text is placed and applying the effect to the layer.

Remember that most image layer effects created in ImageReady are visible in the Layers palette in Photoshop. You can therefore create layer effects in both ImageReady and Photoshop, and have the effects available in either application.

Note: *A few layer effects are not transferable between the ImageReady and Photoshop applications. The Gradient or Pattern effects in ImageReady, for example, are not editable in Photoshop and therefore are not available in the Photoshop Layers palette.*

Now you'll add a drop shadow effect to the text layer that you just created.

1 In the Layers palette, select the layer for the type you just entered.

2 At the bottom of the Layers palette, click the Effects button (⨍) to display the Effects pop-up menu.

3 Choose Drop Shadow from the Effects pop-up menu. The drop shadow is added to the image, and the Drop Shadow options appear in the Layer Options/Effects palette.

4 In the Layer Options/Effects palette, change the opacity to 40%, the distance to 7, the blur to 7, and the angle to 130°.

Effects applied to a layer are applied to all elements in the layer, even if only a few elements are selected.

In the Layers palette, notice the Type layer now indicates the Drop Shadow effect for that layer. You can change a layer effect after it has been set. Click the Drop Shadow effect icon in the Layers palette, and then make changes to the Drop Shadow options in the Layer Options/Effects palette.

When you apply one or more effects to a layer, a list of all effects applied to that layer is displayed below the layer name. To display or hide the effects, click the triangle next to the effects symbol for that layer.

5 Choose File > Save to save your changes.

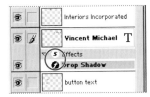

Click the triangle next to the effects for that layer to display a list of effects.

Using Photoshop to revise an image

If you want to add a drop shadow to the sculpture image in your Web page, you should erase the image's colored background. You can best remove the background using the background eraser tool in Adobe Photoshop. All the erasers allow you to selectively erase areas of an image.

Next you'll use the Jump To command to change to Adobe Photoshop to edit the image.

1 In ImageReady, choose File > Open, and select 001.psd (the original sculpture image) from the Tour1>T1_Start folder.

2 With the 001.psd image active, choose File > Jump To > Adobe Photoshop 5.5, choose Update when prompted to save the 003.psd file, and then close it.

The 001.psd image is now active and selected.

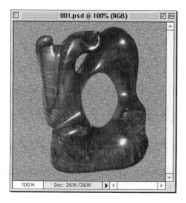

3 Choose Window > Show Brushes, and select the 65 pixel brush from the Brush palette.

4 Select the background eraser tool ( ) in the toolbox. It is hidden beneath the eraser tool ( ). Position the pointer on the visible tool, and drag to highlight the background eraser.

5 Double-click on the background eraser tool icon to display the Background eraser Options palette. Select Discontiguous, and set the Tolerance to 50.

6 In the main window, click on any part of the background color and hold down the mouse button. Drag the crosshair over the background to erase the background color. Notice that the sculpture image is not affected by the brush as long as you do not touch the sculpture with the crosshair.

Dragging with the background eraser to selectively erase the background color

Continue to erase the background until all of the background color is gone. Make sure that the crosshair does not touch the brown sculpture image while you are erasing the background.

Note: *If at any point you notice pixel debris in your image, erase it using the eraser tool.*

Now that the background is gone, you can add a drop shadow to the image. You can add the drop shadow in either Photoshop or ImageReady, because most layer effects that you add in one application are usable in the other application. In this example, you'll add the drop shadow in Photoshop.

7 Choose Layer > Effects > Drop Shadow, and then click OK in the Drop Shadow dialog box to apply the effect.

Image with drop shadow effect applied

8 Choose File > Save to save the changes.

9 Choose File > Jump To > Adobe ImageReady, and choose Update when prompted.

You will now delete the layer containing the old sculpture image and replace it with the new sculpture image.

10 Click anywhere in the window of the 003.psd Web page to make it active.

11 Select the layer containing the old sculpture image, and drag it to the Delete Layer icon (🗑) at the bottom of the palette.

12 With the selection tool, select the new sculpture image in 001.psd, and drag to place it in the green area where the old image was placed.

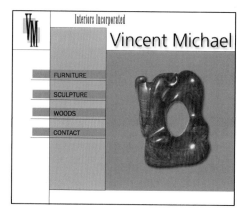

Notice that a new layer containing the new sculpture image is created in the Layers palette. You can also see that the drop shadow effect applied in Photoshop is visible as an effect in the new layer. You can edit the drop shadow just as if it were a drop shadow created in ImageReady.

Drawing and styling a button

Now you can create a button that the Web page viewers will use to bring up an order form. You will create the button on its own layer, so that you can more easily apply effects to it.

Since you want to make the new button match the colors of the existing buttons on the Web page, the first step will be to sample a color from the Web page using the eyedropper tool.

The eyedropper tool samples color from wherever you click in the active image and sets the current foreground color to the sampled color. It is the easiest method for copying colors from one part of an image to another.

1 Select the eyedropper tool ( ), and then click on any of the green buttons on the left of the Web page to sample the color.

2 Select the ellipse tool ( ), which is hidden beneath the rectangle tool ( ) in the toolbox. Click on the rectangle tool, and drag to select the ellipse tool.

3 Click in the lower left of the main window, below the button that says Contact, and drag to create an oval button.

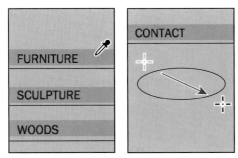

Sample a color using the eyedropper tool, and then
drag with the oval tool to create a new button.

You will name this layer Order Button so that you will know later on that this is the layer on which you created the button.

4 Select the new layer and double-click to bring up the Layers Option palette. Type **Order Button** in the name field, and press Enter or Return.

Now, to make the button appear three-dimensional, you will add a bevel and emboss effect to the button.

5 In the Layers palette, click the Effects button ( ) to display the Effects pop-up menu.

6 Choose Bevel and Emboss from the Effects pop-up menu.

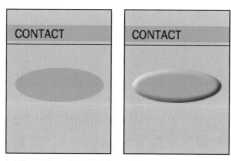

Adding a Bevel and Emboss effect creates a 3-D appearance.

Now you'll add some text to the order button using the text tool.

7 Select the text tool (T).

8 In the toolbox, click the Default Foreground/Background Color button (▣) to select black as the foreground color.

9 If the type palette is not visible, choose Window > Show Type.

10 In the Type palette, enter a value of 18 in the Size box.

11 Click with the I-beam/insertion point in the oval button where you want the text to appear. (Don't worry if the positioning isn't perfect—you can move the text later with the move tool.)

12 Type **ORDER NOW!**

13 Select the move tool (▶✛). Click the text, and then drag to position the text in the center of the button.

Repositioning text on button with move tool

14 Choose File > Save to save your changes.

Applying a style

To make your button stand out more, you can add a texture and some effects. For example, the bevel and emboss effect gives it a more three-dimensional look, and a wood-style texture will tie it into the theme of your furniture maker.

You could apply these effects one by one, but it would be a tedious process—you would have to change the settings on each effect to make them look good together. Instead, you can apply them both at once, using a *style*. Styles are one or more effects that you can save and later apply to layers in any ImageReady document. You can create your own styles, or you can choose from a variety of preprogrammed styles.

In the example, you will use a preprogrammed style called Button-wood that contains a bevel effect and a wood-grain pattern. All of the effects contained within a particular style are displayed in the Styles palette.

1 If the Styles palette is not visible, choose Window > Show Styles. Choose Large Swatch from the Styles palette menu.

2 Select the Button-wood style name.

3 In the Layers palette, select the Order Button layer.

4 Do one of the following to apply the style:

• Double-click the style name in the Styles palette.

• Drag the style from the Styles palette to the Layers palette, and drop it on the Order Button layer.

• Drag the style from the Styles palette directly to the order button in the main window.

Button-wood style applied

Slicing a page

You can use *slices* in ImageReady to divide a document into smaller files. Each slice is an independent file, containing its own individual optimization settings, color palettes, URLs, roll over effects, and animation effects. You can use slices for faster download speeds and increased image quality when working with documents that contain mixed images, or text and images.

Slices are assembled in an HTML table in the document's HTML file. By default, the document starts with one slice that comprises the entire document. You can then create more slices in the document—ImageReady will automatically make additional slices to complete the full table in the HTML file.

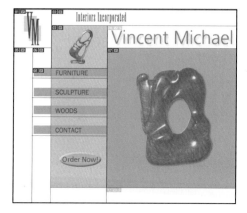

Slices that you create are called *user-slices*. Slices that ImageReady creates automatically are called *auto-slices*.

You will create a slice from one of the Web page buttons, so that you can then define a rollover effect for it. For example, one type of rollover effect would take place when the viewer rolls the mouse pointer over a defined area in the image.

1 Choose the slice tool (✐) from the toolbox. Notice that all of the slices in the image are now visible.

2 Position the pointer at the upper left corner of the Sculpture button. Drag to create a slice around the button.

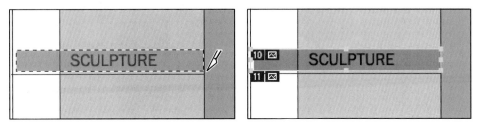

Creating a slice with the slice tool automatically creates other slices in the image.

In the example, the slice is numbered 10, although you may see a different number on your screen if you have created a slice in some other part of the image.

Assigning a URL to a button

Now that you have created slices, you can use the Slice palette to link the Order Now button to an order form. In the example, you will link the button to the Adobe Systems URL (where, if the artist was not imaginary, you would find an order form for the sculptures).

Once you've created a slice and assigned a URL to it, the viewer of the Web site simply clicks on the slice in a Web browser to jump to the defined URL. After you have assigned a URL to the slice, you can preview how the jump works using the Preview In Browser command. See "Previewing in a browser" on page 41.

You can assign a URL to a slice using the Slice palette. In this example, you will use the Order Now button that you created and assign a URL to its slice.

1 Select the slice tool (✏), and draw a slice rectangle around the Order button.

2 If the Slice palette is not visible, choose Window > Show Slice.

Assigning a URL to the selected slice

3 In the Slice palette, enter **http://www.adobe.com** in the URL text box, or choose the URL from the URL pop-up menu.

4 Choose File > Save to save your changes.

Creating a rollover effect

Rollover effects are among the most powerful features of ImageReady, allowing you to create effects that are triggered when the mouse is moved in relation to part of the image within a slice. For example, if the mouse is moved over the image, or if the mouse button is clicked on the image, these can activate an effect.

It is important to keep in mind the relationship of rollover states to the Layers palette. Any changes to the image that are initiated using the Layers palette—such as layer visibility, layer effects, layer position, blend mode, and opacity—are visible only in the rollover state that is currently selected.

In contrast, any changes to the image that are not initiated through the Layers palette— such as image adjustments or using brushes on the image—are visible across *all* rollover states. This is an important point to keep in mind when creating either rollover effects or animations, as you'll see later in the Tour.

The first rollover effect will be a highlight that will only show when the mouse is rolled over a selected part of the image.

In the example, you will apply a rollover effect that will be triggered when a pointer is positioned over the Sculpture button. The button will be highlighted with a different color when the rollover occurs.

You will apply the rollover effect to only the Sculpture button by first selecting the slice that contains the Sculpture button.

1 Select the slice selection tool ($\mathbf{k_H}$).

2 If the Sculpture button is not already selected, click on the slice that contains the button to select it.

3 Choose Window > Show Rollover if the Rollover palette is not currently visible.

Notice that in the Rollover palette, the first thumbnail shows the button in its current state with the word Normal above it.

4 Do one of the following:

• Click the New button (🔲) at the bottom of the Rollover palette.

• Choose New State from the Rollover palette menu.

A duplicate thumbnail appears with the word Over at the top of the thumbnail.

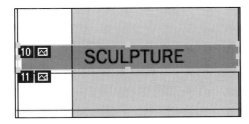
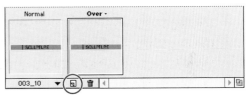

Selecting a slice with the slice selection tool   *Click the New Rollover icon to create a new rollover state.*

Any changes that you now make in your image through the Layers palette will appear in the finished Web page only when the viewer's mouse pointer is over the selected slice.

5 If the Layers palette is not visible, choose Window > Show Layers.

6 In the Layers palette, select the layer called Button Text. This is the text layer associated with the Sculpture button.

7 Choose Select > Create Selection from Slice to create a selection from the Sculpture button slice.

8 Choose Layer > New > Layer via Copy to copy the selection to its own layer.

9 Double-click on the new layer to bring up the Layer Options dialog box.

10 In the name field, type **Sculpture Highlight**.

11 Click OK.

12 Choose Edit > Fill. In the Fill dialog box, select the following options: White, 100% opacity, Normal mode, and Preserve Transparency, and then click OK.

To preview the effect of the rollover, you can click on the Normal thumbnail and then on the Over thumbnail in the Rollover palette. The main window reflects the changes in the different rollover states.

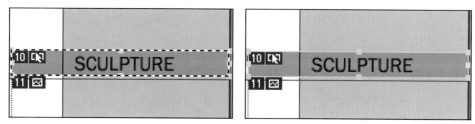

Creating a selection from a slice to create a rollover highlight

To create more interactivity with the viewer, you can also create a *secondary rollover effect* when the mouse is rolled over the button. A secondary rollover effect is an effect that is triggered by a mouse event in one slice, but that takes place in a different slice of the document.

In the example, you will create an animated montage of photographs that begins when the mouse button is rolled over the Sculpture button.

13 In the Rollover palette, click the Over thumbnail to select the rollover state.

You are now ready to create an animation which will be activated when the mouse is rolled over the Sculpture button.

Creating an animation

It's easy to create animated images using ImageReady. An animation is a sequence of images, or frames. Each frame differs slightly from the preceding frame, creating the illusion of movement when the frames are viewed in quick succession.

You start with a single image and create a sequence of animation frames, applying changes to frames to create the appearance of movement in the animation file.

If you create an animation using the Normal rollover state, the file is saved as an animated GIF, and the animation is automatically played when loaded by the browser. If you create an animation in another rollover state, the animation is only played when the rollover effect takes place.

In this example, you will place three sculpture images into the Web page and create the animation so that they appear to fade from one to another. You will place the animation images in slice #3 (the orange area above the green buttons at the upper left of the screen).

1 If the Rollover palette is not visible, choose Window > Show Rollover.

2 Select the slice selection tool (⯈).

3 Click on the Sculpture button to select the Sculpture button slice.

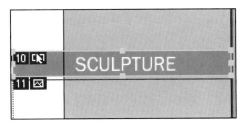

Selecting the Sculpture button slice

4 Do one of the following:

• Click the Hide Slice button (⬚) in the toolbox.

• Choose Slices > Hide Slices.

The slice lines are now hidden around each individual slice. This makes it easier to view images in the main window.

5 In the Rollover palette, click the Over thumbnail to select the rollover state. This ensures that the animation you create will play *only* when the mouse pointer is rolled over the Sculpture button.

6 Do one of the following:

• Select the Animation tab in the Rollover palette.

• Choose Window > Show Animation.

The Animation palette appears, displaying a thumbnail of the entire Web page.

7 Choose Window > Show Layers if the Layers palette is not visible.

The Layers palette displays the layer settings for the current frame of the animation palette. You apply changes to the layers in each frame to create animation effects.

As with the rollover states, changes made through the Layers palette will only take effect for the selected frame.

You will place three different sculpture images into the Web page. Each sculpture image will be placed on its own layer.

8 Choose File > Place, and in the Place dialog box, click Choose.

9 Navigate to the Tour1_Start folder, select the 004.psd file, and click Open.

10 Click OK in the Place dialog box.

The first sculpture image appears in the Web page window. Now you will move the image into place in the space above the buttons.

11 Choose the move tool (⊹).

12 Click on the new sculpture image, and drag into place above the Furniture button.

The first animation layer in place

13 Choose File > Place, and click Choose in the Place dialog box.

14 Navigate to the Tour1_Start folder, select the 005.psd file, and click Open. Then click OK to place the image.

15 Drag the new sculpture image into place directly over the first animation sculpture.

16 Follow steps 13 through 15 to place a third sculpture image from the 006.psd file on top of the previous two sculpture images.

17 Choose New Frame (▣) from the Animation palette menu. A new thumbnail appears, with the number 2 in the upper left corner.

18 In the Layers palette, click the eye icons next to layers 004.psd and 006.psd to make them invisible. Now you should see only the 005.psd sculpture.

19 Choose New Frame (▣) from the Animation palette menu. A new thumbnail appears, with the number 3 in the upper left corner.

20 In the Layers palette, click the eye icon next to the 005.psd layer to make the layer invisible. Now click the eye column next to the 006.psd layer to make it visible.

 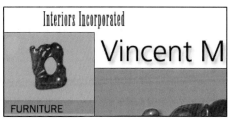

Use the Layers palette to make the 005.psd layer visible in frame 2 and the 006.psd layer (bottom) visible in frame 3.

21 Click frame 1 in the Animation palette, and click the eye icons next to layers 006.psd and 005.psd to make them invisible. Layer 004.psd should still be visible.

22 Choose File > Save to save your changes.

You should now have three animation frames. Test your new animation by clicking the Play button (▷) at the bottom of the Animation palette. Click the Stop button (□) to stop the animation.

Tweening frames to create smooth animation effects

Now you can fine tune the animation so the images flow smoothly into one another.

You use *tweening* to quickly create a series of frames that vary in layer opacity, position, or effects, to create animation effects such as fading in or out, or moving an element across a frame.

In this section you'll use the Tween command to create new frames between the animations, each of which should fade in or fade out.

1 In the Animation palette, click on frame 1 to select it, and then shift-click on frame 2 to add to the selection. These are the two frames that you will Tween between.

2 Select Tween from the Animation palette.

3 In the Tween dialog box, choose All Layers; Select Opacity, and deselect Position and Effects; choose Selection from the Tween With pop-up menu; enter **2** in the Frames to Add box; and then click OK.

ImageReady generates two new frames between the first and second frames, showing a progressive fade between the images.

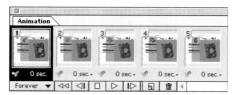

Creating a fade out effect using the Tween command

4 Select frames 4 and 5 and repeat steps 2 and 3 to create a fade between these frames.

You should now have a total of 7 frames in your animation, each showing a fadeout between the last image in the animation.

Now you're ready to preview the animation in ImageReady.

5 Click the Play button (▷) in the Animation palette. Notice that the animation moves quite slowly; the animation will move in real time when viewed in a browser.

6 When you have finished viewing the animation, click the Stop button (□).

Setting delay and saving an animation

You can specify delay time for individual frames using the Delay timer pop-up menu on each frame. By default, all frames are set to a delay time of 0 seconds.

1 In the Animation palette menu, choose Select All Frames.

2 Click the 0 sec text beneath any of the frames in the Animation palette, and choose 0.1 sec from the pop-up menu.

3 Click the Play button (▷) to view the animation again with the new delay time.

When you have finished viewing, click the Stop button (□).

4 Now you will set the delay for a single frame. Select frame 1 in the Animation palette, click the 0.1 sec text beneath the frame, and choose 0.5 sec from the pop-up menu. Do the same to add a 0.5 sec delay to frames 4 and 7.

5 Choose File > Save to save your changes.

You can view the animation using the Preview in Browser command, as described in "Previewing in a browser" on page 41. When previewing, the animation begins when the mouse pointer is rolled over the Sculpture button.

Optimizing images

Earlier in the Tour you learned the basics of how to select optimization settings to compress the file size. Now, you will set optimization settings using slices, so that you can change optimization settings for different parts of the image.

The advantage of setting optimization options for each slice in your document is that you can set the best options for each graphic independently. A photograph in the document might use certain compression options, while text or graphic images may use a completely different set of options. In this way, you can maximize the image quality for the document while minimizing the download time.

You can choose the file format and compression settings for a selected slice in the Optimize palette.

1 Select the slice selection tool (), and click on the largest slice containing the sculpture photograph. You will optimize this photograph as a JPEG.

2 If the Optimize palette is not visible, choose Window > Show Optimize.

3 In the Optimize palette, choose JPEG Medium from the Settings pop-up menu.

Now you will choose a different set of optimization settings for another slice.

4 Select the slice containing the Sculpture button. You will optimize this slice as a GIF.

5 In the Optimize palette, choose GIF 64 No Dither from the Settings pop-up menu. As you can see, this shortcut sets the options in the other settings for the Optimize palette to 64 Colors, No Dither, and Selective palette.

6 In the document window, click the Optimized tab to view the optimized image.

Comparing original and optimized images

The easiest way to compare compression and image quality settings is to use the 2-Up and 4-Up tabs. You can see these tabs both in the main window of ImageReady, and also in the Save for Web dialog box in Photoshop.

The 2-Up and 4-Up options allow you to view multiple optimized versions at the same time to help you make decisions regarding image quality and download times.

First you will compare the original image and the optimized image using the 2-Up tab.

1 In the main window, click the 2-Up tab (2-Up). The original image appears in the left panel, and the optimized version appears in the right panel. The optimization information appears below each image pane.

2 Select the zoom tool ( ), and click on the optimized image for a close up view of the image quality. You can then compare the image to the original to see if the quality is acceptable for the optimization settings selected.

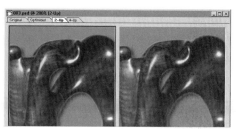

Using the zoom tool to compare quality in the 2-Up optimization format

3 For even more choices, click the 4-Up tab (4-Up).

The 4-Up view provides a number of optimization alternatives that are automatically generated by ImageReady. You can compare the image quality and download times for each optimized image, and select the optimization scheme that works best for your document.

You can also click on an image pane to select it and change the settings in the Optimize palette. The new settings are applied instantly—this provides an excellent way to test new optimization settings without having to open your browser.

4 Select an image pane by clicking on it.

Now you will save the optimized version you selected.

Note: *You can try out even more settings in the 2-Up or 4-Up views by choosing Slices > Show Slices. This command lets you view slices in each image pane. Each slice can then be given different optimization settings.*

5 Choose File > Save Optimized.

6 In the Save Optimized dialog box, name the new file **WebPage.htm**, click the Save HTML File and Save Images options, and click Save. ImageReady will save all of the optimized images as well as an HTML file containing all the necessary code. The viewer's Web browser will then reassemble the page and display the rollover effects and animation.

You can also save the original, uncompressed file with the optimization information stored for later use, using the Save As command. The Save As command automatically saves an original version of the file, while retaining the current optimization settings.

Previewing in a browser

Once you've created the optimized images in ImageReady, you can easily preview the image in a Web browser.

1 Choose File > Preview In, and choose a browser from the submenu. When you install ImageReady, all browsers on your system are added to the Preview in submenu.

You can add other browsers to the submenu after ImageReady is installed. To do this place a shortcut (Windows) or an alias (Mac OS) for the browser in the Preview In folder in the Helpers folder, located in the ImageReady application folder.

Note: *If desired, you can also launch your browser separately and open the WebPage.htm file that you saved in the previous section.*

2 With the Browser launched, use the mouse to roll the pointer over the Sculpture button. The button should highlight in white, and the animation at the top of the screen should begin running while the pointer is over the button.

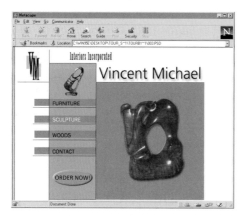

3 Position the pointer over the Order Now! button, and click the button. The Adobe Web site (www.adobe.com) should now appear in the browser window.

Congratulations! You've completed the Web tour for Photoshop 5.5. Continue experimenting by creating more files, or try creating new effects and optimization levels for the file that you have just created.

Basic Tour

A Tour of Photoshop 5.5 Basics

This interactive tour of Adobe Photoshop, adapted from the Adobe Photoshop 5.0 User Guide, provides an overview of key features of the program. A movie version of the tour is also available on the Photoshop 5.5 CD. More detailed instructions on how to use the features in this tour are provided in individual lessons throughout this book.

Projects in Adobe Photoshop or ImageReady can begin in a variety of ways. Most projects start with a scanned image, stock digital art, or artwork created with a drawing program, such as Adobe Illustrator®. Some images can also be created from scratch within Adobe Photoshop. For this tour, you'll use files that were created from all of these sources.

The tour will take about 45 minutes to complete. The tour is designed to be done in Adobe Photoshop, but information on using similar functionality in Adobe ImageReady is included where appropriate. The key features covered in this tour are also available in ImageReady, with small differences as noted.

1 Start Adobe Photoshop.

2 Choose File > Open, and open the files Tour.psd, CD.psd, and Horn.psd, located in the Lessons/Tour2/T2_Start folder. Arrange the windows so that you can work with them easily.

3 Click the title bar of the Tour.psd file to make it active.

Selecting

You modify part of an image by first selecting that area. You'll begin the tour by making selections in images using the selection tools. (If you make a mistake at any point in the tour, simply choose Edit > Undo, and try again.)

First you'll make a simple selection, and drag an image from one file to another.

1 Click the title bar of the CD.psd window to make it active.

2 Hold down the mouse button on the rectangular marquee tool (⬚) in the toolbox, and drag to the elliptical marquee tool (◯). Click in the upper left corner of the image's gray background, and begin dragging diagonally. Then hold down Shift to change the elliptical selection to a circular selection, and drag to the bottom right corner of the image.

3 When the selection border matches the outside edge of the CD, release the mouse button, and then release Shift.

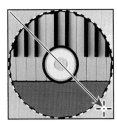

4 Select the move tool (▸₊) in the toolbox, position it within the selection border, and drag the CD onto the Tour.psd window. The CD is now part of that file.

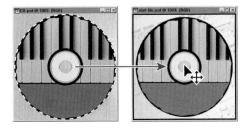

Now you'll resize the CD.

5 Choose Edit > Free Transform. Move the pointer onto one of the corner handles. Hold down Shift, and drag a corner handle to shrink the CD to about three-fourths its current size. Holding down Shift constrains the image's proportions as you resize it.

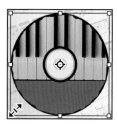 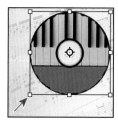

6 Move the pointer outside the selection handles, and drag clockwise to rotate the CD about 30°. Press Enter (Windows) or Return (Mac OS) to apply the transformation to the CD.

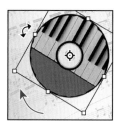

Note: You can also use the Numeric Transform dialog box to transform a selection using specific numeric values.

Next you'll make a selection with the magic wand tool, which selects areas based on how similar they are in color.

7 Select the magic wand tool (✳); then click the title bar of the Horn.psd window to make it active.

8 Click the white background in the upper right corner of the image to select it. Notice that not all the white background was selected.

9 Choose Select > Similar to add the rest of the background to the selection. You've now selected everything except the horn.

10 Choose Select > Inverse. The Inverse command selects everything that wasn't selected—in this case, the horn.

11 Hold down Control (Windows) or Command (Mac OS), position the pointer within the selection marquee, and drag the horn onto the Tour.psd window. (Holding down Control/Command temporarily changes the current tool to the move tool.) Move the horn to the bottom left corner of the image.

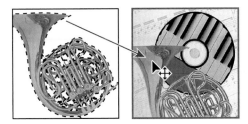

12 Choose File > Save.

13 Close the CD.psd and Horn.psd files.

You've tried out some basic selection tools. Photoshop provides advanced selection tools not available in ImageReady, including sophisticated masking techniques and the ability to create complex and precise selections from paths. For more practice selecting, see Lesson 2, "Working with Selections"; Lesson 7, "Basic Pen Tool Techniques"; and Lesson 5, "Masks and Channels."

Layers

Photoshop and ImageReady let you organize artwork on separate transparent layers so that you can easily construct composite images and experiment with various effects.

1 Click the Layers palette tab to bring the palette to the front, or if the Layers palette is not visible on your screen, choose Window > Show Layers. Click the minimize/maximize box (Windows) or resize box (Mac OS) at the top of the Layers palette to expand the palette.

Notice that this file has several layers, each named and with a *thumbnail*, or miniature representation, of the image on that layer. Photoshop automatically created separate layers for the CD image (Layer 1) and horn image (Layer 2) when you brought them into the Tour file. In addition, the background (Photoshop) and the Notes layer were already in the file.

When you open files in ImageReady, Layer 0 is the equivalent of the Photoshop background. ImageReady does not support backgrounds used in Photoshop and converts them to a normal layer.

In Photoshop, the background is the first layer of an image and is analogous to the base layer of a painting. You cannot change the stacking order of a background or apply a blending mode or opacity (unless you convert it to a normal layer.) In ImageReady, the first layer of an image is a normal layer, with no special properties.

From the Layers palette you can display or hide layers in the image.

2 Click the eye icon column to the far left of the Notes layer to display the layer. Then try clicking the eye icon for Layer 2 to hide the layer, and again to redisplay it.

By changing the order of layers, you can restack images in the artwork.

3 Drag Layer 2 (the horn layer) until it's between Layer 1 (the CD layer) and the background on the Layers palette. Release the mouse button to set Layer 2 in its new position. The horn now appears behind the CD in the artwork.

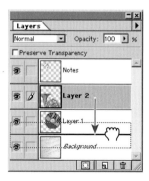

4 Click Layer 1 in the Layers palette to make it the active layer. The layer is highlighted and a paintbrush icon appears next to the layer thumbnail, indicating that your changes now will affect artwork only on that layer.

5 Select the move tool (◂₊). Then drag the CD to the top right corner of the artwork. Because the CD is on its own layer, you can move it separately from artwork on other layers.

Now you'll adjust the opacity of Layer 1.

6 Select Layer 1 in the Layers palette, and drag the opacity slider to 40%. You can now see other layers through the CD.

By specifying *blending modes*, you can determine how one layer interacts with another.

7 Choose Multiply from the mode menu at the top left of the Layers palette. Notice how the CD blends with the layers below it.

Adding type

Now you're ready to create and manipulate some text. You will create the text with the type tool, which places the text on its own type layer. You will then edit the text and apply special effects to its layer.

1 Select the type tool (T), and click the image in the upper right corner.

In Photoshop, the Type Tool dialog box appears. If you're working in ImageReady, the program adds a type layer (T) to the Layers palette, indicated by the T icon.

2 Select a font by entering a point size in the Size and Leading boxes (we used 22-point Lucida® Sans Bold with 43-point leading):

• In Photoshop, use the Font menu in the Type Tool dialog box.

• In ImageReady, click the Type palette tab to bring it forward, or choose Window > Show Type, and use the Type palette.

3 Select the right alignment option in the Type Tool dialog box or Type palette.

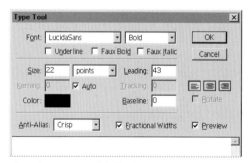

Photoshop Type Tool dialog box   *ImageReady Type palette*

4 Type **MEZZO PIANO** in two lines in the large text box at the bottom of the dialog box (Photoshop) or in the upper right of the image (ImageReady).

5 Select a color for the type:

• In Photoshop, click the color box on the left side of the dialog box, select a color from the color picker, and click OK.

• In ImageReady, select a color from the Color palette by dragging in the color bar or dragging the R, G, and B sliders.

6 Resize "PIANO":

• In Photoshop, select "PIANO," and enter a larger point size in the Type Tool dialog box.

• In ImageReady, click in the image beneath the type to select its baseline, and enter a larger point size in the Size box in the palette.

7 Position the type on the image:

• In Photoshop, with the Type Tool dialog box still displayed, move the pointer into the image area. Notice that the pointer temporarily changes to the move tool. You can now reposition the text. When the text looks the way you want it, click OK in the dialog box. The text is automatically placed in the Layers palette on a new type layer, marked with a T icon.

• In ImageReady, click beneath the type in the image to select its baseline. Then drag the type to reposition it.

Adding layer effects

You can enhance any layer by adding a shadow, glow, bevel, or emboss special effect from the program's assortment of layer effects, as well as a new color fill effect. ImageReady also includes pattern and gradient layer effects, as well as styles—sets of one or more layer effects.

You can also apply a combination of layer effects to the same layer. Here you'll apply the Drop Shadow and Bevel and Emboss layer effects to the type.

1 Make sure that the MEZZO PIANO type layer is active. Then choose Layer > Effects > Drop Shadow.

In ImageReady, you can also add layer effects by clicking the Effects button at the bottom of the Layers palette.

2 In the dialog box, change the opacity to 60% and set the angle to 150°.

3 Now choose Bevel and Emboss from the menu at the top of the dialog box.

4 In the new dialog box, click Apply. Then change the opacity for both Highlight and Shadow to 50%, select Inner Bevel for Style, set Blur to 2 pixels, and click OK. The drop shadow and bevel and emboss effects are now applied to the type.

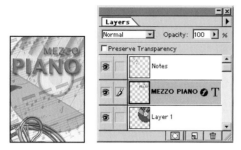

It's easy to change text on a type layer and ensure that any layer effects applied will automatically track changes made to the layer. You can see how this works by changing the wording of your text.

5 Double-click the T icon on the Mezzo Piano layer in the Layers palette.

6 Select the word "PIANO" and change it to "FORTE":

• In Photoshop, use the Type Tool dialog box.

• In ImageReady, drag over the type in the image to select it, and then type the change.

Notice how the layer effects are applied to the new word.

7 If you like, try applying other layer effects to the text. When you have finished, click OK.

8 Choose File > Save.

Filters

To quickly add special effects to your artwork, you can choose from a wide variety of filters. In this part of the tour, you'll apply some filters to transform the background.

The Photoshop filters also appear in ImageReady. In addition, most plug-in filters developed for Photoshop by non-Adobe software developers are compatible with ImageReady.

1 Click the background in the Layers palette to make it active.

2 Choose Filter > Distort > Wave. In the dialog box, set Number of Generators to 3, Maximum Wavelength to 350, Minimum Amplitude to 1, and Maximum Amplitude to 20. Click OK.

3 Choose Filter > Brush Strokes > Angled Strokes, and click OK to accept the default settings.

4 Then choose Filter > Fade Angled Strokes. In the dialog box, set the opacity to 50%, select Multiply for the mode, and click OK.

Note: *ImageReady does not have a Fade Filter command.*

The Fade Angled Strokes Explore some additional filters if you like.

Painting

With the painting tools, you can add color to your artwork using preset swatches, colors you create, or colors you sample from existing art. Now you'll paint part of the background using the paintbrush tool.

1 Double-click the paintbrush tool ( ), and make sure that the opacity in the Paintbrush Options palette is set to 100%.

Note: Each tool in Photoshop has its own Options palette, which you can display by double-clicking the tool in the toolbox.

2 Choose Window > Show Brushes, and click the 35-pixel brush from the bottom row of the Brushes palette.

Now you'll paint arcs of four different colors over the bell of the French horn. The first color is white, which you'll select through the toolbox color selection box. This box sets the foreground color, the color you paint with, and the background color, the color used when you erase part of an image. The default colors are black for foreground and white for background.

3 Click the Switch Colors icon ( ) in the upper right corner of the color selection box to make the foregound color white.

4 With the background selected, paint a white arc over the bell of the French horn.

You can use the eyedropper tool to select additional colors by sampling (copying) them from artwork in the image. You'll use a keyboard shortcut to access the eyedropper when selecting colors for the next three arcs.

5 Hold down Alt (Windows) or Option (Mac OS) to temporarily change from the paint-brush tool to the eyedropper tool. Then click a yellow note in the image. The foreground color in the color selection box switches to the same yellow as in the note, indicating that you can now paint with this color.

6 Release the Alt/Option key, change the opacity in the Options palette to 80%, and paint a yellow arc just above the first white arc.

7 Now hold down Alt/Option, and click a red note to change the foreground color to red. Release the Alt/Option key, change the opacity in the Options palette to 60%, and paint a red arc above the yellow arc.

8 Repeat the process, but this time sample the foreground color from a green note, change the opacity to 40%, and paint a green arc.

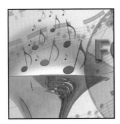

Next you'll use the History palette to remove the paint you just applied. The History palette records changes you make to the image and lets you step back through recent changes. Using this palette, you can return to an earlier version of the image and continue working from that point.

9 To display the History palette, choose Window > Show History.

10 Click Fade Angled Strokes in the history list. The image reverts to the way it looked right after you applied the Fade Angled Strokes filter.

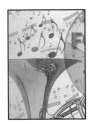

You can now continue working from this version of the image. All changes past Fade Angled Strokes will be deleted, and new changes will be recorded in their place.

Next you'll try out a gradient fill in Photoshop to "paint" or blend between two colors on the background of the image.

(ImageReady does not have a gradient tool. However, you can add gradients to an entire layer using a layer gradient effect. If you've been following the tour in ImageReady, you can save your file and skip to the next section.)

11 Choose Window > Show Swatches, and click a blue swatch to set your foreground color. Then double-click the linear gradient tool (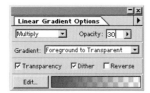), and in the Gradient Tool Options palette choose Foreground to Transparent for the gradient, 30% for the opacity, and Multiply for the mode.

12 Drag the gradient tool from the top left to the bottom right corner of the background to set the beginning and end of the gradient.

13 Choose File > Save.

Retouching

Adobe Photoshop provides a full range of tools for retouching images, including dodge and burn tools, as well as features for adjusting color, tone, contrast, hue, and saturation. Many basic color correction tools are also available in ImageReady, including Levels, Auto Levels, Brightness/Contrast, Hue/Saturation, Desaturation, Invert, Variations, and the Unsharp Mask filter.

You'll use a few of the Photoshop retouching tools to do some basic color correction and editing on an image.

1 Click Layer 2 in the Layers palette to make it active.

2 To set the basic contrast and tonal range between the highlights and shadows in the horn, choose Image > Adjust > Levels.

3 In the dialog box, select the Preview option, and then drag the left and right triangles inward to where the first spikes of the dark and light ends of the histogram's color range begin.

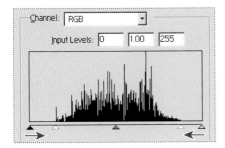

4 Click OK to apply the changes and extend the tonal range of the image.

Notice that the midtones in the horn are still not right; they need to be more red. To correct the color, you'll use the Color Balance command. (ImageReady doesn't have a Color Balance command.)

5 Choose Image > Adjust > Color Balance. A dialog box appears for adjusting the mixture of colors in the image.

6 Select the Preview option in the dialog box, drag the top slider away from Cyan toward Red, and click OK. The horn turns more red.

Tip: To replicate adjusting the color balance by adding red, choose Image > Adjust > Variations, click Midtones to adjust the middle tones of the image, click the More Red thumbnail preview, and click OK.

Now you'll remove a scratch on the horn with the rubber stamp tool. This tool lets you sample part of an image and then paint with a copy of the sampled area.

7 Double-click the rubber stamp tool (🖫) to display its Options palette, and select the Aligned option. Then choose a small feathered brush in the second row of the Brushes palette.

8 Place the rubber stamp tool over the horn next to the scratch. Hold down Alt (Windows) or Option (Mac OS), and click to sample this area. Release the Alt/Option key. Then drag the rubber stamp tool to paint over the scratch.

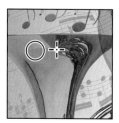

9 Choose File > Save.

Actions

The Actions palette lets you combine a set of commands into a single command or *action* and then execute the action on a single file or multiple files within a folder. With the Actions palette, you can record, play, edit, and delete commands to easily automate common techniques.

Adobe Photoshop offers some ready-made actions you can run on a file or set of files. You'll use one of these actions to add a vignette effect to the image. But first, to get the best results from the vignette, you'll flatten the file's layers into one layer. Then you'll make a selection to set the vignette's border.

While ImageReady also features actions and an Actions palette, actions created in Photoshop are incompatible with ImageReady.

1 Choose Layer > Flatten Image.

2 Hold down the mouse button on the elliptical marquee tool, and drag to the rectangular marquee tool. Then click approximately 1/8-inch in from the upper left corner of the image, and drag diagonally to 1/8-inch in from the lower right corner.

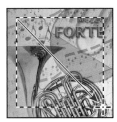

You can now apply the vignette action.

3 To display the Actions palette, choose Window > Show Actions.

4 In the Actions palette, open the Default Actions folder by clicking the folder arrow. Then select Vignette (selection) by clicking its name.

5 Click the Play button (▷) at the bottom of the palette.

6 Accept the default feather radius of 5 pixels in the Feather Selection dialog box, and click OK.

The action is then run on the image, creating the vignette.

7 When the action is complete, choose Layer > Flatten Image, and in the dialog box click OK to discard the hidden layers.

Saving the file

Because you may want to return to a version of the file with all its layers intact, you can use the Save As command to save the flattened file with a new name.

Choose File > Save As, name the file **Tour2.psd**, and save it in the Lessons/Tour2 folder.

You can save files in various formats, depending on how you plan to use the file. For example, you can save a file in JPEG format for display on the World Wide Web.

For more information on file formats, see Chapter 14 in the Photoshop 5.0 User Guide or "Saving and Exporting Images" in Photoshop 5.0 online Help.

Congratulations, you've finished the tour.

For an illustration of the finished artwork, see the color signature.

Lesson 1

1 | Getting to Know the Work Area

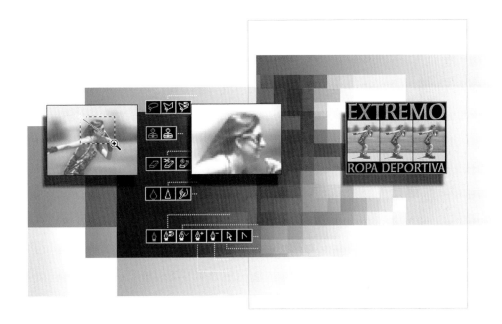

As you work with Adobe Photoshop and Adobe ImageReady, you'll discover that there is often more than one way to accomplish the same task. To make the best use of both applications' extensive editing capabilities, you first must learn to navigate the work area.

In this introduction to the work area, you'll learn how to do the following:

- Open an Adobe Photoshop file.

- Select tools from the toolbox.

- Use viewing options to enlarge and reduce the display of an image.

- Work with palettes.

- Use online Help.

This lesson will take about an hour to complete. The lesson is designed to be done in Adobe Photoshop, but information on using similar functionality in Adobe ImageReady is included where appropriate.

Copy the Lesson01 folder onto your hard drive.

Starting Adobe Photoshop and opening files

When you start Adobe Photoshop, the menu bar, the toolbox, and four palette groups appear on the screen.

1 So that you can see the application's default settings, delete the Adobe Photoshop preferences file to restore the application's default palettes and command settings. For step-by-step instructions on how to delete the preferences file, see "Restoring default preferences" on page 4.

2 Double-click the Adobe Photoshop icon to restart Adobe Photoshop.

Both Photoshop and ImageReady work with bitmapped, digitized images (that is, continuous-tone images that have been converted into a series of small squares, or picture elements, called *pixels*). You can create original artwork in Adobe Photoshop, or you can get images into the program by scanning a photograph, a slide, or a graphic; by capturing a video image; or by importing artwork created in drawing programs. You can also import previously digitized images—such as those produced by a digital camera or by the Kodak® Photo CD process.

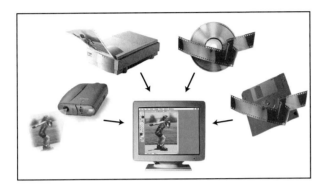

For information on the kinds of files you can use with Adobe Photoshop, see "About file formats" in Chapter 14 of the Photoshop 5.0 User Guide or in "Saving and Exporting Images" of Photoshop 5.0 online Help.

3 Choose File > Open, and open the 01Start.psd file, located in the Lessons/Lesson01 folder.

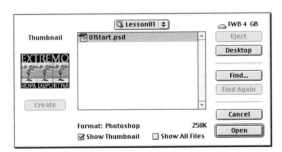

Using the tools

The toolbox contains selection tools, painting and editing tools, foreground and background color selection boxes, and viewing tools. This section introduces the toolbox and shows you how to select tools. As you work through the lessons, you'll learn more about each tool's specific function.

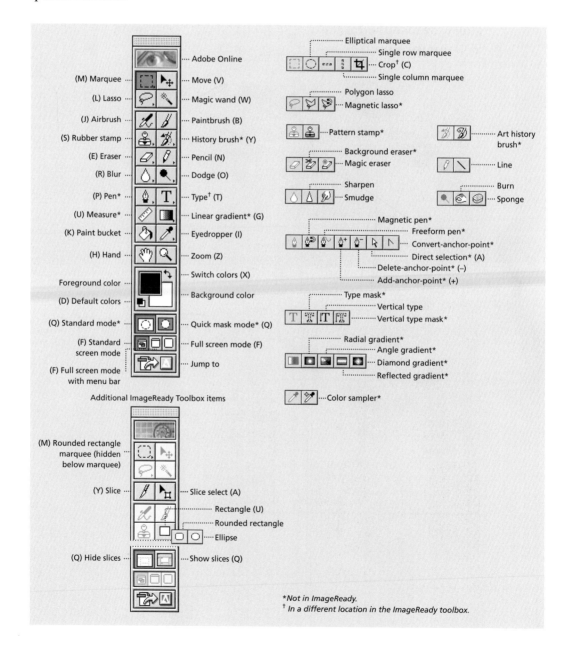

Additional ImageReady Toolbox items

*Not in ImageReady.
† In a different location in the ImageReady toolbox.

For an illustration of the tools, see figure 1-1 in the color signature.

Like most Adobe products, the work areas of Photoshop and ImageReady consist of a menu bar at the top of the work area, a floating toolbox on the left, floating palettes on the right and bottom, and one or more document windows, which you open manually.

Together Photoshop and ImageReady provide a consistent and integrated set of tools for producing sophisticated graphics for print and for the Web. ImageReady includes many tools that will already be familiar to users of Photoshop 5.0.

1 To select a tool, you can either click the tool in the toolbox, or you can press the tool's keyboard shortcut. For example, you can press M to select the marquee tool from the keyboard. Selected tools remain active until you click a different tool.

2 If you don't know the keyboard shortcut for a tool, position the mouse over the tool until its name and shortcut are displayed.

Photoshop and ImageReady use the same keyboard shortcut keys for corresponding keys, with the exceptions of Q, U, and A:

• *In Photoshop, press Q to switch between Quick mask mode and Standard mode; in ImageReady, press Q to show or hide slices.*

• *In Photoshop, press U for the measure tool; in ImageReady, press U for the rectangle, rounded rectangle, and ellipse drawing tools.*

• *Photoshop does not use A; in ImageReady, press A to select a slice.*

All keyboard shortcuts are also listed in the Quick Reference section of online Help. You'll learn how to use online Help later in this lesson.

Some of the tools in the toolbox display a small triangle at the bottom right corner, indicating the presence of additional hidden tools.

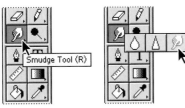

Name and
shortcut displayed   Hidden tools

3 Select hidden tools in any of the following ways:

• Click and hold down the mouse button on a tool that has additional hidden tools. Then drag to the desired tool, and release the mouse button.

• Hold down Alt (Windows) or Option (Mac OS), and click the tool in the toolbox. Each click selects the next hidden tool in the hidden tool sequence.

• Press Shift + the tool's keyboard shortcut repeatedly until the tool you want is selected.

Note: When you click a viewing tool to change the screen display of an image, you must return to the Standard screen mode to see the default work area displayed.

*Standard
screen mode*

Viewing images

You can view your image at any magnification level to 1600% from 0.28% (Photoshop) or 12.5% (ImageReady). Adobe Photoshop displays the percentage of an image's actual size in the title bar. When you use any of the viewing tools and commands, you affect the *display* of the image, not the image's dimensions or file size.

Using the View menu

To enlarge or reduce the view of an image using the View menu, do one of the following:

• Choose View > Zoom In to enlarge the display of the 01Start image.

• Choose View > Zoom Out to reduce the view of the 01Start image.

Each time you choose a Zoom command, the view of the image and the surrounding window are resized. The percentage at which the image is viewed is displayed in the Title bar and at the bottom left corner of the Adobe Photoshop window.

View percentage

You can also use the View menu to fit an image to your screen.

1 Choose View > Fit on Screen. The size of the image and the size of your monitor determine how large the image appears on-screen.

2 Double-click the zoom tool in the toolbox to return to a 100% view.

Using the zoom tool

In addition to the View commands, you can use the zoom tool to magnify and reduce the view of an image.

1 Click the zoom tool ($\mathcal{Q}$) in the toolbox to select the tool, and move the tool pointer onto the Work01 image. Notice that a plus sign appears at the center of the zoom tool.

2 Position the zoom tool over one of the skaters in the Work01 image, and click. The image is magnified to a 200% view.

3 With the zoom tool selected and positioned in the image area, hold down Alt (Windows) or Option (Mac OS). A minus sign appears at the center of the zoom tool ($\mathcal{Q}$).

4 Click once; the view of the image is reduced to a 100% view.

You can also drag a marquee with the zoom tool to magnify a specific area of an image.

5 Drag a marquee around the head of one of the skaters using the zoom tool.

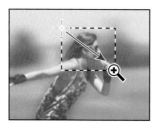

Area selected   *Resulting view*

The percentage at which the area is magnified is determined by the size of the marquee you draw with the zoom tool. (The smaller the marquee you draw, the larger the level of magnification.)

Note: You can draw a marquee with the zoom-in tool to enlarge the view of an image, but you cannot draw a marquee with the zoom-out tool to reduce the view of an image.

You can use the zoom tool to quickly return to a 100% view, regardless of the current magnification level.

6 Double-click the zoom tool in the toolbox to return the Work01 file to a 100% view.

Because the zoom tool is used frequently during the editing process to enlarge and reduce the view of an image, you can select it from the keyboard at any time without deselecting the active tool.

7 To select the zoom tool from the keyboard, hold down spacebar+Ctrl (Windows) or spacebar+Command (Mac OS). Zoom in on the desired area, and then release the keys.

8 To select the zoom-out tool from the keyboard, hold down spacebar+Ctrl+Alt (Windows) or spacebar+Command+Option (Mac OS). Click the desired area to reduce the view of the image, and then release the keys.

Scrolling an image

You use the hand tool to scroll through an image that does not fit in the active window. If the image fits in the active window, the hand tool has no effect when you drag it in the image window.

1 Resize the image window to make it smaller than the image.

2 Click the hand tool in the toolbox. Then drag in the image window to bring another skater into view. As you drag, the image moves with the hand.

3 Like the zoom tool, you can select the hand tool from the keyboard without deselecting the active tool.

4 First, click any tool but the hand tool in the toolbox.

5 Hold down the spacebar to select the hand tool from the keyboard. Drag to reposition the image. Then release the spacebar.

6 Double-click the zoom tool in the toolbox to return the 01Start image to a 100% view.

Note: *To return the window to its original size at 100% view, select Resize Windows to Fit in the Zoom Options palette, and then double-click the zoom tool.*

Using the Navigator palette

The Photoshop Navigator palette lets you scroll an image at different magnification levels without scrolling or resizing an image in the image window. (ImageReady does not have a Navigator palette.)

1 Make sure that the Navigator palette is at the front of the palette group. (If necessary, click the Navigator palette tab, or choose Window > Show Navigator.)

2 In the Navigator palette, drag the slider to the right to about 200% to magnify the view of the skater. As you drag the slider to increase the level of magnification, the red outline in the Navigator window decreases in size.

3 In the Navigator palette, position the pointer inside the red outline. The pointer becomes a hand.

Dragging slider to 200%   *200% view of image*   *View in Navigator palette*

4 Drag the hand to scroll to different parts of the image.

You can also drag a marquee in the Navigator palette to identify the area of the image you want to view.

5 With the pointer still positioned in the Navigator palette, hold down Ctrl (Windows) or Command (Mac OS), and drag a marquee over an area of the image. The smaller the marquee you draw, the greater the magnification level in the image window.

Using the Info bar

The Info bar is positioned at the lower left corner of the application window (Windows) or of the image window (Mac OS). In Photoshop, you can choose from a pop-up menu to display information about a file's size, resolution, view, and positioning on the printed page. In ImageReady, you can choose to display information on the image dimensions, watermark strength, number of undos, download times, and the original and optimized file size. You can also use the ImageReady Info bar to change the view of an image.

Photoshop Info bar

ImageReady Info bar

1 Position the pointer over the triangle in the bottom border of the program window (Windows) or image window (Mac OS).

By default, the image's file size appears. The first value indicates the size if saved as a flattened file with no layer data, the second value indicates the size if saved with all layers and channels.

2 Hold down the mouse button to display the pop-up menu.

You can choose to display the amount of RAM used to process images, how efficiently Photoshop is operating and whether it's using the scratch disk (an Efficiency of less than 100%), and the amount of time it took to complete the last operation. You can also choose to display the selected tool.

💡 *In ImageReady, use the Info bar to change the view of an image by choosing a preset zoom percentage from the percentage pop-up menu at the bottom left of the image window. For complete information on the ImageReady Info bar options, see "Looking at the Work Area" in the ImageReady 2.0 online Help.*

Working with palettes

Palettes help you monitor and modify images. By default, they appear in stacked groups. To show or hide a palette as you work, choose the appropriate Window > Show or Window > Hide command. Show displays the selected palette at the front of its group; Hide conceals the entire group.

Changing the palette display

You can reorganize your work space in various ways. Experiment with several techniques:

• To hide or display all open palettes and the toolbox, press Tab. To hide or display the palettes only, press Shift+Tab.

• To make a palette appear at the front of its group, click the palette's tab.

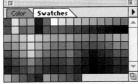

Click the Swatches tab to move it to the front.

• To move an entire palette group, drag its title bar.

• To rearrange or separate a palette group, drag a palette's tab. Dragging a palette outside of an existing group creates a new group.

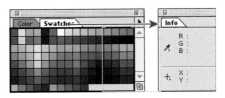

Palettes are grouped.   *Click the palette tab, and drag the palette to separate from group.*

• To move a palette to another group, drag the palette's tab to that group.

• To display a palette menu, position the pointer on the triangle in the upper right corner of the palette, and hold down the mouse button.

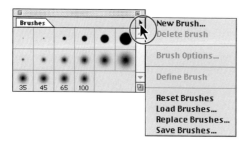

• To change the height of a palette (except the Color, Options, or Info palette), drag its lower right corner. To return the palette to default size, click the minimize/maximize box (Windows) or the resize box (Mac OS) in the right of the title bar. (A second click collapses the palette group.)

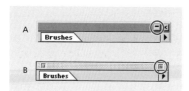

Click to collapse or expand palette.
A. *Windows* **B.** *Mac OS*

• To collapse a group to palette titles only, Alt-click the minimize/maximize box (Windows) or Option-click the resize box (Mac OS). Or double-click a palette's tab. You can still access the menu of a collapsed palette.

🔆 *In ImageReady, to show or hide options for palettes that include hidden options (the Optimize, Color, Type, Layer Options, and Slice palettes), click the Show Options button (◆) on the palette tab to cycle through palette displays, or choose Show Options or Hide Options from the palette menu.*

For the Web: Viewing hexadecimal values for colors in the Info palette

In Photoshop, hexadecimal values for colors are displayed in the Info palette when you select Web Color Mode for one or both color readouts. In ImageReady, hexadecimal values for colors are displayed automatically in the right side of the Info palette, next to RGB color values. The Photoshop and ImageReady Info palettes also display other information, depending on the tool being used.

To view hexadecimal color values in the Photoshop Info palette:

1. *Choose Window > Show Info or click the Info palette tab to view the palette.*

2. *Choose Palette Options from the palette menu.*

3. *Under First Color Readout, Second Color Readout, or both, choose Web Color from the Mode menu.*

4. *Click OK.*

The Info palette displays the hexadecimal equivalents for the RGB values of the color beneath the pointer in the image.

–From the Adobe Photoshop 5.5 User Guide Supplement, Chapter 4, "Optimizing Images for the Web." A similar topic can be found in Adobe ImageReady 2.0 online Help.

Setting the positions of palettes and dialog boxes

The positions of all open palettes and movable dialog boxes are saved by default when you exit the program. Alternatively, you can always start with default palette positions or restore default positions at any time:

• To reset palettes to the default positions, choose File > Preferences > General. Click Reset Palette Locations to Defaults.

In ImageReady, you can also choose Window > Reset Palettes.

• To start always with the preset palette and dialog box positions, choose File > Preferences > General. Deselect Save Palette Locations. The change takes effect the next time you start Adobe Photoshop.

Using context menus

In addition to the menus at the top of your screen, context menus display commands relevant to the active tool, selection, or palette.

To display context menus, position the pointer over the image or over an item in a palette list. Then click with the right mouse button (Windows), or press Control and hold down the mouse button (Mac OS).

Here we've used the blur tool. The Sample Size options are displayed in the tool's context menu. (You access these same options by double-clicking the tool to display its Options palette.)

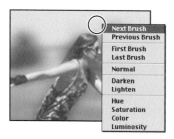

Using online Help

For complete information about using palettes, tools, and the application features, you can use online Help.

Adobe Photoshop and Adobe ImageReady each include complete documentation in online Help plus keyboard shortcuts, full-color galleries of examples, and more detailed information about some procedures.

Online Help is easy to use, because you can look for topics in several ways:

• Scanning a table of contents.

• Searching for keywords.

• Using an index.

• Jumping from topic to topic using related topic links.

First you'll try looking for a topic using the Contents screen.

1 Display online Help:

• In Windows, press F1 to display the Help Contents menu, choose Help > Contents, or choose another topic from the Help menu.

• In Mac OS, choose Help > Help Topics.

Two windows appear: the Topics window for the Photoshop 5.0 online Help system (all of the information in the Photoshop 5.0 User Guide) plus the documentation of features new to Photoshop 5.5 included in the Photoshop 5.5 User Guide Supplement.

When you're using ImageReady, the ImageReady 2.0 Help window appears. The ImageReady help system includes complete documentation of all ImageReady features.

2 Drag the scroll bar or click the arrows to navigate through the contents. The contents are organized in a hierarchy of topics, much like the chapters of a book. Each book icon represents a chapter of information in Help.

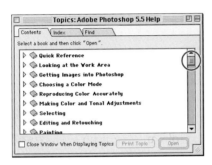 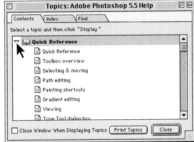

3 Position the pointer on the Quick Reference book, and click to display its contents.

4 Locate the Toolbox overview topic, and double-click to display it. An illustration of the toolbox and toolbar shortcut information appears.

The online Help system is interactive. You can click any red underlined text, called a *link*, to jump to another topic. The pointer icon indicates links and appears when you move the mouse pointer over a link or a hotspot.

5 Position the pointer over a tool in the toolbox, and click. The tool topic appears. At the top of the tool topic, click Next to display the next topic. You can continue to click Next or Previous to display the individual tool topics. You can also click Print to print the topic.

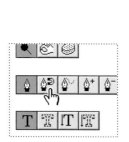

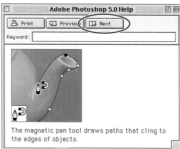

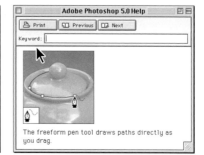

Click on a tool.   *The tool topic appears.*   *Show the next tool topic.*

6 When you have finished browsing the topics, click the Close box to close the topic and return to the toolbox overview.

💡 *In Windows, you can also use context-sensitive Help. Press Shift+F1 (a question mark appears next to the pointer), and choose a command or click in a palette to display the appropriate Help topic. Or with a dialog box open, press F1 to display the Help topic for that dialog box.*

Using keywords, links, and the index

If you can't find the topic you are interested in by scanning the Contents page, then you can try searching using a keyword.

1 Move the pointer to the Keyword text box, and begin typing **Correcting mistakes**. Notice that as soon as you type "cor," the entire phrase appears in the text box. Press Enter or Return to go to that topic.

2 Read through the topic, and if desired, click some of the links to go to the related topics. When you have finished browsing, click the Close box to close the topic window.

You can also search for a topic using the index.

3 In the Topics window, click Index to display index entries. These entries appear alphabetically by topic and subtopic, like the index of a book.

4 In the text box under the instructions in step 1, type the word **background**. Notice that entries for "background" appear as you begin typing. Add an *s* to the entry to change it to **backgrounds**. Then find the subentry "adding" and select it. (You may have to double-click "*backgrounds*" to display the subentries.)

5 Click Display to display the entry.

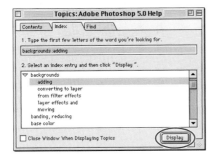

6 When you have finished browsing the topics, click the Close box to close the topic window and return to the toolbox overview.

Using the online galleries

As you work with the Help system, you will find full-color galleries of examples associated with several topics. Some of these galleries are not included in the printed user guide. Throughout online Help, you will find full-color illustrations of various Photoshop features.

1 In the online Help Topics window, click the Find tab. In the empty text box under step 1, type the word **gallery**. Notice that you can refine your search by choosing an option from the pop-up menus to the left. Click Search.

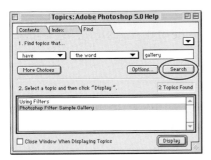

2 In the list that appears, select "Photoshop Filter Sample Gallery," and click Display. (You can also double-click the entry to display it.)

3 Click one of the links to display the filter topic. Use the Next and Previous buttons to browse the topic.

 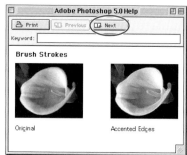

Try looking at another gallery.

4 Click the Find tab again, and type **blending**. In the list that appears, select one of the following:

• Click "Selecting a blending mode," and then click Display.

• Double-click "Specifying layer blending modes" to display the topic. (You may have to scroll to find the topic.) Then click Display.

5 In the topic that appears, click the mode names to see examples of the effects.

6 When you have finished, click the Close box to close the topic. Then click the Help Close box to exit Help.

Using Adobe online services

Another way to get information on Adobe Photoshop or on related Adobe products is to use the Adobe online services. If you have an Internet connection and a Web browser installed on your system, you can access the U.S. Adobe Systems Web site (at www.adobe.com) for information on services, products, and tips pertaining to Photoshop.

Adobe Online provides access to up-to-the-minute information about services, products, and tips for using Adobe products.

1 If you have an Internet connection and an Internet browser installed, choose File > Adobe Online, or click the icon at the top of the toolbox.

2 Click Update to download the latest information, or if you are accessing Adobe Online from Photoshop for the first time or want to change your configuration settings, click Configure.

3 If you clicked Configure in step 2, select configuration options in the Configure dialog box and then click OK:

• In the Update pop-up menu, select an option for updating Adobe Online.

• Select Always Trust Adobe for Authenticating Adobe Online Downloads to enable downloading from Adobe Online.

When you set up Adobe Online to connect to your Web browser, Adobe can either notify you whenever new information is available or automatically download that information to your hard disk. If you choose not to use the Adobe automatic download feature, you can still view and download new files whenever they are available from within the Adobe Online window.

• Select Use Default Browser Proxy Settings (Windows) or Use Internet Config Settings (Mac OS) to use the Internet configuration currently used by your system, or enter new proxy and port settings to be used by ImageReady.

♡ *In ImageReady in Mac OS only: Click Browser to select the browser to be used by ImageReady to access Adobe Online.*

4 Click an area of interest to open the relevant page from the Adobe Web site.

You can easily find information specifically on Photoshop and ImageReady—including tips and techniques, galleries of artwork by Adobe designers and artists around the world, the latest product information, and troubleshooting and technical information. Or you can learn about other Adobe products and news.

5 When you have finished browsing the Adobe page, close the browser and exit it.

Jumping to ImageReady

Now you'll switch to ImageReady. Jumping between the applications lets you use the full feature sets of both applications when preparing graphics for the Web or other purposes, yet still maintain a streamlined workflow. Jumping to another application also saves you from having to close the file in Photoshop and reopen it in the other application.

1 Click the Jump To icon (⬚⬚) in the toolbox. The ImageReady application starts.

You can jump between Photoshop and ImageReady to transfer an image between the two applications for editing, without closing or exiting the originating application. You can also jump to other graphics-editing applications from Photoshop or ImageReady, and jump to HTML editing applications from ImageReady. When you jump to another application, the file remains open in Photoshop or ImageReady while you work in the destination application.

2 Click the Jump To icon in the toolbox, or choose File > Jump To > Adobe Photoshop to return to Photoshop.

If you had made changes to the file in ImageReady, you would be prompted to update the file. You can set Photoshop and ImageReady to automatically update an image that has been modified in a jumped-to application, or you can update the file manually.

Each time an image in Photoshop or ImageReady is updated with changes made in a jumped-to application, a single history state is added to the Photoshop or ImageReady History palette. You can undo the update in Photoshop or ImageReady as you do other states in the History palette. For more information, see "Undoing changes" on page 145 in Lesson 4 of this book.

3 Choose File > Save. Close the file.

You're ready to begin learning how to create and edit images.

Making colors consistent between Photoshop and ImageReady

RGB color display can vary between Photoshop and ImageReady. In Photoshop, you can select from several RGB color spaces when editing images. As a result, images created in Photoshop may use an RGB color space that differs from the monitor RGB color space used by ImageReady. New color management features in ImageReady enable you to adjust RGB color display during image preview to compensate for differences between Photoshop and ImageReady.

In Photoshop, all preview options except Uncompensated are affected by the settings in the Photoshop RGB Setup dialog box. In ImageReady, the Photoshop Compensation preview option is the only one that will communicate with Photoshop's color management system.

To adjust RGB color display in ImageReady to match color display in Photoshop:

Choose View > Preview > Photoshop Compensation.

ImageReady's Photoshop Compensation feature is available only when viewing images saved in Photoshop format from Photoshop 5.0 or later, with both RGB profile embedding and Display Using Monitor Compensation turned on in Photoshop's Profile Setup dialog box.

–From the Photoshop 5.5 User Guide Supplement, Chapter 3, "Using Photoshop and ImageReady Together." A similar topic can be found in ImageReady 2.0 online Help.

Review questions

1 Describe two ways to change your view of an image.

2 How do you select tools in Photoshop or ImageReady?

3 How do you switch between Photoshop and ImageReady?

4 Describe two ways to get more information about Photoshop and ImageReady.

5 Describe two ways to create images in Photoshop and ImageReady.

Review answers

1 You can select commands from the View menu to zoom in or out of an image, or to fit it to your screen; you can also use the zoom tools in the toolbox and click or drag over an image to enlarge or reduce the view. In addition, you can use keyboard shortcuts to magnify or reduce the display of an image. You can also use the Navigator palette to scroll an image or change its magnification without using the image window.

2 To select a tool, you can either click the tool in the toolbox, or you can press the tool's keyboard shortcut. For example, you can press M to select the marquee tool from the keyboard. A selected tool remains active until you click a different tool.

3 You can click the Jump To icon in the toolbox or choose File > Jump To to switch between Photoshop and ImageReady.

4 Adobe Photoshop contains online Help, with all the information in the Photoshop 5.0 User Guide and Photoshop 5.5 User Guide Supplement, plus keyboard shortcuts and some additional information and full-color illustrations. Photoshop also includes a link to the Adobe Systems home page for additional information on services, products, and tips pertaining to Photoshop. ImageReady 2.0 also contains online Help and a link to the Adobe home page.

5 You can create original artwork in Adobe Photoshop or ImageReady, or you can get images into the program by scanning a photograph, a slide, or a graphic; by capturing a video image; or by importing artwork created in drawing programs. You can also import previously digitized images—such as those produced by a digital camera or by the Kodak Photo CD process.

Lesson 2

2 | Working with Selections

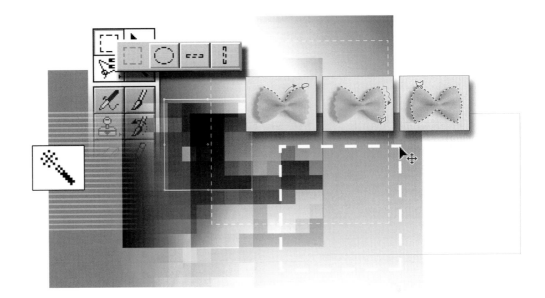

Learning how to select areas of an image is of primary importance—you must first select what you want to affect. Once you've made a selection, only the area within the selection can be edited. Areas outside the selection are protected from change.

In this lesson, you'll learn how to do the following:

- Select parts of an image using a variety of tools.

- Reposition a selection marquee.

- Deselect a selection.

- Move and duplicate a selection.

- Constrain the movement of a selection.

- Choose areas of an image based on proximity or color of pixels.

- Adjust a selection with the arrow keys.

- Add to and subtract from selections.

- Rotate, scale, and transform a selection.

- Combine selection tools.

- Crop an image.

This lesson will take about 40 minutes to complete. The lesson is designed to be done in Adobe Photoshop, but information on using similar functionality in Adobe ImageReady is included where appropriate.

If needed, remove the previous lesson folder from your hard drive, and copy the Lesson02 folder onto it.

Tool overview

In Adobe Photoshop, you can make selections based on size, shape, and color using four basic sets of tools—the marquee, lasso, magic wand, and pen tools. You can reposition your selections using the move tool. You can also use the magic eraser tool to make selections in much the same way you use the magic wand tool.

Note: In this lesson, you will use the marquee, lasso, magic wand, and move tools; for information on the pen tools, see Lesson 7, "Basic Pen Tool Techniques."

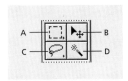

A. Marquee tool
B. Move tool
C. Lasso tool
D. Magic wand tool

The marquee and lasso tool icons contain hidden tools, which you can select by holding down the mouse button on the toolbox icon and dragging to the desired tool in the pop-up menu.

The *rectangular marquee tool* (⬚) lets you select a rectangular area in an image. The *elliptical marquee tool* (○) lets you select elliptical areas. The *rounded rectangle marquee tool* (⬚) in ImageReady lets you select rectangular areas with rounded corners. The *single row and single column marquee tools* (⚬⚬) (⚬) let you select a 1-pixel-high row and 1-pixel-wide column. You can also use the *crop tool* (⌗) to crop an image.

The *lasso tool* (⬭) lets you make a freehand selection around an area. The *polygon lasso tool* (⬭) lets you make a straight-line selection around an area. The *magnetic lasso tool* (⬭) in Photoshop lets you draw a freehand border that snaps to the edges of an area.

The *magic wand tool* (⬭) lets you select parts of an image based on the similarity in color of adjacent pixels. This tool is useful for selecting odd-shaped areas without having to trace a complex outline using the lasso tool.

ImageReady includes the basic marquee selection tools, the lasso and polygon lasso tools, and the magic wand tool familiar to users of Photoshop. For added convenience in working with common shapes, ImageReady adds an additional marquee selection tool: the rounded rectangle marquee tool.

Getting started

Before beginning this lesson, restore the default application settings for Adobe Photoshop. See "Restoring default preferences" on page 4.

You'll start the lesson by viewing the final Lesson file to see what you'll accomplish.

1 Restart Adobe Photoshop.

2 Click Cancel to exit the color management dialog box that appears.

3 Choose File > Open, and open the 02End.psd file, located in the Lessons/Lesson02 folder. An image of a face, constructed using various types of fruits and vegetables, is displayed.

4 When you have finished viewing the file, either leave the End file open on your desktop for reference, or close it without saving changes.

For an illustration of the finished artwork for this lesson, see the gallery at the beginning of the color section.

Now you'll open the start file and begin the lesson.

5 Choose File > Open, and open the 02Start.psd file, located in the Lessons/Lesson02 folder on your hard drive.

Selecting with the rectangular marquee tool

You'll start by practicing selection techniques using the rectangular marquee tool.

1 Click the rectangular marquee tool () in the toolbox.

2 Drag it diagonally from the top left to the bottom right corner of the melon to create a rectangular selection.

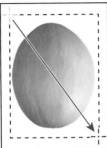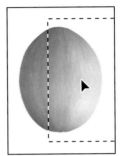

Initial selection   *Marquee tool placed within selection*   *Selection border repositioned*

You can move a selection border after you've created it by positioning the tool within the selection and dragging. Notice that this technique changes the location of the selection border; it does not affect the size or shape of the selection.

3 Place the marquee tool anywhere inside the selection surrounding the melon. The pointer becomes an arrow with a small selection icon next to it.

4 Drag to reposition the border around the melon.

Note: Repositioning techniques for selection borders work with any of the marquee, lasso, and magic wand tools.

If you are still not happy with the selection after repositioning it, you can deselect it and redraw it.

5 Choose Select > Deselect, or click anywhere in the window outside the selection border to deselect the selection.

6 Reselect the melon using the rectangular marquee tool.

   To back up one action at any point in the lesson, choose Edit > Undo. In ImageReady, you can set the number of undos in the ImageReady preferences. (The default is 32.)

Selecting with the elliptical marquee tool

Next you'll use the elliptical marquee tool to select eyes for the face. Note that in most cases, making a new selection replaces the existing selection.

1 Select the zoom tool (🔍), and click twice on the blueberry to zoom in to a 300% view.

2 Hold down the mouse button on the rectangular marquee tool, and drag to the elliptical marquee tool (⬭).

3 Move the pointer over the blueberry, and drag it diagonally from the top left to the bottom right edge of the blueberry to create a selection. Do not release the mouse button.

Repositioning a selection border while creating it

If a selection border isn't placed exactly where you want it, you can adjust its position and size while creating it.

1 Still holding down the mouse button, hold down the spacebar, and drag the selection. The border moves as you drag.

2 Release the spacebar (but not the mouse button), and drag again. Notice that when you drag without the spacebar, the size and shape of the selection change, but its point of origin does not.

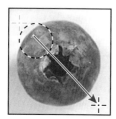  

Incorrect point of origin   *Corrected point of origin*   *Adjusted border*
(Click and drag)   *(Spacebar depressed)*   *(Spacebar released)*

3 When the selection border is positioned and sized correctly, release the mouse button.

Selecting from a center point

Sometimes it's easier to make elliptical or rectangular selections by drawing a selection from the center point of the object to the outside edge. Using this method, you'll reselect the blueberry.

1 Choose Select > Deselect.

2 Position the marquee tool at the approximate center of the blueberry.

3 Click and begin dragging. Then without releasing the mouse button, hold down Alt (Windows) or Option (Mac OS) and continue dragging the selection to the blueberry's outer edge. Notice that the selection is centered over its starting point.

4 When you have the entire blueberry selected, release the mouse button first and then Alt/Option.

If necessary, adjust the selection border using one of the methods you learned earlier.

Moving a selection

Now you'll use the move tool to move the blueberry onto the carrot slice to create an eye for the face. Then you'll duplicate and move the selection to make a second eye.

1 Make sure that the blueberry is selected. Then click the move tool (‖+), and position the pointer within the blueberry's selection. The pointer becomes an arrow with a pair of scissors to indicate that dragging the selection will cut it from its present location and move it to the new location.

2 Drag the blueberry onto the carrot slice.

*Move tool placed
within blueberry
selection*

*Blueberry moved onto
carrot slice*

3 Choose Select > Deselect.

4 Choose File > Save.

Moving and duplicating simultaneously

Next you'll move and duplicate a selection simultaneously.

1 Choose View > Fit on Screen to resize the document to fit on your screen.

2 Select the elliptical marquee tool.

3 Drag a selection around the carrot slice containing the blueberry. If necessary, adjust the selection border using one of the methods you learned earlier.

4 Click the move tool, hold down Alt (Windows) or Option (Mac OS), and position the pointer within the selection. The pointer becomes a double arrow, which indicates that a duplicate will be made when you move the selection.

5 Continue holding down Alt/Option, and drag a duplicate of the eye onto the left side of the melon face. Release the mouse button and Alt/Option, but do not deselect the eye.

Holding down Shift when you move a selection constrains the movement horizontally or vertically. Using this technique, you'll drag a copy of the left eye to the right side of the face so that the two eyes are level.

6 Hold down Shift+Alt (Windows) or Shift+Option (Mac OS), and drag a copy of the eye to the right side of the face.

7 Choose File > Save.

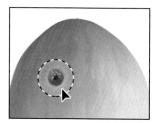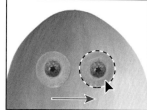

Eye moved onto left side of face   *Duplicate of eye moved with Shift+Alt/Option*

Moving with a keyboard shortcut

Next you'll select the kiwi fruit for the melon's mouth and then move it onto the melon using a keyboard shortcut. The shortcut allows you to temporarily access the move tool instead of selecting it from the toolbox.

1 Select the elliptical marquee tool from the toolbox.

2 Drag a selection around the kiwi fruit using one of the methods you learned earlier.

3 With the marquee tool still selected, hold down Ctrl (Windows) or Command (Mac OS), and position the pointer within the selection. A pair of scissors appears with the pointer to indicate the selection will be cut from its current location.

4 Drag the kiwi mouth onto the face. Do not deselect.

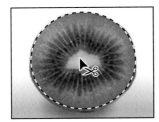
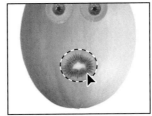

Selection to be cut   Selection moved onto melon

Moving with the arrow keys

You can make minor adjustments to the position of a selection using the arrow keys, which allow you to nudge the selection 1 pixel or 10 pixels at a time.

Note: The arrow keys adjust the position of a selection only if you've already moved the selection or if you have the move tool selected. If you try the arrow keys on a selection that has not yet been moved, they will adjust the selection border, not the part of the image that is selected.

1 Press the Up Arrow (⬆) key a few times to move the mouth upward. Notice that each time you press the arrow key, the mouth moves in 1-pixel increments. Experiment with the other arrow keys to see how they affect the selection.

Sometimes the border around a selected area can distract you as you make adjustments. You can hide the edges of a selection temporarily without actually deselecting and then display the selection border once you've completed the adjustments.

2 Choose View > Hide Edges. The selection border around the mouth disappears.

3 Now hold down Shift, and press an arrow key. Notice that the selection moves in 10-pixel increments.

4 Use the arrow keys to nudge the mouth until it is positioned where you want it. Then choose View > Show Edges.

5 Choose File > Save.

Copying selections or layers

You can use the move tool to copy selections as you drag them within or between images. Or you can copy and move selections using the Copy, Copy Merged, Cut, and Paste commands. Dragging with the move tool saves memory because the Clipboard is not used as it is with the Copy, Copy Merged, Cut, and Paste commands.

Keep in mind that when a selection or layer is pasted between images with different resolutions, the pasted data retains its pixel dimensions. This can make the pasted portion appear out of proportion to the new image. Use the Image Size command to make the source and destination images the same resolution before copying and pasting.

Photoshop and ImageReady contain several copy and paste commands:

- *The Copy command copies the selected area on the active layer.*
- *The Copy Merged command makes a merged copy of all the visible layers in the selected area.*
- *The Paste command pastes a cut or copied selection into another part of the image or into another image as a new layer.*
- *The Paste Into command (Photoshop) pastes a cut or copied selection inside another selection in the same image or different image. The source selection is pasted onto a new layer, and the destination selection border is converted into a layer mask.*

–From the Adobe Photoshop 5.0 User Guide, Chapter 7, "Selecting." A similar topic can be found in ImageReady 2.0 online Help.

Selecting with the magic wand

The magic wand tool lets you select adjacent pixels in an image based on their similarity in color. You'll use the magic wand tool to select the pear tomato, which you'll use as a nose for the face.

1 Double-click the magic wand tool (✎) in the toolbox to select the tool and display its Options palette.

Note: *Most tools in the toolbox come with their own Options palettes, which allow you to change the way the tools work.*

In the Magic Wand Options palette, the Tolerance setting controls how many similar tones of a color are selected when you click an area. The default value is 32, indicating that 32 similar lighter tones and 32 similar darker tones will be selected.

2 For Tolerance, enter **50** to increase the number of shades that will be selected.

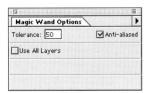

3 Click the magic wand tool anywhere within the pear tomato. Most of it will be selected.

4 To select the remaining area of the pear tomato, hold down Shift, and click the unselected areas. Notice that a plus sign appears with the magic wand pointer, indicating that you're adding to the current selection.

Initial selection   *Adding to selection*   *Complete selection*
                        (Shift key depressed)

5 When the pear tomato is completely selected, hold down Ctrl (Windows) or Command (Mac OS), position the pointer within the selection, and drag the tomato nose onto the melon face.

6 Choose Select > Deselect.

7 Choose File > Save.

Selecting with the lasso tool

You can use the lasso tool to make selections that require both freehand and straight lines. You'll select a bow tie for the face using the lasso tool this way. It takes a bit of practice to use the lasso tool to alternate between straight-line and freehand selections—if you make a mistake while you're selecting the bow tie, simply deselect and start again.

1 Select the zoom tool, and click twice on the bow tie pasta to enlarge its view to 300%.

2 Select the lasso tool (⌒). Starting at the top left corner of the bow tie pasta, drag to the right to create a freehand outline across the curves at the top of the bow tie. Continue holding down the mouse button.

3 To select the right edge of the bow tie, hold down Alt (Windows) or Option (Mac OS), release the mouse button, and then begin outlining with short, straight lines by clicking along the edge. (Notice that the pointer changes from the lasso icon to the polygon lasso icon.) When you reach the bottom right corner of the bow tie, do not release the mouse button.

Freehand outline with lasso tool

Straight-line outline with polygon lasso tool

Completed selection (outline crosses starting point)

4 Release Alt/Option, and drag to the left to create a freehand outline across the bottom of the bow tie. (The pointer returns to the lasso icon.)

5 Hold down Alt/Option again, and click the mouse button along the left edge of the bow tie to draw straight lines.

6 To complete the selection, make sure that the last straight line crosses the start of the selection, release Alt/Option, and then release the mouse button.

7 Choose View > Fit on Screen to resize the document to fit on your screen.

8 Hold down Ctrl (Windows) or Command (Mac OS), and drag the bow tie selection to the bottom of the melon face.

9 Choose File > Save.

Adding and subtracting selections

Holding down Shift while you are selecting an area adds to the current selection. Holding down Alt (Windows) or Option (Mac OS) subtracts from the selection. Now you'll use these techniques with the lasso tool to perfect a rough selection of the mushroom image. The mushroom will become a hat for the melon face.

1 Select the zoom tool, and click twice on the mushroom to enlarge its view to 300%.

2 Select the lasso tool, and drag a rough outline around the mushroom (include some of the area outside the mushroom and some of the stem).

3 Hold down Shift. A plus sign appears with the lasso tool pointer.

4 Drag the lasso tool around an area you want to add to the selection. Then release the mouse button. The area is added to the current selection.

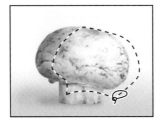  

Initial selection   *Adding to selection*   *Result*
                              (Shift key depressed)

Note: If you release the mouse button while drawing a selection with the lasso tool, the selection closes itself by drawing a straight line between the starting point and the point where you release the mouse. To create a more precise border, end the selection by crossing the starting point.

Next you'll remove, or subtract, part of the selection.

5 Hold down Alt (Windows) or Option (Mac OS). A minus sign appears with the lasso tool pointer.

6 Drag the lasso tool around an area you want to remove from the selection. Then repeat the process until you've finished removing all the unwanted parts of the selection.

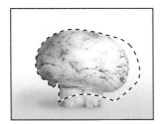  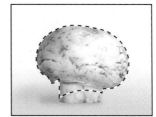

Selection   *Subtracting from selection*   *Result*
                           (Alt/Option depressed)

7 Choose View > Fit on Screen.

8 To move the mushroom hat onto the melon head, hold down Alt+Ctrl (Windows) or Option+Command (Mac OS), and drag a copy of the mushroom to the top of the melon.

9 Choose File > Save.

Selecting with the magnetic lasso

You can use the magnetic lasso tool in Photoshop to make freehand selections of areas with high-contrast edges. When you draw with the magnetic lasso, the border automatically snaps to the edge you are tracing. You can also control the direction of the tool's path by clicking the mouse to place occasional fastening points in the selection border. (There is no magnetic lasso tool in ImageReady.)

You'll now make an ear for the melon face by using the magnetic lasso to select the red part of the grapefruit slice.

1 Select the zoom tool, and click the grapefruit slice to zoom in to a 200% view.

2 Hold down the mouse button on the lasso tool in the toolbox, and drag to the magnetic lasso tool (🔾) to select it.

3 Now click once at the lower left corner of the red flesh of the grapefruit slice, release the mouse button, and begin tracing the outline of the flesh by dragging to the right over the curved upper edge. Notice that the tool snaps to the edge and automatically puts in fastening points.

If you think the tool is not following the edge closely enough (in low-contrast areas), you can place your own fastening point in the border by clicking the mouse button. You can add as many fastening points as you feel are necessary. You can also remove fastening points and back up in the path by pressing Delete and moving the mouse back to the last remaining fastening point.

4 When you reach the lower right corner of the grapefruit flesh, double-click the mouse button, which signals the magnetic lasso tool to return to the starting point and close the selection. Notice that the tool automatically follows the remaining edge of the flesh as it completes the border.

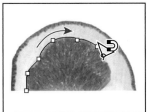 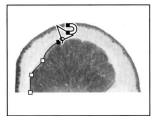 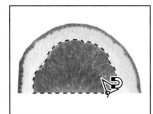

Laying down fastening points   *Removing fastening points*   *Double-clicking at corner to close path*

You can now move the selected part of the grapefruit next to the melon.

5 Double-click the hand tool (✋) to fit the image on-screen.

6 Click the move tool, and drag the grapefruit ear to the middle of the left side of the melon face. Do not deselect.

7 Choose File > Save.

Softening the edges of a selection

You have two ways to smooth the hard edges of a selection.

Anti-aliasing smooths the jagged edges of a selection by softening the color transition between edge pixels and background pixels. Since only the edge pixels change, no detail is lost. Anti-aliasing is useful when cutting, copying, and pasting selections to create composite images. Anti-aliasing is available for the lasso, polygon lasso, magnetic lasso, elliptical marquee, and magic wand tools. (Double-click the tool to display its Options palette.) You must specify this option before using these tools. Once a selection is made, you cannot add anti-aliasing.

Feathering blurs edges by building a transition boundary between the selection and its surrounding pixels. This blurring can cause some loss of detail at the edge of the selection. You can define feathering for the marquee, lasso, polygon lasso, or magnetic lasso tool as you use the tool, or you can add feathering to an existing selection. Feathering effects become apparent when you move, cut, or copy the selection.

• To use anti-aliasing, double-click the marquee, lasso, polygon lasso, or magnetic lasso tool to display its Options palette. Then select Anti-aliased in the Options palette for the selected tool.

• To define a feathered edge for a selection tool, double-click the marquee, lasso, polygon lasso, or magnetic lasso tool to display its Options palette. Then enter a Feather value in the Options palette. This value defines the width of the feathered edge and can range from 1 to 250 pixels.

• To define a feathered edge for an existing selection, choose Select > Feather. Then enter a value for the Feather Radius, and click OK.

–From the Adobe Photoshop 5.0 User Guide, Chapter 7, "Selecting." A similar topic can be found in ImageReady 2.0 online Help.

Transforming a selection

Next you'll use the Free Transform command to rotate and scale the melon's left ear, and then you'll duplicate and flip a copy to create a right ear.

1 Choose Edit > Free Transform. A bounding box appears around the ear selection.

2 To rotate the ear, position the pointer outside a corner handle until you see a double-headed arrow, and then drag in the direction you want the ear to rotate. Notice that the ear rotates around the selection's center point (⬦).

3 To scale the ear, position the pointer directly on one of the corner handles, and drag to reduce the size of the ear. To scale the ear proportionately, hold down Shift as you drag.

4 To reposition the ear, place your pointer within the bounding box, but not on the center point, and drag. (If you place the pointer on the center point and drag, you will move the center point.)

[?] For information on working with the center point in a transformation, see "Transforming objects in two dimensions" in Chapter 8 of the Photoshop 5.0 User Guide or "Editing and Retouching" of Photoshop 5.0 online Help. A similar topic can be found in ImageReady 2.0 online Help.

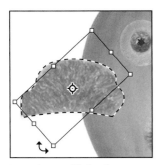 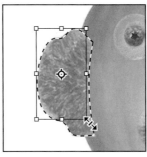 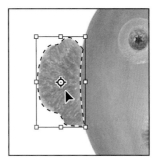

Dragging outside border to rotate ear   *Dragging on corner to scale ear*   *Dragging within border to reposition ear*

💡 *If you don't like the results of a Free Transform, press the Escape key and start over.*

5 When you have the ear positioned correctly, press Enter (Windows) or Return (Mac OS) to apply the transformation. The ear remains selected.

Now you'll move a copy of the ear to the right side of the face, flip the ear horizontally, and fine-tune its placement.

6 Position the pointer within the ear selection, hold down Shift+Alt (Windows) or Shift+Option (Mac OS), and drag a copy of the ear to the right side of the face.

7 Choose Edit > Transform > Flip Horizontal.

8 If necessary, place the pointer within the selection, and drag to reposition it next to the melon face.

9 If necessary, choose Edit > Free Transform, rotate the ear to fit the right side of the face, and press Enter (Windows) or Return (Mac OS) to complete the transformation.

10 Choose File > Save.

Combining selection tools

As you already know, the magic wand tool makes selections based on color. If an object you want to select is on a solid-colored background, it can be much easier to select the object and the background and then use the magic wand tool to subtract the background color, leaving the desired object selected.

You'll see how this works by using the rectangular marquee tool and the magic wand tool to select radish eyebrows for the face.

1 Hold down the mouse button on the elliptical marquee tool, and drag to the rectangular marquee tool.

2 Drag a selection around the radishes. Notice that some of the white background is included in the selection.

At this point, the radishes and the white background area are selected. You'll subtract the white area from the selection, resulting in only the radishes being selected.

3 Click the magic wand tool in the toolbox; then hold down Alt (Windows) or Option (Mac OS). A minus sign appears with the magic wand pointer.

4 Click anywhere in the white area surrounding the radishes. Now only the radishes are selected.

Initial selection   *Subtracting from selection with*   *Result*
Alt/Option magic wand

5 To duplicate and move the radish eyebrow to the melon face, hold down Alt+Ctrl (Windows) or Option+Command (Mac OS), and drag the radish above the left eye on the melon face. Do not deselect.

Left eyebrow placed with Alt+Ctrl/Option+ Command

Right eyebrow placed with Shift+Alt+Ctrl/ Shift+Option+Command

Right eyebrow flipped horizontally

6 Hold down Shift+Alt+Ctrl (Windows) or Shift+Option+Command (Mac OS), position the pointer within the selection, and drag to duplicate and reposition another eyebrow above the right eye.

7 Choose Edit > Transform > Flip Horizontal to adjust the right eyebrow. If you like, reposition the eyebrow using any of the methods you've learned.

8 Choose File > Save.

Cropping the completed image

To complete the artwork, you'll crop the image to a final size.

In both Photoshop and ImageReady, you can use either the crop tool or the Crop command to crop an image. In ImageReady, you can decide whether to delete or discard the area outside of a rectangular selection or whether to hide the area outside of the selection. In ImageReady, you can also use the Trim command to discard a border area around the edge of the image, based on transparency or edge color.

   In ImageReady, use the Crop command or the crop tool set to Hide when creating animations with elements which move from off-screen into the live image area.

1 Choose the crop tool ( ) from the toolbox, or press C to switch from the current tool to the crop tool. The crop tool is located in the hidden tools palette under the marquee tool.

Note: *In ImageReady, the crop tool is next to the type tool—it is not hidden.*

2 Move the pointer into the image window, and drag diagonally from the top left to the bottom right corner of the completed artwork to create a crop marquee.

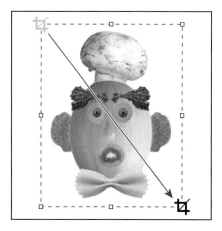

3 If you need to reposition the crop marquee, position the pointer anywhere inside the marquee and drag.

4 If you want to resize the marquee, drag a handle.

5 When the marquee is positioned where you want it, press Enter (Windows) or Return (Mac OS) to crop the image.

6 Choose File > Save.

The fruit-and-vegetable face is complete.

For the Web: Creating evenly spaced buttons for a Web page

One of the most common tasks when designing Web pages is to create a column of buttons which are used to link to other pages in the Web site. Using a background grid in Adobe Photoshop, you can quickly create identical and evenly spaced buttons from selections using the rectangular marquee tool. These buttons can then be stylized in ImageReady in preparation for the Web. Here's a way to create the column of buttons, and then to add a style to create the illusion of three-dimensional buttons.

1 Start Adobe Photoshop, and choose File > New. Name the new file, size it to fit the buttons you want to create (we chose 3 inches wide by 4.5 inches tall), choose the Transparent option, and click OK.

2 Choose File > Preferences > Guides and Grid. Set the Gridlines Every option to the height of your planned buttons (we chose 0.5 inches), the Subdivisions option to 1, and click OK.

Note: *Grids are only available in Photoshop.*

3 To make the grid visible, choose View > Show Grid.

4 Choose View > Snap to Grid if the command is not already selected. (Snap to Grid is selected if there is a check mark next to the command.)

5 Select the rectangular marquee tool (▢), and draw a rectangular selection one grid line high by four grid lines wide (or as wide as you want your buttons to be). Notice that the marquee snaps to the nearest grid line.

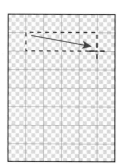

6 Choose Window > Show Color.

7 Choose Web Color Sliders from the Color palette menu to ensure that you will choose a Web-safe color for your button.

8 Select a color in the Color palette. (We chose blue.)

9 Select the paint bucket tool (🖌), and click on the rectangle to paint it.

10 To duplicate the rectangle, hold down the Shift+Ctrl+Alt keys (Windows) or the Shift+Command+Option keys (Mac OS), and drag two grid lines down from the original rectangle. (Holding Ctrl+Alt/Command+Option as you drag duplicates the selection. Holding Shift constrains the newly created rectangle along the horizontal or (in this case) vertical axis). Repeat this process to add the third and fourth rectangles. You should now have four buttons spaced evenly by two grid lines each.

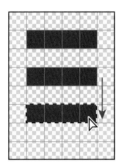

11 Choose File > Save to save your new buttons.

12 Click the Jump To button at the bottom of the toolbox to jump to the ImageReady application.

13 Choose Window > Show Styles.

14 In the Style palette, apply a style to your rectangles (we chose shiny red buttons). To apply the style, drag from the Style palette onto any of the buttons in the main window and release the mouse button. The button style is automatically applied to all of the buttons on the layer.

If you want, you can now add text to the buttons using the text tool (T). When you are finished, save your artwork. You can now use the buttons in your Web page design.

Review questions

1 Once you've made a selection, what area of the image can be edited?

2 How do you add to and subtract from a selection?

3 How can you move a selection while you're drawing it?

4 When drawing a selection with the lasso tool, how should you finish drawing the selection to ensure that the selection is the shape you want?

5 How does the magic wand tool determine which areas of an image to select? What is tolerance, and how does it affect a selection?

Review answers

1 Only the area within the selection can be edited.

2 To add to a selection, hold down Shift, and then drag or click the active selection tool on the area you want to add to the selection. To subtract from a selection, hold down Alt (Windows) or Option (Mac OS), and then drag or click the active selection tool on the area you want to remove from the selection.

3 Without releasing the mouse button, hold down the spacebar, and drag to reposition the selection.

4 To make sure that the selection is the shape you want, end the selection by dragging across the starting point of the selection. If you start and stop the selection at different points, Photoshop or ImageReady draws a straight line between the start point of the selection and the end point of the selection.

5 The magic wand selects adjacent pixels based on their similarity in color. The Tolerance setting determines how many shades of color the magic wand will select. The higher the tolerance setting, the more shades the magic wand selects.

PROFESSIONAL 72 mm

Lesson 3

In this lesson, you'll learn how to do the following:

- Organize your artwork on layers.
- Create a new layer.
- View and hide layers.
- Select layers.
- Remove artwork on layers.
- Reorder layers to change the placement of artwork in the image.
- Apply modes to layers to vary the effect of artwork on the layer.
- Link layers to affect them simultaneously.
- Apply a gradient to a layer.
- Add text and layer effects to a layer.
- Save a copy of the file with the layers flattened.

This lesson will take about 40 minutes to complete. The lesson is designed to be done in Adobe Photoshop, but information on using similar functionality in Adobe ImageReady is included where appropriate.

If needed, remove the previous lesson folder from your hard drive, and copy the Lesson03 folder onto it.

Organizing artwork on layers

Every Photoshop file contains one or more *layers*. New files are generally created with a *background*, which contains a color or an image that shows through the transparent areas of subsequent layers. You can view and manipulate layers with the Layers palette. ImageReady files do not contain backgrounds but do contain layers.

All new layers in an image are transparent until you add artwork (pixel values). Working with layers is analogous to placing portions of a drawing on sheets of acetate: Individual sheets of acetate may be edited, repositioned, and deleted without affecting the other sheets, and when the sheets are stacked, the entire drawing is visible.

Note: ImageReady does not support backgrounds. If you jump from Photoshop to ImageReady, your background will be converted to an ImageReady layer (Layer 0). If you make changes in ImageReady and then jump back to Photoshop, Layer 0 remains a layer—it does not convert back to a background.

For complete information on backgrounds and converting backgrounds to layers, see Chapter 11 in the Photoshop 5.0 User Guide or "Using Layers" in Photoshop 5.0 online Help. A similar topic can be found in ImageReady 2.0 online Help.

Getting started

Before beginning this lesson, restore the default application settings for Adobe Photoshop. See "Restoring default preferences" on page 4.

You'll start the lesson by viewing the final Lesson file to see what you'll accomplish.

1 Restart Adobe Photoshop.

2 Click Cancel to exit the color management dialog box that appears.

3 Choose File > Open, and open the 03End.psd file, located in the Lessons/Lesson03 folder.

4 When you have finished viewing the file, either leave the End file open on your desktop for reference, or close it without saving changes.

For an illustration of the finished artwork for this lesson, see the gallery at the beginning of the color section.

Now, you'll open the start file and begin the lesson by working with the image as you learn about the Layers palette and layer options.

5 Choose File > Open, and open the 03Start.psd file, located in the Lessons/Lesson03 folder on your hard drive.

Creating and viewing layers

Now you'll create a new layer in the 03Start.psd file by bringing in an image from another file.

1 Choose File > Open, and open the Clock.psd file in the Lesson03 folder.

Clock image in Clock.psd   *Clock image moved into 03Start.psd*

2 Select the move tool (➤✛). Then hold down Shift and drag the image in Clock.psd into the 03Start.psd file. Place it on top of the image of the keyboard. (Holding down Shift when dragging artwork into a new file centers the art on the new file's image.) The clock now appears on its own layer, Layer 1, in the 03Start.psd file's Layers palette.

3 Close the Clock.psd file.

4 If the Layers palette is not visible on your screen, choose Window > Show Layers. If you want to expand the Layers palette, click the minimize/maximize box (Windows) or the resize box (Mac OS) at the top of the palette.

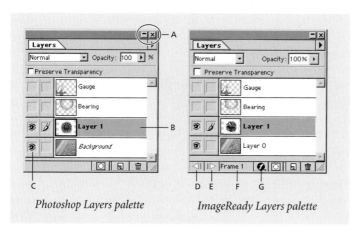

Photoshop Layers palette   *ImageReady Layers palette*

A. *Minimize/maximize or resize box* **B.** *New layer (clock image) added to palette*
C. *Show/hide column* **D.** *Previous animation frame button* **E.** *Next animation frame button* **F.** *Current animation frame* **G.** *Effects menu*

You can use the Layers palette to hide, view, reposition, delete, rename, and merge layers. The Layers palette displays all layers with the layer name and a thumbnail of the layer's image. The thumbnail is automatically updated as you edit the layer.

You will now use the Layers Options dialog box to rename Layer 1 with a more descriptive name.

5 In the Layers palette, double-click Layer 1.

6 In the Layer Options dialog box, type the name **Clock,** and click OK. Layer 1 is now renamed Clock in the Layers palette.

The Layers palette shows that 03Start.psd contains three layers in addition to the Clock layer, some of which are visible and some of which are hidden. The eye icon (👁) to the far left of a layer name in the palette indicates that the layer is visible. You can hide or show a layer by clicking this icon.

7 Click the eye icon next to the Clock layer to hide the clock. Click again to redisplay it.

Creating a layered image

Adobe Photoshop lets you create up to 100 layers in an image, each with its own blending mode and opacity. However, the amount of memory in your system may put a lower limit on the number of layers possible in a single image. Newly added layers appear above the selected layer in the Layers palette. You can add layers to an image in a variety of ways:

- *By creating new layers or turning selections into layers.*
- *By converting a background to a regular layer or adding a background to an image.*
- *By pasting selections into the image.*
- *By creating type using the horizontal type tool or vertical type tool.*

–From the Adobe Photoshop 5.0 User Guide, Chapter 11,"Using Layers." A similar topic can be found in ImageReady 2.0 online Help.

Selecting and removing artwork on a layer

Notice that when you moved the clock image onto the keyboard in 03Start.psd, you also moved the white area surrounding the clock. This opaque area blocks out part of the keyboard image, since the clock layer sits on top of the keyboard, or background.

Now you'll remove the white area from around the clock image on the Clock layer.

1 Make sure that the Clock layer is selected. To select the layer, click the layer name in the Layers palette. The layer is highlighted, and a paintbrush icon appears to the left of the layer name, indicating the layer is active.

2 To make the opaque areas on this layer more obvious, hide the keyboard by clicking the eye icon in the Layers palette to the left of the background name. The keyboard image disappears, and the clock appears against a checkerboard background. The checkerboard indicates transparent areas on the active layer.

3 Now click and hold down the mouse button on the eraser tool in the toolbox. Drag to the magic eraser (), and release the mouse button.

In ImageReady, the magic eraser is the default eraser tool. You can just click this tool to select it.

4 Click the white area surrounding the clock. Notice that the checkerboard fills in where the white area had been, indicating this area is now transparent also.

5 Turn the background back on by clicking the eye icon column next to its name. The keyboard image now shows through where the white area on the Clock layer was removed.

Opaque white area   *Opaque area erased*   *Background turned on*

Rearranging layers

The order in which the layers of an image are organized is called the *stacking order*. The stacking order of layers determines how the image is viewed—you can change the order to make certain parts of the image appear in front of or behind other layers.

Now you'll rearrange layers in the 03Start.psd file so that the clock image moves in front of the other images in the file.

1 Make the Gauge and Bearing layers visible by clicking the eye icon column next to their layer names. Notice that the clock image is partly covered up by the other images in the file.

Making all layers visible   *Result*

2 In the Layers palette drag the Clock layer up to position it at the top of the palette. When you see a thick black line above the Gauge layer, release the mouse button. The Clock layer moves to the top of the palette's stacking order, and the clock image appears in front of the other images.

Repositioning Clock layer   *Result*

Changing the opacity and mode of a layer

The clock image now blocks out any images that lie on layers below it. You can reduce the opacity of the clock layer, which allows other layers to show through it. You can also apply different blending modes to the layer, which affect how the clock image blends with the layers below it. You can also apply blending modes to layers in ImageReady.

1 With the Clock layer selected press the arrow next to the Opacity text box in the Layers palette, and drag the slider to 50%. The clock becomes partially transparent, and you can see the layers underneath. Note that the change in opacity affects only the image areas on the Clock layer.

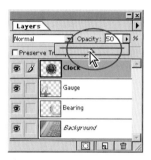
Changing opacity

Result

2 Next try applying some blending modes to the Clock layer to see their effects. Choose Difference and then Darken from the mode menu (to the left of the Opacity text box), and notice the effect on the clock image. Then select the Screen mode (the mode we used for our example) and change the opacity to 90%.

Changing mode and opacity

Result

3 Choose File > Save.

 For complete information on blending modes, see "Selecting a blending mode" in Chapter 9 of the Photoshop 5.0 User Guide or in "Painting" of Photoshop 5.0 online Help. A similar topic can be found in ImageReady 2.0 online Help.

Specifying layer options

The layer options let you change a layer's name and opacity and control how the pixels in the layer blend with the layers underneath. It's important to remember that the opacity and blending modes chosen for a specific layer interact with the opacity and mode settings for the tools you use to paint and edit the pixels on the layer.

For example, suppose you are working on a layer that uses the Dissolve mode and an opacity of 50%. If you paint on this layer using the paintbrush tool set to Normal mode with an opacity of 100%, the paint will appear in Dissolve mode with a 50% opacity because this is the maximum the layer can display. On the other hand, suppose you are working on a layer created using Normal mode and 100% opacity. If you use the eraser tool with an opacity of 50%, only 50% of the paint will disappear as you erase.

–From the Adobe Photoshop 5.0 User Guide, Chapter 11, "Using Layers." A similar topic can be found in ImageReady 2.0 online Help.

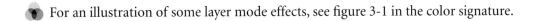 For an illustration of some layer mode effects, see figure 3-1 in the color signature.

Linking layers

An efficient way to work with layers is to link two or more of them together. By linking layers, you can move and transform them simultaneously, thereby maintaining their alignment with each other. ImageReady supports layer linking.

Now you'll now link the Clock and Bearing layers, and then reposition, scale, and rotate them together.

1 Select the move tool, and drag the clock to the bottom right corner of the collage so that just the top half of the clock face is visible.

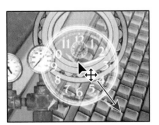

Dragging clock image   *Result*

2 With the Clock layer active in the Layers palette, click the small box to the right of the eye icon for the Bearing layer. A link icon appears in the box, indicating that the Bearing layer is linked to the Clock layer. (The active or selected layer does not display a link icon when you create linked layers.)

3 Position the move tool in the image window, and drag toward the top margin of the image. The clock and bearing images move simultaneously.

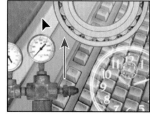

*Linking Clock layer to
Bearing layer*

Moving layers simultaneously

Now you'll try scaling and rotating the linked layers by using the Free Transform command.

4 Choose Edit > Free Transform. A transformation bounding box appears around the clock face.

5 To rotate the clock, position the pointer outside one of the handles until you see a double-headed arrow, drag the face clockwise, and then release the mouse button. The bearing rotates as well.

6 Hold down Shift, drag on a handle of the bounding box, and scale the clock and bearing to a smaller size.

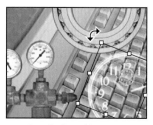

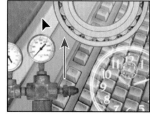

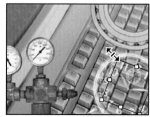

Rotating clock and bearing   *Scaling clock and bearing*   *Repositioning clock and bearing*

7 If necessary, position the pointer inside the bounding box, and drag to reposition the two images.

8 Press Enter (Windows) or Return (Mac OS) to apply the transformation changes.

Adding a gradient to a layer

Next you'll create a new layer and add a gradient effect to it. You can add a layer to a file with the New Layer command, which creates a transparent layer with no artwork on it. If you then add a special effect to the layer, such as a gradient, the effect is applied to any layers stacked below the new layer.

In ImageReady, which does not have a gradient tool, you could apply a Gradient/Pattern layer effect from the Layers palette.

Note: The Gradient/Pattern effects that you apply in ImageReady are not displayed when you view the file in Photoshop. However, the effects are preserved in the image. An alert icon in Photoshop indicates that the effects are present on the layer. The pattern and gradient effects are not altered in Photoshop unless you rasterize the layer on which the effects are applied.

For complete information on layers and layer effects, see Chapter 11 in the Photoshop 5.0 User Guide or "Using Layers" in Photoshop 5.0 online Help; also "Using Layers" in Chapter 3 of the Photoshop 5.5 User Guide Supplement or in "Using Photoshop and ImageReady Together" of Photoshop 5.5 online Help. Similar topics can be found in ImageReady 2.0 online Help.

1 In the Layers palette, click the background to make it active.

2 Choose New Layer from the Layers palette menu.

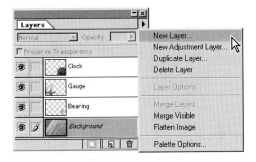

3 In the New Layer dialog box, type the name **Gradient**, and click OK. The Gradient layer appears above the background in the Layers palette.

You can now apply a gradient to the new layer. A gradient is a gradual transition between one or more colors. You control the type of transition using the gradient tool.

4 Double-click the linear gradient tool (▨) in the toolbox to select the tool and its Options palette.

5 In the Options palette, choose Foreground to Transparent for the type of Gradient.

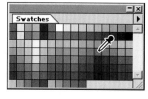

Gradient Options palette   *Swatches palette*

6 Click the Swatches palette tab to bring it to the front of its palette group, and select a shade of purple that appeals to you.

7 With the Gradient layer active in the Layers palette, drag the gradient tool from the right to the left margin of the image.

The gradient extends over the width of the layer, starting with purple and gradually blending to transparent, and affects the look of the keyboard on the layer below it. Because the gradient partially obscures the keyboard, you'll now lighten the effect by changing the Gradient layer's opacity.

8 In the Layers palette, change the opacity for the Gradient layer to 60%. The full keyboard shows through the gradient.

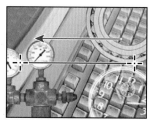

Dragging gradient tool   *Gradient at 100% opacity*   *Gradient at 60% opacity*
(right to left)

Adding text

Now you're ready to create and manipulate some type. You'll create text with the type tool, which places the text on its own type layer. You'll then edit the text and apply a special effect to that layer. ImageReady also has type creation and manipulation features, but it uses a palette to display type options, rather than a dialog box.

Using type in Photoshop and ImageReady

Photoshop and ImageReady let you add horizontal and vertical type to an image. You can specify the font, leading, kerning, tracking, baseline, style, size, and alignment of the type and edit its characters. You can also create type in double-byte fonts, enabling you to create designs that include Chinese, Japanese, and Korean text (if you have the correct system software installed on your computer). In Photoshop, you can also create selection borders in the shape of type.

New type features in both Photoshop and ImageReady allow you to select an anti-aliasing option for type, apply simulated styles to type, and turn off fractional character widths to improve the appearance of small type displayed at low resolution.

To enter type, you begin by selecting a type tool and clicking in the image to set an insertion point. In Photoshop, you use the Type Tool dialog box to enter the text and specify formatting attributes. The type appears in the image on a new type layer when you close the dialog box. (You can also preview type in the image while working in the Type Tool dialog box.)

In ImageReady, you use the type tool to enter the type directly onto a new type layer created when you click the type insertion point. The type appears in the image on the new type layer as you work with the type tool. You use the Type palette in ImageReady to specify type attributes.

–From the Photoshop 5.5 User Guide Supplement, Chapter 3, "Using Photoshop and ImageReady Together."

Now you'll add text to the image with the type tool.

1 In the Layers palette, click the Clock layer to make it active.

2 Select the type tool (**T**), and click the image in the upper left corner.

3 Click the color box on the Type Tool dialog box, select a beige color from the color picker, and click OK.

4 Choose a font from the Font menu in the dialog box, and enter a point size in the Size text box (we used 70-point Helvetica* Neue Condensed Heavy). Make sure the Strong option is selected in the Anti-Alias menu.

💡 *In ImageReady, use the Type palette to change the type settings.*

5 Type **Z2000** in the large text box at the bottom of the dialog box. The text is automatically placed on a new layer in the upper left corner of the image where you clicked.

Now you'll leave the dialog box open while you reposition the text in the image.

💡 *ImageReady places the type directly on the layer as you type, rather than in a dialog box.*

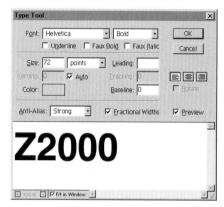

The Type Tool dialog box.

The text as it appears in the image.

6 Move the cursor into the image area, where the cursor temporarily changes to the move tool, and reposition the text.

7 When the text is placed where you want it, click OK. Notice that the Layers palette now includes a layer named Z2000 with a T icon next to the name, indicating it is a type layer.

For the Web: Ensuring Readability On-Screen

A monitor's resolution is much coarser than what even the least expensive inkjet or laser printer can produce, so a common publication-preparation problem to avoid is hard-to-read type. Text that looks fine on paper often does not look good on-screen. Fortunately, since you design electronic publications on-screen, you get a very good idea as you create your publications how readable their text is. Just be sure to check the on-screen text at actual size (if you have to zoom in, you know it's too hard for your readers to read). Be sure to proof the document in your browser so you will be able to view the same text quality that your readers will see.

Here are some basic guidelines for choosing readable typefaces for on-screen use:

Typeface Selection *Choose a simple font designed for on-screen use. Sans serif typefaces usually work better on screen than serif faces, because a monitor cannot easily reproduce the serif font's details. Serif text is generally easier to read in printed documents because the serifs give more visual clues on what letters are being used. (Serifs are those little bars and curves that extend from the ends of letters; "sans" is French for "without," so sans serif means "without serifs.") Sans serif fonts with subtle changes in the characters' strokes (the lines and curves that comprise a character) are usually as hard to read on-screen as are serif fonts, so be cautious about using delicate sans serif fonts for on-screen publications. Instead, consider squared, simple serifs and even-stroke sans serifs in online publications, using fonts specifically designed for on-screen viewing whenever possible.*

Text size *Use larger sizes than what you would use in print. Typically, use 12-point type for body text in electronic publications. Remember that fine differences in point size are difficult to distinguish on-screen, so avoid sizes like 11.5 and 13 points—they are too close to 12-point type.*

Text Spacing *Use more leading (line spacing) online than in print. Instead of the common 2 points of extra leading for print, use 4 or 6 extra points for on-screen publications. So, for 12-point text, you would ideally have 16- or 18-point leading on-screen.*

–From the Official Adobe Electronic Publishing Guide, Chapter 3, "Preparing Text and Graphics."

Adding a layer effect

You can enhance a layer by adding a shadow, glow, bevel, or emboss special effect from a collection of automated layer effects. These effects are easy to apply and link directly to the layer you specify.

Adding layer effects in Photoshop and ImageReady

You add layer effects in Photoshop by choosing Layer > Effects and selecting an effect from the submenu. You specify options for layer effects using the Effects dialog box.

You add layer effects in ImageReady by clicking the Effects button (◉) at the bottom of the Layers palette and choosing an effect from the Effects menu. You specify options for layer effects using the Layer Options/Effects palette. (You can also add effects in ImageReady by using the Layer > Effects menu.) Photoshop and ImageReady have numerous effects that you can apply in any combination to a layer.

- *The Drop Shadow effect adds a shadow that falls behind the contents on the layer.*

- *The Inner Shadow effect adds a shadow that falls just inside the edges of the layer contents, giving the layer a recessed appearance.*

- *The Outer Glow and Inner Glow effects add glows that emanate from the outside or inside edges of the layer contents.*

- *The Bevel and Emboss effects add various combinations of highlights and shadows to a layer.*

- *The new Color Fill applies a solid fill to a layer.*

- *In ImageReady, the Gradient/Pattern effect applies a pattern or color gradient fill to a layer.*

Gradient and Pattern layer effects that you apply in ImageReady are not displayed when you view the file in Photoshop. However, the effects are preserved in the image. An alert icon (◉) in Photoshop indicates that the effects are present on the layer. The pattern and gradient effects are not altered in Photoshop, unless you rasterize the layer on which the effects are applied.

–From the Photoshop 5.5 User Guide Supplement, Chapter 3, "Using Photoshop and ImageReady Together."

Layer effects are handled differently in ImageReady and Photoshop. In ImageReady, a layer effect can be applied from the Layer > Effect submenu. You can also click the Effects button at the bottom of the Layers palette, and select an effect from the pop-up menu. As mentioned earlier, ImageReady treats gradients and patterns as layer effects, giving ImageReady an extra layer effect (Gradient/Pattern) in the Layers palette Effect menu.

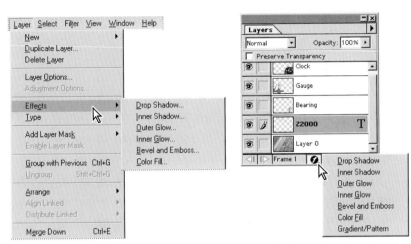

Accessing layer effects in Photoshop

Accessing layer effects from the ImageReady Layers palette

A major difference between Photoshop and ImageReady is that ImageReady layer effects are controlled using the Layer Options/Effects palette (located directly above the Layers palette) rather than with dialog boxes. In ImageReady, individual effects can also be hidden temporarily by clicking the eye icon in the Layers palette or copied to other layers by dragging the effect onto the destination layer.

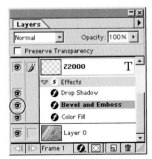

ImageReady layers can contain multiple effects, which can be shown or hidden individually.

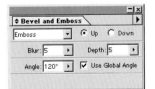

The Layer Effects/Options palette controls all effect settings in ImageReady.

Now you'll apply a bevel and emboss layer effect to the type.

1 With the Z2000 type layer still active, choose Layer > Effects > Bevel and Emboss.

2 In the Effects dialog box, change the Highlight opacity to 20%. Then click the Highlight color box, and select a color from the color picker (we used a light blue).

3 Change the Shadow opacity to 40%. Click the Shadow color box, and select a color from the color picker (we used black).

4 Choose Emboss from the Style pop-up menu, and click OK to apply the layer effect to the text.

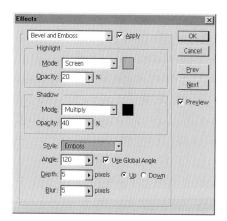 

Layer effects are automatically applied to changes you make to a layer. You can edit the text and watch how the layer effect tracks the change.

5 Double-click the Z2000 type layer in the Layers palette.

6 In the Type Tool dialog box, select "Z2000," and change it to **Z999**.

💡 *In ImageReady, you can make the change directly on the type layer.*

7 Reselect the new text in the dialog box, enter a larger point size in the Size text box (we used 90 points), and click OK. Note that the layer effect is applied to the text both as you type the new text and when you change to the larger font size.

💡 *In ImageReady, change the size by selecting a size from the pop-up menu in the Type palette.*

8 Choose File > Save.

Flattening and saving files

When you have edited all the layers in your image, you can make a copy of the file with the layers flattened. Flattening a file's layers merges them into a single background, greatly reducing the file size. You shouldn't flatten an image until you are certain you're satisfied with all your design decisions, however. In most cases, you should retain a copy of the file with its layers intact, in case you later need to edit a layer. ImageReady also lets you flatten images to reduce file size.

To save a flattened version of the file, you will use the Save a Copy command.

1 Choose File > Save a Copy.

ImageReady has no Save a Copy command. Instead, choose Flatten Image from the Layers palette menu, and then choose File > Save As to save the flattened version of the file under a different name.

2 In the dialog box, type the name **Flat03.psd**, and select the Flatten Image option.

3 Click Save. The Save a Copy command saves a flattened version of the file while leaving the original file and all its layers intact. Your collage of business images is now complete.

Review questions

1 What is the advantage of using layers?

2 How do you hide or show individual layers?

3 How can you make artwork on one layer appear in front of artwork on another layer?

4 How can you manipulate multiple layers simultaneously?

5 When you've completed your artwork, what can you do to a file to minimize its size?

Review answers

1 Layers allow you to edit different parts of an image as discrete objects.

2 The eye icon to the far left of the layer name in the Layers palette indicates that a layer is visible. You can hide or show a layer by clicking this icon.

3 You can make artwork on one layer appear in front of artwork on another layer by dragging the layer name in the Layers palette or by using the Layer > Arrange > Bring to Front command.

4 You can link the layers you want to adjust by selecting one of the layers in the Layers palette, and then clicking the square box to the left of the Layer name of the layer to which you want to link it. Once linked, both layers can be moved, rotated, and resized together.

5 You can flatten the image, which merges all the layers onto a single background.

Lesson 4

4 Painting and Editing

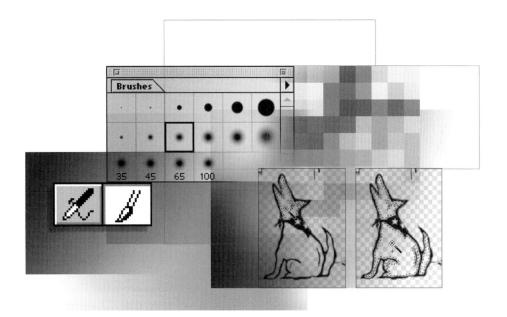

Adobe Photoshop and Adobe ImageReady
let you create original artwork or retouch
existing artwork in lots of different ways.
You can select from many painting tools
and fill commands that let you add and
manipulate color.

In this lesson, you'll learn how to do the following:

• Use the painting tools to create original artwork and to apply various painting effects to existing artwork.

• Understand the relationship between a painting tool, its Options palette, and its brush size.

• Select paint colors from the Color palette, the Swatches palette, and the color picker.

• Select options for the painting tools to enhance the behavior of the tools.

This lesson will take about 90 minutes to complete. The lesson is designed to be done in Adobe Photoshop, but information on using similar functionality in Adobe ImageReady is included when appropriate.

If needed, remove the previous lesson folder from your hard drive, and copy the Lesson04 folder onto it.

Getting started

Before beginning this lesson, restore the default application settings for Adobe Photoshop. See "Restoring default preferences" on page 4.

You'll start the lesson by viewing the final Lesson file to see what you'll create.

1 Restart Adobe Photoshop.

2 Click Cancel to exit the color management dialog box that appears.

3 Choose File > Open, and open the 04End.psd file, located in the Lessons/Lesson04 folder.

4 When you have finished viewing the file, either leave the End file open on your desktop for reference, or close it without saving changes.

Now you'll open the start file, a black-and-white line drawing of the coyote, which you'll color using painting tools and their options.

Choose File > Open, and open the 04Start.psd file, located in the Lessons/Lesson04 folder on your hard drive.

For the Web: Selecting Web-safe colors

Web-safe colors are the 216 colors common to the Windows and Mac OS 8-bit (256-color mode) color palettes. Selecting Web-safe colors for an optimized image ensures that the colors will not dither in a browser. Browser dither occurs when a Web browser using 8-bit color attempts to simulate colors that appear in an optimized image but not in the browser's color palette.

Photoshop and ImageReady provide several ways for you to select Web-safe colors for an image. You can select colors that appear in the image and shift the colors to the closest Web palette equivalents. You can select Web-safe colors from the Adobe color picker or from the Color palette. You can also specify a tolerance level to automatically shift colors to the closest Web palette equivalents.

–From the Adobe Photoshop 5.0 User Guide Supplement, Chapter 3, "Using Photoshop and ImageReady Together."
A similar topic can be found in ImageReady 2.0 online Help.

Painting and filling images with color

In this lesson, you'll explore many ways to add and manipulate color in an image.

Tools for applying color include the line, paintbrush, airbrush, and pencil tools. The workflow for applying and tracking color uses a Color palette, a Swatches palette, and the foreground and background color boxes.

You can also use a wide variety of editing and retouching tools and various commands and filters for making changes to existing colors in an image and applying special effects. You can choose from several tools for retouching images: the rubber stamp tool, the smudge tool, the blur and sharpen tools, and the dodge, burn, and sponge tools. Two tools, the history brush and the art history brush, let you paint with data from the History palette. (ImageReady does not have a history or an art history brush.)

The drawing and editing tools use the Brushes palette and its various options, including blending modes.

In addition to the drawing and painting tools shared with Photoshop, ImageReady has additional tools for drawing basic shapes on an image—the rectangle tool (□), the rounded rectangle tool (◯), and the ellipse tool (◯). Useful for creating buttons, these tools create bitmap shapes (not vector objects).

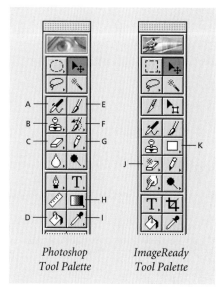

Photoshop
Tool Palette

ImageReady
Tool Palette

A. Airbrush B. Rubber stamp C. Eraser
D. Paint bucket E. Paintbrush F. History brush
G. Pencil H. Gradient I. Eyedropper
J. Magic Eraser K. Basic Shapes

You'll start simply by experimenting with the painting tools.

1 To get an idea of how easy it is to paint, click any of the painting tools in the toolbox to select the tool.

2 Click or drag in the image to paint.

Notice that your paint strokes are black, the default *foreground color.*

The foreground color is used to paint, to fill selections, and as the beginning color for gradient fills. The *background color* (white by default) appears when you delete pixels in a transparent area of color and as the ending color for gradient fills. Think of the background color as the canvas behind a painting—when you remove paint, the canvas shows through.

The current foreground and background colors are shown in the *color selection boxes* in the toolbox.

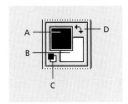

A. *Foreground color*
B. *Background color*
C. *Default colors*
D. *Switch colors*

3 Position the pointer over the color ramp in the Color palette (the pointer becomes the eyedropper tool), and click to select another color.

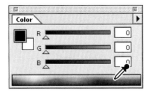

You can choose the foreground and background colors in many ways. In addition to using the color ramp and Color palette, you can also use the color picker, the eyedropper tool, or the Swatches palette. You'll learn about the painting colors and selecting them later in this lesson.

4 To display a non-Web color alert, choose Web Color Sliders from the Color palette menu. If you choose a non-Web color, an alert cube appears above the color ramp on the left side of the Color palette. Click the alert cube to select the closest Web color.

If no alert cube appears, the color you chose is Web-safe.

In ImageReady, choose any Slider option from the Color palette menu to display a non-Web color alert. Then drag around the alert icon to select other close Web colors.

5 Now double-click a different painting tool in the toolbox to select it and display its options.

Clicking any tool in the toolbox once selects the tool. Double-clicking the tool displays its Options palette. In addition, the Brushes palette displays a set of brushes for the various painting and editing tools. When you paint or edit, typically you first select a color. Then you select a tool and specify its options and brush, using the tool's Options palette and Brushes palette. You'll try out different options as you work through this painting and editing lesson.

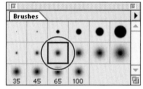

Selected tool   Options palette   *Current brush size*

6 Change the opacity of the paint by entering a different value in the Opacity text box in the Options palette, and select a different size brush in the Brushes palette.

You can choose how painting and editing tools apply and alter color in many ways:

• Display the tool pointer as a brush of a specific size and a specific shape.

• Change the size and shape of the brush.

• Control the distance between brush strokes or the angle of a brush stroke.

• Change the opacity of the color the tool applies.

• Change the color the tool applies. (You can even paint with patterns or with previous versions of the image.)

• Make paint fade out as you paint with a tool.

• Create all kinds of special effects by changing how the color applied by the tool blends with other pixels in the image.

7 If you have a small screen and you want to make it easier to work with the palettes and select color, you can click the Brushes palette tab and drag the palette to another location on-screen. This separates the palette from the Color/Swatches/Brushes palette group so that it stays visible as you work.

8 Try out the painting tool and settings in the image, clicking or dragging to apply paint.

When you've finished experimenting with the painting tools, you'll delete your work so far and start over.

For the Web: Previewing color for cross-platform display

If you're preparing images for display on the Web, you must consider how the colors of your image will appear on a computer monitor. RGB color display on a computer monitor varies with the operating system used by the computer. For example, the same image will appear darker on a Windows system than on a Macintosh system (because the standard RGB color space is darker in Windows than in Mac OS).

New color management features in Photoshop and ImageReady enable you to compensate for cross-platform differences in RGB color display during image preview. These options adjust color display only. No changes are made to pixels in the image.

To adjust RGB color display for cross-platform variations:

In Photoshop or ImageReady, choose View > Preview, and choose an option for adjusting the color display:

- *Macintosh RGB (Windows) to view the image with color simulating Mac OS color display.*

- *Windows RGB (Mac OS) to view the image with color simulating Windows color display.*

- *Uncompensated RGB to view the image with no color adjustment.*

The most effective way to use the Preview commands is through multiple views. For example, if you're working on Windows, choose View > Preview > Standard Windows Color for the original view. Then choose View > New View, and then choose View > Preview > Standard Macintosh Color for the new view. Choose Window > Tile. Now you can instantly see how corrections will appear on both platforms.

–From the Photoshop 5.5 User Guide Supplement, Chapter 3, "Using Photoshop and ImageReady Together." A similar topic can be found in ImageReady 2.0 online Help.

Undoing changes

You'll use the History palette to remove the paint you just applied so that you can restore the image to how it looked when you first opened it.

1 Click the History tab in the History/Actions palette group to display the History palette. If the palette group isn't visible, choose Window > Show History.

The History palette lets you undo changes and step back through recent changes. Unlike the Undo command, which undoes only the last performed operation, the History palette lets you undo a series of tool operations or commands, called *states*. Each state is listed with the name of the tool or command used to change the image, with the oldest state at the top of the list, followed by more recent states. Using this palette, you can return to an earlier version of the drawing and continue working from that point. ImageReady also has a History palette, but it functions somewhat differently than in Photoshop.

The list shows that several changes to the drawing have already been recorded, ending with the most recent changes.

2 Click the snapshot at the top of the History palette list to display the state of the image when you first opened it and before you painted it. The subsequent open and painting states in the History palette are dimmed.

In ImageReady, the History palette records changes made only to the original version of an image. The palette does not include an original state of the image.

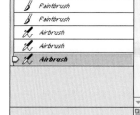

Photoshop History palette   ImageReady History palette

You can select a previous state of the image in the History palette and change the image to redisplay your work up to that point in the image and to continue editing the image from that state. When you change the image in a selected state, all states that come after the selected one are eliminated by default. You can select the Allow Non-Linear History option to make changes to a selected state without deleting subsequent states. (ImageReady does not have this option.)

Note: If you jump between Photoshop and ImageReady, history states aren't copied to the jumped-to application. Instead, each time you update an image with changes in the jumped-to application, a single history state is added to the Photoshop or ImageReady History palette. You can undo the update as you do other states in the History palette.

3 Select any of the painting states in the History palette, and watch the effect on the image.

As soon as you start working in the image again, any states after the selected state in the History palette are deleted. For now, you'll continue to work from the state when you first opened the image.

4 Click the snapshot in the History palette again to select the image's original state.

The ImageReady History palette doesn't contain a snapshot or the original state. To select the image's original state, choose File > Revert; the palette now contains only the Revert state.

You can use the Revert command to reverse all changes made to the image since it was last saved.

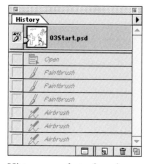

History snapshot selected
in Photoshop

The image reverts to the way it looked when you first opened it. All states but the snapshot at the top of the History palette are dimmed. Continuing your work from this point will clear all painting from the image.

You can also use the eraser tool ($\mathscr{Q}$) with the Erase to History option selected.

The History palette lets you undo tool operations and commands, but it does not reset tool options. To return to the default tool options, you must use the Reset All Tools command.

Note: *ImageReady does not include the Erase to History option or the Reset All Tools command.*

5 In the currently displayed tool Options palette, click the arrow to the right of the palette name, and select Reset All Tools from the pop-up menu. Click OK.

You are now ready to proceed with the lesson. As you work with the painting tools to create the drawing, keep in mind that you don't have to select the "right" colors or exactly replicate the drawing. As you just saw, it's easy to undo your work.

Setting up a painting or editing tool

Before you start painting the coyote with the paintbrush tool, first you'll make some decisions about how you want the tool to apply color. You'll soon be able to select options for the painting and editing tools effortlessly as you switch between the array of tools.

The painting and editing tools all work in a similar way, so once you've set up one tool, you'll know generally how to set up any of the other painting and editing tools. You select a color that the tool will apply, set the tool pointer display if desired, and then select the tool's brush size and any options.

Any time you're deciding which painting tool to use, consider their differing effects:

• The paintbrush tool (⟋) creates soft strokes of color.

• The airbrush tool (⟋) applies gradual tones to an image, simulating traditional airbrush techniques. The edges of the stroke are more diffused than those created with the paintbrush tool. The pressure setting for the airbrush tool determines how quickly the spray of paint is applied.

• The pencil tool (⟋) creates hard-edge freehand lines.

• The history brush (⟋), available in Photoshop only, paints with the selected state or snapshot on the History palette.

• The art history brush (⟋), available in Photoshop only, paints stylized strokes using the source data from a specified history state or snapshot and lets you simulate the texture of painting with different colors and artistic styles. For information on using the tool, see "On your own: Painting with the art history brush" on page 235.

Selecting foreground and background colors

You'll start by selecting a painting color. You can easily select another color as you paint.

1 Click the Swatches palette tab to bring the palette to the front of its group. (If the palette is not visible, choose Window > Show Swatches.)

The Swatches palette contains 122 color swatches from the default palette. To select a foreground color, click the desired swatch. When you click a color swatch, the new color appears in the foreground color selection box in the toolbox.

2 Click a brown swatch; the foreground box in the toolbox is updated to reflect the change.

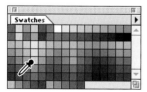

Using the Brushes palette

Now you'll choose a medium-sized brush for your painting. The brush sizes and shapes available for painting and editing appear in the Brushes palette. Brush settings are retained for each painting or editing tool.

1 Select the paintbrush tool (✐) in the toolbox.

2 To display the Brushes palette, choose Window > Show Brushes. You can click the Brushes palette tab any time to bring the palette to the front of its group. The default brush size for the paintbrush tool is highlighted.

3 Click a medium-sized brush in the middle row.

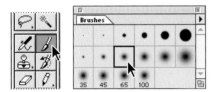

Paintbrush tool and medium-sized brush selected

Using the Options palette

You'll specify an opacity setting for the paintbrush tool to determine the transparency of brush strokes—the lower the value, the more transparent the paint. This is only one of the options you can specify for a painting or editing tool by using its Options palette. You'll learn about other options later.

1 Double-click the paintbrush tool in the toolbox to display its Options palette. The default opacity setting in the Paintbrush Options palette is 100%.

Simply clicking any tool in the toolbox selects the tool. Double-clicking the tool displays its Options palette. Generally, each painting and editing tool has its own options and brushes that you specify in the Options palette and Brushes palette, respectively.

2 Experiment with changing the opacity level of paint in either of these ways:

• By dragging the Opacity slider in the painting tool's Options palette. (Click the arrowhead next to the Opacity text box to display the Opacity slider.)

- By typing a number on your keypad. If you type a number from 1 to 9, the opacity changes in 10% increments; type **0** for 100%. (If you want to set the opacity to an increment other than 10%, type the 2-digit number quickly.)

Dragging the Opacity slider   *Typing a new Opacity value*

Note: *In Windows, the NumLock key must be on to use the keypad to set brush opacity.*

3 When you've finished experimenting, return the opacity setting to 100%.

Painting within a selection

As you saw at the beginning of the lesson, you can paint anywhere in an image, simply by not making a selection. Now you'll confine painting to a selection you'll make with the magic wand tool. When you select an area, any painting you do affects only the area within the selection. By selecting the area within the coyote first, you won't get any paint outside the edges of the selection.

1 In the toolbox, click the magic wand tool ( ).

2 Click within the coyote's body. Then hold down Shift, and click within the coyote's head and tail. Continue clicking until you've selected all the area within the coyote's body.

Magic wand selection   *Selection extended*

Before you begin painting, you'll create a new layer on which to paint so that you can edit your painting repeatedly without affecting the line drawing.

3 To open the Layers palette, choose Window > Show Layers. Click the New Layer button at the bottom of the Layers palette. To rename the layer, double-click the layer, enter the name **Painting**, and then click OK.

Note: This new layer is empty. So if you try to select anything on this layer with the magic wand tool, you'll select the entire layer.

4 In the toolbox, double-click the paintbrush tool to select its Options palette. Check to make sure that the opacity setting is 100%.

5 Using the brown color you selected earlier, paint a few areas within the coyote selection (don't fill in the selection completely).

New Layer button   *Painting layer*

By default, transparency (the absence of color or pixels) is indicated by a checkerboard pattern. Notice that where you applied the brown paint at an opacity level of 100%, the checkerboard is no longer visible. (Later you'll learn how to turn this gray pattern off if you want to.)

6 Now click the arrowhead next to the Opacity text box in the Paintbrush Options palette to display the Opacity slider, and drag the Opacity slider to about 60%.

7 Select another shade of brown (or any other color you like), and continue painting within the selection until you've painted the entire selection.

As you paint, notice the tool's *hotspot*, the point from which the tool's action begins.

By default, when you select a tool and move it into the image window, the pointer becomes an icon for the size brush selected in the Brushes palette. This Brush Size cursor is helpful for seeing the actual size of the painting tool in pixels. You can also change the tool's cursor to a precise or tool-shaped hotspot, using the Painting Cursors options in the Display & Cursors preferences.

Note: Caps Lock, if set, displays a precise cursor and overrides the default Brush Size option.

8 Choose View > Hide Edges to hide the selection border.

Notice that where you painted with the brown color at 60% opacity, part of the checkerboard shows through, indicating partial transparency.

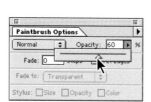

Opacity set to 60%

Showing edges of selection border

Now you'll soften and blur the paint you've applied to the coyote using a filter. ImageReady has all of the filters available in Photoshop.

9 Choose Filter > Blur > Gaussian Blur.

10 Make sure that the Preview option is turned on. Then experiment by dragging the Radius slider to the right. The higher the value in the Radius text box, the more blurred the colors in the selection. Click OK to apply the blur.

Gaussian Blur filter applied   Result

11 Choose Select > Deselect to deselect everything.

If you deselect first and then apply the filter, the blurring applies to the entire image, not just the selection.

Now you'll change the order of the layers so that the black outline of the coyote appears on top of the brown paint you've applied.

12 In the Layers palette, drag the Painting layer down to position it below the Drawing layer.

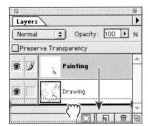

*Positioning Painting layer below
Drawing layer*

At this point, you'll turn off the checkerboard so you can easily see the changes you make.

13 Choose File > Preferences > Transparency & Gamut. For Grid Size, choose None. Then click OK.

Gray checkerboard transparent grid   *White transparent grid*

You can also choose a color for the transparent grid display. Don't confuse this color with the background or with actual color added to an image, however.

Creating hard-edged lines with the pencil tool

Next you'll try out the pencil tool, adding lines to the artwork and closing up the cactus to make it easier to select.

1 In the toolbox, click the Default Colors icon to return the foreground and background colors to their defaults—black and white, respectively.

Resetting default colors

2 Click the pencil tool in the toolbox to select it.

3 In the Brushes palette, select a small brush from the top row.

Notice that the brush selection for the pencil tool consists only of hard-edged brushes. The pencil tool draws only with hard edges.

4 Drag with the pencil tool to close the bottom of the cactus.

5 Draw another line for the horizon. Make the horizon line appear behind the cactus, running from the left side of the drawing to the base of the mountains.

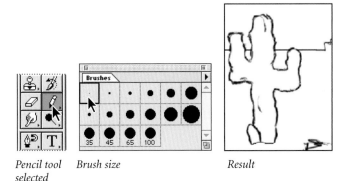

Pencil tool   *Brush size*   *Result*
selected

Painting with a watercolor effect

Next you'll paint the mountain using the Wet Edges option of the paintbrush tool. This option creates a watercolor effect by building up (darkening) the edges of brush strokes. (ImageReady does not have the Wet Edges option.)

To choose colors for the mountains, you'll use the Adobe Photoshop Color Picker. The color picker lets you select the foreground or background color from a color spectrum or enter values to define a color. It is also used to choose custom color systems, such as PANTONE® or Focoltone® colors.

1 To open the color picker, click the foreground color box in the toolbox.

The swatch in the top right of the Color Picker dialog box indicates the current foreground color.

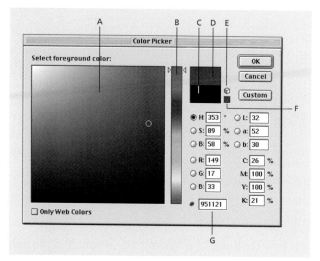

A. *Color field* B. *Color bar* C. *Current foreground color swatch*
D. *New foreground color swatch* E. *Non-Web color alert cube*
F. *Web color equivalent* G. *Web Color mode hexadecimal value*

When you select a color that is not in the 216 Web-safe color palette, an alert cube appears in the Color Picker dialog box and in the Color palette. The closest color is displayed next to the cube. To select the closest Web color, click the alert cube that appears in the Color Picker dialog box or the Color palette.

In addition, in Web Color mode, you can specify a color as a hexadecimal value in the # field. You can then copy the color to the Clipboard and paste it into an HTML document.

2 Drag the triangles along the color bar to find a color range that appeals to you for painting the mountains.

When the default is set to other than black, dragging updates the swatch at the right side of the dialog box. The top half of the swatch displays the new color, and the bottom half of the swatch displays the previous foreground or background color.

3 To select a different shade of the new color, click the desired shade in the color field at the left side of the color picker. Click OK to close the color picker.

The foreground color box in the toolbox shows the new color.

4 Double-click the paintbrush tool to display its Options palette. Turn on the Wet Edges option. Set the Opacity to 100%.

5 Click the Brushes palette tab to bring the Brushes palette forward. Select a medium-sized, soft-edged brush from the middle row.

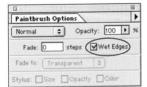
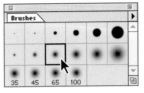

Wet Edges paintbrush option   *Medium-sized soft brush*

6 Move the paintbrush into the window, and begin painting the mountains. Don't worry if you paint a little outside the edges of the mountains. You'll have a chance to clean up any stray paint in the next section.

If you'd like to paint with some straight lines, hold down Shift as you drag the paintbrush.

If paint doesn't appear where you expected, check to make sure that:

- You're painting within the selection and on the correct layer (Painting).

- You selected the desired tool (here, the paintbrush tool).

- You chose the desired options and brush. (Some options, such as Fade, may cause paint to become transparent.)

Whenever a painting or editing tool doesn't perform as you expect it to, you should check all of these possibilities.

7 Use the sliders or color bar in the Color palette, or use the Swatches palette to select different foreground colors to add different colors to the mountains as you paint.

Painting mountains   *Painting with different foreground colors*

You can also reverse the foreground and background colors by clicking the Switch Colors icon (↨) in the toolbox. (Clicking the Default Colors icon (▇) returns the foreground color to black and the background color to white.)

8 In the Paintbrush Options palette, turn off the Wet Edges option.

You won't use this option again in this lesson. Because the last used setting for each brush is retained, you must turn off this option so that the paintbrush won't continue to paint with it.

9 Choose File > Save to save your work.

Erasing

Now you'll use the eraser tool to touch up mistakes you may have made. It's better to think of the eraser tool as returning transparency rather than "erasing" colored pixels. (In Photoshop, you can also use the eraser to return an area of an image to its previously saved state.)

1 Click the eraser tool (✐) in the toolbox, and move the pointer into the image area. By default, the eraser is the same shape and size as the default paintbrush.

2 In the Brushes palette, select a small, hard-edged brush from the top row.

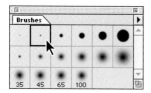

When you switch tools, the last brush settings you set for a painting or editing tool are retained.

3 Drag the eraser tool over any area around the mountains where you want to get rid of any stray paint.

Filling with the paint bucket tool

Now you'll select the cactus and fill it with color. A quick way to fill a selection with color is by clicking it with the paint bucket tool.

1 In the Layers palette, make sure that the Painting layer is the active layer.

2 In the toolbox, double-click the lasso tool (⌀) to display its Options palette.

3 In the Lasso Options palette, enter a value of **3** in the Feather text box.

4 Create a rough selection around the cactus, using the cactus as a guide.

5 End the selection by crossing the starting point.

6 Click the paint bucket tool (⌀) in the toolbox. This tool fills a selection or image with flat color.

7 In the Swatches palette, select a light green color.

8 Click inside the cactus selection to fill it with color.

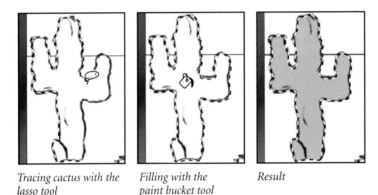

Tracing cactus with the lasso tool   *Filling with the paint bucket tool*   *Result*

9 Choose Select > Deselect.

Using custom brushes

To finish painting the cactus, you'll use some custom brushes and add texture. To use custom brushes, you load the brushes into the Brushes palette, and then select a brush shape. ImageReady lets you load and use custom brushes, but not create them.

1 Select the paintbrush tool in the toolbox.

2 Choose Load Brushes from the Brushes palette menu. Remember that you must load the brushes in the application in which you'll use them.

3 In the Lesson04 folder, select Assorted.abr, and then click Open to add the custom brushes to the Brushes palette.

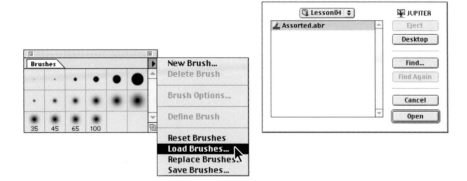

Note: For this lesson, we've placed the custom brushes in the Lesson04 folder. For future reference, the custom brushes are located in the Photoshop subdirectory under Goodies/Brushes.

4 In the eighth row of the Brushes palette, click the far right brush to select the texture brush.

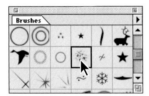

5 In the Swatches palette, select a lighter green or yellow color to add texture.

6 Using the brush tool, click inside the cactus to add texture.

To complete the cactus texture, you'll add some spines.

7 In the toolbox, click the Default Colors icon to return the foreground color to its default of black.

8 In the Brushes palette, click to select the fourth brush in the ninth row—a spiny-shaped brush.

9 Click at the edges of the cactus to add prickles.

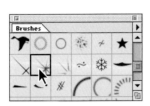 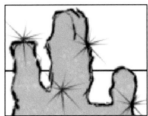

Selecting spiny custom brush   *Result*

10 Choose Select > Deselect.

11 Choose File > Save to save your work.

Airbrushing and smudging

Now you'll paint the clouds using the airbrush tool.The airbrush tool applies paint in the same way as a traditional airbrush. The default pressure for the airbrush tool is 50%, but the rate at which you drag the tool also influences the density of the paint. The more slowly you drag, the more dense the application of the paint.

To choose colors for the clouds, you'll select them from the Swatches palette and from the existing colors in the border of the drawing. Choosing a color within an image is called *sampling* a color. You can save sampled colors for future use by storing them in the Swatches palette.

1 In the Layers palette, make sure that the Painting layer is the active layer (so that you can paint without affecting the line drawing).

2 In the Brushes palette, select a small soft-edged brush from the second row of brushes.

3 Double-click the airbrush tool ( ) to display its Options palette. Notice that the default pressure for the airbrush tool is 50%.

4 In the Swatches palette, click a gray swatch, and paint a portion of the clouds using the airbrush. Don't worry if you paint a bit outside the outlines of the clouds.

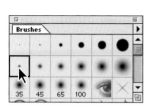

Brush selected in palette   *Airbrush applied to clouds*

Next you'll sample a color from the border of the image to add as a color for the clouds.

5 With the airbrush tool still selected, hold down Alt (Windows) or Option (Mac OS). The pointer becomes the eyedropper (✐). (You can also select the eyedropper tool in the toolbox. But you must remember to reselect the airbrush tool when you have finished.)

Note: Although you can always select the eyedropper tool from the toolbox to sample a color, you can also select the eyedropper tool using Alt (Windows) or Option (Mac OS) whenever a painting tool is selected.

6 Click the eyedropper in the green border to sample the green color and to make it the new foreground color.

Sampling color from the border   *Color applied to clouds*

7 Release Alt/Option. The pointer becomes the airbrush tool again. Continue painting the clouds with the airbrush tool.

Before you select another color, you'll save the green color in the Swatches palette.

8 Click the Swatches palette tab.

9 Position the pointer in the blank area at the bottom of the Swatches palette. The pointer becomes a paint bucket.

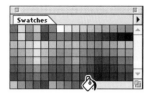
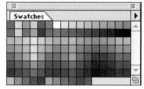

Paint bucket in Swatches   Color added
palette

10 Click the paint bucket in the blank area; the green color is added to the Swatches palette.

Note: You don't have to save a sampled color to work with it—you've done it here just to learn how to save colors in the Swatches palette. To remove a swatch from the Swatches palette, Ctrl-click (Windows) or Command-click (Mac OS) the swatch. Holding down Ctrl/Command turns the paint bucket pointer into the scissors pointer, and clicking removes the swatch.

11 Finish painting the clouds using either sampled colors or colors from the Swatches palette.

As a final touch, you'll use the smudge tool to smudge the colors in the clouds. The smudge tool moves and mixes different-colored pixels as you drag.

12 Select the smudge tool (🖐), located under the blur tool in the hidden tools palette. To select a hidden tool, you position the pointer on the visible tool and drag to highlight the tool you want.

13 In the Brushes palette, select a smaller soft brush from the second row.

14 Drag the tool in the clouds to create swirls.

Smudge tool   Mixed color
selected in palette

The smudge tool uses a default opacity of 50% to softly mix colors. You can increase the opacity to make the effect more pronounced.

15 Choose File > Save to save your work.

Creating gradients

In the next part of the lesson you'll use the gradient tools and painting modes to continue painting the coyote image. The gradient tools let you apply a gradual transition between multiple colors. The gradient pull-out menu in the toolbox includes five different tools. You'll use the radial gradient tool to apply a gradient to the sun that shades concentrically from the starting point to the ending point. The gradient tools aren't available in ImageReady, but ImageReady includes a number of automated effects that you can apply to layers, including gradients.

1 In the Layers palette, make sure that the Painting layer is the active layer. You'll continue to work on this layer.

2 Using the zoom tool (🔍), drag over the sun to zoom in on that part of the image.

3 Select the ellipse marquee tool (◯) hidden under the rectangular marquee tool, and double-click to display its Options palette. (To select a hidden tool, you position the pointer on the visible tool and drag to the tool you want.)

To fill only part of the image, you must select the desired area first. Otherwise the gradient fill is applied to the entire active layer.

4 In the Marquee Options palette, enter a value of **2** in the Feather text box. Feathering blurs the edges of a selection.

5 Hold down Alt (Windows) or Option (Mac OS), and then drag from the center point of the sun to the outside edge to create a circular selection.

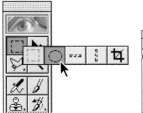

Elliptical marquee tool selected

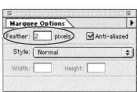

Feather: 2

Selecting from center

6 Select and double-click the radial gradient tool. Remember that to select a hidden tool, you position the pointer on the visible tool and drag to the tool you want.

7 In the Radial Gradient Options palette, select Orange, Yellow, Orange from the Gradient pop-up menu. Set the opacity to 50% or 60%.

8 In the image, drag from the center of the sun to the outside edge to apply the gradient.

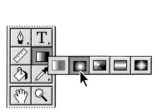 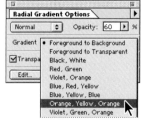 

Radial gradient tool selected   *Orange, Yellow, Orange option*   *Applying gradient from center*

9 Choose Select > Deselect to deselect everything.

10 Double-click the zoom tool in the toolbox to zoom out of the image.

About the Photoshop gradient tools

The gradient tools create a gradual blend between multiple colors. You can choose from existing gradient fills or create your own. You draw a gradient by dragging in the image from a starting point (where the mouse is pressed) to an ending point (where the mouse is released). The starting and ending points affect the gradient appearance according to the gradient tool used.

The gradient pull-out menu in the toolbox includes these tools:

• *Linear gradient shades from the starting point to the ending point in a straight line.*

• *Radial gradient shades from the starting point to the ending point in a circular pattern.*

• *Angular gradient shades in a counterclockwise sweep around the starting point.*

• *Reflected gradient shades using symmetric linear gradients on either side of the starting point.*

• *Diamond gradient shades from the starting point outward in a diamond pattern. The ending point defines one corner of the diamond.*

–From the Adobe Photoshop 5.0 User Guide, Chapter 9, "Painting."

Creating soft-edged effects

You can use the Fade option with any of the painting tools (the paintbrush, airbrush, or pencil tools) to cause paint to fade to the background color or to fade to transparent over the length of a brush stroke. You'll use this option with the paintbrush tool again to create rays around the sun. (ImageReady does not have the Fade option.)

First you'll learn another way to select a foreground color using the Color palette. The Color palette contains sliders and a color bar that let you change the foreground and background colors. The current foreground and background colors are displayed in the Color palette; the swatch with the outline determines which swatch is selected.

1 In the Layers palette, make sure that the Painting layer is the active layer. You'll continue to work on this layer.

2 Click the Color palette tab to bring it to the front of the palette group. Make sure that the swatch in the top left corner of the Color palette is selected. When a swatch is selected, it has a border.

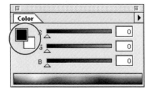

Active swatch (foreground color)

Note: *If the swatch is already selected and you click it, you'll open the color picker. If necessary, click Cancel to close the color picker.*

You can select colors in the Color palette either by dragging the sliders or by dragging through the color bar at the bottom of the palette. You'll select a color from the color bar.

3 Position the pointer in the color bar; the pointer becomes an eyedropper.

Just to see what happens, drag the eyedropper through the color bar to see how the foreground box changes color as you drag. Select a reddish-brown color from the color bar to paint the rays around the sun.

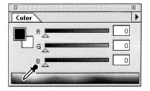
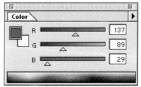

Dragging eyedropper pointer   *Result*
in the color bar to select a color

4 Double-click the airbrush tool in the toolbox to display its Options palette. Enter a value of **15** in the Fade text box. In the Fade To menu, make sure that Transparent is selected so the paint will fade to transparency.

The value you enter in the Fade text box determines how long the painting tool will apply paint before it begins to fade. The higher the value you set, the longer the brush paints before beginning to fade. Turning on the Fade option lets you select an option from the Fade To menu.

5 In the Brushes palette, select a small, soft-edged brush.

6 Position the pointer in the window, and drag to draw rays around the sun. You'll notice that they begin to fade as you drag.

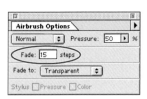
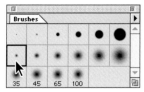

Fade option: 15 steps   *Small, soft-edged brush*   *Drawing with airbrush tool*

Painting with gradients and modes

You'll continue trying out different blending modes to use as a background sky for the artwork. You'll work on the Painting layer that you created at the start of the lesson.

1 Make sure that the Painting layer is active—selecting it, if necessary, in the Layers palette. Make sure that the Preserve Transparency option is off.

2 Select the rectangular marquee tool ({⁻}) in the toolbox. Drag a selection marquee from the horizon line to the top of the image.

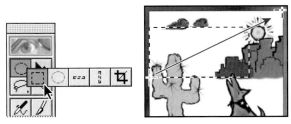

Sky selected with rectangular marquee tool

Now you'll apply a gradient to the sky. As you saw when you applied a radial gradient, a gradient blends from one color to another over the length of a selection. You can choose from several predefined gradients in the Gradient Options palette. You can also create your own gradients.

3 In the toolbox, position the pointer on the radial gradient tool, and drag to the right to select the linear gradient tool (▨) from the hidden tools.

Photoshop includes five gradient tools, which differ in the point from which they blend colors. The linear gradient tool blends colors from the starting point to the ending point in a straight line.

4 In the Gradient Tool Options palette, for Gradient select Foreground to Background. A sample of the gradient you select appears at the bottom of the Gradient palette. If desired, change the opacity to 80% or 90%.

5 Select Violet, Green, Orange from the Gradient pop-up menu. Make sure that Transparency, Dither, and Reverse are deselected.

6 Using the gradient tool, drag downward from the top of the image to the horizon line to apply the linear gradient.

The gradient is applied on top of the cactus and mountains, saturating them with color. You'll undo the gradient so that you can see what happens when you reverse the order of the colors.

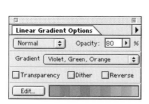 

7 Choose Edit > Undo to undo the gradient.

8 In the Gradient Options palette, select an opacity of 60%, and select the Reverse option to reverse the order in which the colors are applied (from orange, to green, and then to violet).

9 Drag from the top of the image down to the horizon line to apply the gradient.

You'll undo the gradient again so that you can change its mode and see the effect.

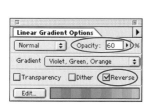 

10 Choose Edit > Undo.

11 In the Linear Gradient Options palette, choose Behind from the mode menu.

In the Behind mode, paint is applied only to the transparent part of a layer to give the appearance of painting behind existing objects. This mode works only in layers with Preserve Transparency off and is analogous to painting on the back of transparent areas in a sheet of acetate.

12 Using the gradient tool, drag from the top of the image downward to the horizon line. The gradient now appears behind the mountains and cactus for a more realistic sky.

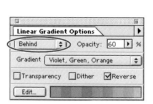

When using a blending mode, it's helpful to think in terms of the following colors when visualizing an effect:

- The *base color* is the original color in the image.

- The *blend color* is the color being applied with the painting or editing tool.

- The *result color* is the color resulting from the blend.

You can set blending modes for layers as well as for painting tools. Painting modes affect only the paint applied by a selected tool; layer modes affect the entire layer.

Try out other painting modes to see their effect.

For complete information on the blending modes, see "Selecting a blending mode" in Chapter 9 of the Photoshop 5.0 User Guide or in "Painting" of Photoshop 5.0 online Help. A similar topic can be found in ImageReady 2.0 online Help. For a gallery illustration of the blending modes, see Photoshop 5.0 online Help or ImageReady 2.0 online Help.

For an illustration of different blending modes applied to brush strokes, see figure 4-1 in the color signature.

13 When you are satisfied with the results, choose Select > Deselect.

Painting with texture

Now you'll paint in the desert floor by painting behind the existing fill and gradients.

1 Make sure that the Painting layer is still active. You'll continue working on this layer.

2 Using the rectangular marquee tool (⬚), drag a selection marquee to select the desert floor.

3 In the Swatches palette, select a light brown or tan color for desert sand.

Now you'll set options to paint behind the coyote and cactus.

4 In the Paintbrush Options palette, choose Behind from the palette's mode menu.

5 Select the paintbrush tool in the toolbox; in the Brushes palette, select a large, soft brush from the second row.

6 Drag to paint in the desert floor.

7 Choose Select > Deselect.

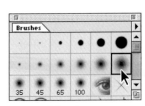

Large, soft brush   *Behind mode*

As you just saw, in Behind mode, any paint is applied behind existing paint. You can paint freely without affecting existing artwork. Painting modes differ from layer modes: Painting modes, like painting tool options, affect only the paint applied by the selected tool. Layer modes affect the entire layer

8 Choose File > Save.

Setting brush options

You can define a number of options for the default brushes and any brushes you create. For custom brushes, only the spacing and anti-aliased options can be changed.

- *Diameter controls the size of the brush. Enter a value in pixels or drag the slider.*

- *Hardness controls the size of the brush's hard center. Type a number, or use the slider to enter a value that is a percentage of the brush diameter.*

- *Spacing controls the distance between the brush marks in a stroke. To change the spacing, type a number, or use the slider to enter a value that is a percentage of the brush diameter. To paint strokes without defined spacing, deselect this option.*

- *Angle specifies the angle by which an elliptical brush's long axis is offset from horizontal. Type a value in degrees, or drag the horizontal axis in the left preview box.*

- *Roundness specifies the ratio between the brush's short and long axes. Enter a percentage value, or drag the points in the left preview box. A value of 100% indicates a circular brush, a value of 0% indicates a linear brush, and intermediate values indicate elliptical brushes.*

–From the Adobe Photoshop 5.0 User Guide, Chapter 9, "Painting." A similar topic can be found in ImageReady 2.0 online Help.

Defining a brush

To complete the artwork, you'll define a brush to add details to the desert floor. (You can't define a brush in ImageReady.)

1 In the Layers palette, click to select the Drawing layer. Click the eye icon next to the Painting layer to hide that layer.

You'll define a brush using the Drawing layer, which contains only black and white values—that is, fully selected or fully deselected pixels. If you select from the Painting layer, your selection (and thus your brush) will contain gray values; the result will be a brush with partially selected pixels.

2 Select the rectangular marquee tool in the toolbox. Only a rectangular selection can be defined as a brush.

3 Drag to select some rays of the sun.

Selecting black-and-white art from Drawing layer

Now you'll use this part of an image to create a custom brush shape.

4 In the Brushes palette, choose Define Brush from the Brushes palette menu.

The sun-ray selection is added as a new brush to the Brushes palette. Next, you'll set the brush's options.

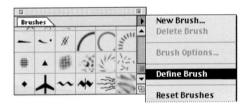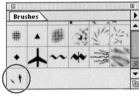

Defining brush   *Result*

5 Double-click the brush in the Brushes palette to select it and set its options.

6 In the Brush Options dialog box, set the spacing to 300%, and click OK.

The amount you set for spacing controls the distance between brush strokes.

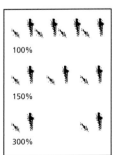

Brush spacing options   *Result*

7 Choose Select > Deselect. Deselecting the rectangular selection also deselects the brush you just defined.

8 Choose Save Brushes from the Brushes palette menu. Name the file **Brushes.abr**, and save the file in the Lessons/Lesson04 folder.

The .abr file extension identifies the file information as brushes. Saving the brush lets you use it in other Photoshop work sessions and in other applications.

💡 *In ImageReady, you can load and use custom brushes created in Photoshop.*

Painting with a custom brush

You can try out the brush you just created.

1 In the Layers palette, click the Painting layer to select it and make it visible. You'll finish working on this layer.

2 Click the paintbrush tool in the toolbox to select it and to reselect the brush you just defined.

3 In the Paintbrush Options palette, set the tool's Opacity to 40%. Choose Normal from the mode menu so that any paint you apply will appear on top of existing paint.

Remember that the painting modes, like painting tool options, affect only the paint applied by the selected tool. Layer modes affect the entire layer.

4 In the Swatches palette, click a dark brown color to contrast with the sand.

5 Using the paintbrush tool, drag to paint in the desert floor.

Another way to add texture to painting is to apply a filter or to use different tools to apply paint on top of paint.

6 Choose File > Save. Close any open files.

You've completed the painting lesson.

For an illustration of the finished artwork in this lesson, see the End Gallery section of the color signature.

For the Web: Painting with Web-safe colors

You can start with any image and convert it to Web-safe colors. This technique in Photoshop shows how to create a loose, painterly effect in images as you paint with Web-safe colors.

1 Start with an RGB image. If the image has layers, either flatten the layers, or select the layer you'll convert and discard the others.

2 Choose Image > Mode > Indexed Color to convert the image to use an indexed-color palette. In the Indexed Color dialog box, select Web for the palette. For Options, select None for Dither. Click OK.

The image colors are converted to indexed, Web-safe colors.

3 Now convert the image back to RGB by choosing Image > Mode > RGB Color. You can apply filters in RGB mode, but not in Indexed Color mode.

4 Arrange your palettes: Click the Color palette tab to display the palette. Click the Swatches palette tab; then drag the palette by its tab to separate the palette from its group so that you can see both the Color and Swatches palette as you work.

 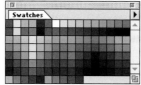

5 Select or load a Web-safe palette, using one of the following techniques:

• From the Color palette pop-up menu, choose Web Color sliders. Choose Make Ramp Web Safe. This option constrains the sliders to select only Web-safe colors.

• From the Swatches palette menu, choose Replace Swatches; select and load the Web Safe palette in the Adobe Photoshop 5.5/Goodies/Adobe Photoshop Only/Color Swatches folder within the Adobe Photoshop application folder.

6 Touch up the image as desired using any of the painting tools set to a hard-edged brush and colors selected from the Color or Swatches palette.

 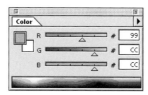

7 To give the image a painterly effect and add texture, experiment with filters that add texture without dithering colors and shifting colors outside the Web palette (For example, try the Dry Brush, Paint Daubs, Dust & Scratches, and Crystallize filters.) Use the eyedropper tool to verify that colors haven't shifted to non-Web-safe colors.

8 Save the file as a GIF or JPEG image either by choosing File > Save for the Web and selecting a file format and optimization setting, or by flattening the image (choose Layer > Flatten Image), choosing File > Save As, and selecting the corresponding file format.

9 Construct and use a Web-safe color palette from a second image containing Web-safe colors (or repeat steps 2 and 3 to convert the colors). Use the eyedropper tool to select colors in your image. Add the new color to the Swatches palette by clicking the cursor in the Swatches palette to add the new color.

For an illustration of the artwork for this section, see the gallery at the end of the color section.

Review questions

1 What is the benefit of making a selection before starting to paint in an area?

2 How are a painting tool, its Options palette, and the Brushes palette related? For example, if you click the paintbrush tool in the toolbox, what effect do the Brushes palette and the Paintbrush Options palette have on the tool?

3 How do painting modes and layer modes differ?

4 How do you create a custom brush?

Review answers

1 Once you've made a selection, you cannot paint outside the boundary of the selection marquee.

2 When you select a painting tool, the Brushes palette displays the size of the painting tool, and the tool's Options palette displays the opacity, the mode, and any other options you may have previously selected. If a tool does not perform the way you expect it to, check the Brushes palette and the tool's Options palette to make sure the options are set the way you want.

3 Painting modes, like painting tool options, affect only the paint applied by the selected tool. Layer modes affect the entire layer.

4 In Photoshop, select the area you want to define as a brush, and then choose Define Brush from the Brushes palette menu. You can then load the brush in ImageReady to paint with it.

Lesson 5

5 Masks and Channels

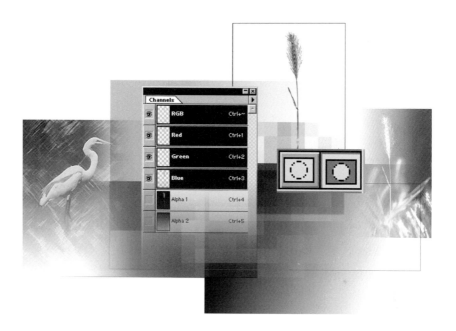

Adobe Photoshop uses masks to isolate and manipulate specific parts of an image. A mask is like a stencil. The cutout portion of the mask can be altered, but the area surrounding the cutout is protected from change. You can create a temporary mask for one-time use, or you can save masks for repeated use.

In this lesson, you'll learn how to do the following:

- Refine a partial selection using a quick mask.

- Save a selection as a channel mask.

- View a mask using the Channels palette.

- Load a saved mask and apply effects.

- Paint in a mask to modify a selection.

- Make an intricate selection using the Extract command.

- Create and use a gradient mask.

This lesson will take about 1 hour and 10 minutes to complete. The lesson is designed to be done in Adobe Photoshop. ImageReady does not contain the advanced masking features available in Photoshop.

If needed, remove the previous lesson folder from your hard drive and copy the Lesson05 folder onto it.

Working with masks and channels

Masks let you isolate and protect parts of an image. When you create a mask from a selection, the area not selected is *masked* or protected from editing. With masks, you can create and save time-consuming selections and then use them again. In addition, you can use masks for other complex editing tasks—for example, to apply color changes or filter effects to an image.

In Adobe Photoshop, you can make temporary masks, called *quick masks*, or you can create permanent masks and store them as special grayscale channels, called *alpha channels*. Photoshop also uses channels to store an image's color information and information about spot color. Unlike layers, channels do not print. You use the Channels palette to view and work with channels. ImageReady does not support channels, except for alpha channels used for PNG transparency.

Getting started

Before beginning this lesson, restore the default application settings for Adobe Photoshop. See "Restoring default preferences" on page 4.

You'll start the lesson by viewing the final lesson file.

1 Restart Adobe Photoshop.

2 Click Cancel to exit the color management dialog box that appears.

3 Choose File > Open, and open the 05End.psd file, located in the Lessons/Lesson05 folder on your hard drive.

4 When you have finished viewing the file, either leave it open on your desktop for reference, or close it without saving changes.

For an illustration of the finished artwork for this lesson, see the gallery at the beginning of the color section.

Creating a quick mask

Now you'll open the Start file and begin the lesson by using Quick Mask mode to convert a selection border into a temporary mask. Later you will convert this temporary quick mask back into a selection border. Unless you save a quick mask as a more permanent alpha channel mask, the temporary mask will be discarded once it is converted to a selection.

You'll begin by making a partial selection of the egret using the magic wand tool, and then you'll edit the selection using a quick mask.

1 Choose File > Open, and open the 05Start.psd file, located in the Lessons/Lesson05 folder on your hard drive.

2 Double-click the magic wand tool ( ) in the toolbox to display its Options palette.

3 Enter a Tolerance value of **12**.

4 Click anywhere in the white area of the egret to begin the selection process.

5 To extend the selection, hold down Shift, and click the magic wand on another white portion of the egret. When you hold down Shift, a plus sign appears next to the magic wand tool. This indicates the tool is adding to the selection.

Magic wand selection   *Selection extended*

The egret is still only partly selected. Now you'll add to this selection using a quick mask.

6 In the toolbox, click the Quick Mask icon. By default you have been working in Standard mode.

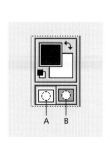 

A. Standard mode   *Quick mask selection*
B. Quick Mask mode   *showing red overlay*

In Quick Mask mode, a red overlay (similar to a piece of *rubylith*, or red acetate, that a print shop uses to mask an image) appears to mask and protect the area outside the selection. You can apply changes only to the unprotected area that is visible and selected. (It's possible to change the color of the red overlay; the color is only a matter of display.)

Note: A partial selection must exist to see the overlay color in Quick Mask mode.

Editing a quick mask

Next you will refine the selection of the egret by adding to or erasing parts of the masked area. You'll use the paintbrush tool to make changes to your quick mask. The advantage of editing your selection as a mask is that you can use almost any tool or filter to modify the mask. (You can even use selection tools.) In Quick Mask mode, you do all of your editing in the image window.

In Quick Mask mode, Photoshop automatically defaults to Grayscale mode. The foreground color defaults to black, and the background color defaults to white. When using a painting or editing tool in Quick Mask mode, keep these principles in mind:

- Painting with white erases the mask (the red overlay) and increases the selected area.

- Painting with black adds to the mask (the red overlay) and decreases the selected area.

Adding to a selection by erasing masked areas

You begin by painting with white to increase the selected area within the egret. This erases some of the mask.

1 To make the foreground color white, click the Switch Colors icon above the foreground and background color selection boxes in the toolbox.

Switch Colors icon

2 Click the paintbrush tool ( ) in the toolbox. Then click the Brushes palette tab, and select a medium brush from the first row of brushes. As you work, you may want to change the size of your brush. Simply click the Brushes palette tab again, and select a different-sized brush. You'll notice that the size of the tool brush pointer changes.

3 As you edit your quick mask, magnify or reduce your view of the image, as needed. When you zoom in, you can work on details of the image. When you zoom out, you can see an overview of your work.

You can zoom in or magnify your view in these ways:

• Select the zoom tool, and click the area you want to magnify. Each click magnifies the image some more. When the zoom tool is selected, you can also drag over the part of the image you want to magnify.

• Select the zoom tool from the keyboard by holding down Ctrl+spacebar (Windows) or Command+spacebar (Mac OS); then release the keys to go back to painting.

You can zoom back out in the following ways:

• Double-click the zoom tool to return the image to 100% view.

• Select the zoom tool. Hold down Alt (Windows) or Option (Mac Os) to activate the zoom-out tool, and click the area of the image you want to reduce.

• Select the zoom-out tool from the keyboard by holding down Alt+spacebar (Windows) or Option+spacebar (Mac OS) and click to reduce the view; then release the keys to go back to painting.

4 Move the paintbrush onto the window, and begin painting over the red areas within the egret's body. As you paint with white, the red areas are erased.

Don't worry if you paint outside the outline of the egret's body. You'll have a chance to make adjustments later by masking areas of the image as needed.

Unedited mask　　　*Painting with white*　　　*Result*

5 Continue painting with white to erase all of the mask (red) in the egret, including its beak and legs. As you work you can easily switch back and forth between Quick Mask mode and Standard mode to see how painting in the mask alters the selected area.

Standard mode

Notice that the selection border has increased, selecting more of the egret's body.

*Edited mask in
Standard mode*

Quick mask selection

 For an illustration of the selection in Standard and Quick Mask modes, see figure
5-1 in the color signature.

If any areas within the body of the egret still appear to be selected, it means that you haven't erased all of the mask.

Selection in Standard
mode

Erasing in Quick Mask
mode

6 Once you've erased all of the red areas within the egret, click the Standard mode icon again to view your quick mask as a selection. Don't worry if the selection extends a bit beyond the egret. You can fix that.

7 If you zoomed in on the image for editing, choose any of the techniques in step 3 to zoom out.

8 Choose File > Save to save your work.

Subtracting from a selection by adding masked areas

You may well have erased the mask beyond the edges of the egret. This means that part of the background is included in the selection. Now you'll return to Quick Mask mode and restore the mask to those edge areas by painting with black.

1 Click the Quick Mask icon to return to Quick Mask mode.

2 To make the foreground color black, click the Switch Colors icon (◼) above the foreground and background color selection boxes in the toolbox. Make sure that the black color box now appears on top. Remember that in the image window, painting with black will add to the red overlay.

3 Choose a brush from the Brushes palette. Select a small brush from the first row of brushes, because you'll be refining the edges of the selection.

4 Now paint with black to restore the mask (the red overlay) to any of the background area that is still unprotected. Only the area inside the egret should remain unmasked. Remember that you can zoom in and out as you work. You can also switch back and forth between Standard mode and Quick Mask mode.

*Painting with black to
restore mask*

⬤ For an illustration of painting in Quick Mask mode, see figure 5-2 in the color signature.

5 Once you're satisfied with your selection, switch to Standard mode to view your final egret selection. Double-click the hand tool (✋) in the toolbox to make the egret image fit in the window.

Using alpha channels

In addition to the temporary masks of Quick Mask mode, you can create more permanent masks by storing and editing selections in alpha channels. You create a new alpha channel as a mask. For example, you can create a gradient fill in a blank channel and then use it as a mask. Or you can save a selection to either a new or existing channel.

An alpha channel has these properties:

- *Each image can contain up to 24 channels, including all color and alpha channels.*

- *All channels are 8-bit grayscale images, capable of displaying 256 levels of gray.*

- *You can add and delete alpha channels.*

- *You can specify a name, color, mask option, and opacity for each channel. (The opacity affects the preview of the channel, not the image.)*

- *All new channels have the same dimensions and number of pixels as the original image.*

- *You can edit the mask in an alpha channel using the painting and editing tools.*

- *Storing selections in alpha channels makes the selections permanent, so that they can be used again in the same image or in a different image.*

–From the Adobe Photoshop 5.0 User Guide, Chapter 10, "Using Channels and Masks."

Saving a selection as a mask

Now you'll save the egret selection as an alpha channel mask. Your time-consuming work won't be lost, and you can use the selection again later.

Quick masks are temporary. They disappear when you deselect. However, any selection can be saved as a mask in an alpha channel. Think of alpha channels as storage areas for information. When you save a selection as a mask, a new alpha channel is created in the Channels palette. (An image can contain up to 24 channels, including all color and alpha channels.) You can use these masks again in the same image or in a different image.

1 To display the Channels palette, choose Windows > Show Channels.

In the Channels palette, you'll see that your image by default already has color information channels—a full-color preview channel for the RGB image and a separate channel for the red, green, and blue channels.

2 With the egret selection still active, choose Select > Save Selection.

In the Save Selection dialog box, the name of your current document appears in the Destination pop-up menu, and New by default appears in the Channel pop-up menu.

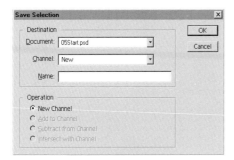

3 Click OK to accept the defaults.

You'll see that a new channel labeled Alpha 1 has been added to the bottom of the Channels palette. All new channels have the same dimensions and number of pixels as the original image. You'll rename this new channel in a moment.

4 Experiment with looking at the various channels individually. Click in the eye icon column next to the channel to show or hide that channel. To show or hide multiple channels, drag through the eye icon column in the palette.

Alpha channel mask visible and selected; other channels hidden

Alpha channels can be added and deleted, and like quick masks, can be edited using the painting and editing tools. For each channel, you can also specify a name, color, mask option, and opacity (which affects just the preview of the channel, not the image).

To avoid confusing channels and layers, think of channels as containing an image's color and selection information; think of layers as containing painting and effects.

If you display all of the color channels plus the new alpha mask channel, the image window looks much as it did in Quick Mask mode (with the rubylith appearing where the selection is masked). It is possible to edit this overlay mask much as you did the quick mask. However, in a minute you will edit the mask channel in a different way.

5 When you have finished looking at the channels, click in the eye icon column next to the RGB channel in the Channels palette to redisplay the composite channel view.

6 Choose Select > Deselect to deselect everything.

7 To rename the channel, double-click the Alpha 1 channel in the Channels palette. Type the name **Egret** in the Channel Options dialog box, and click OK.

Editing a mask

Now you'll touch up your selection of the egret by editing the mask channel. It's easy to miss tiny areas when making a selection. You may not even see these imperfections until you view the saved selection as a channel mask.

You can use most painting and editing tools to edit a channel mask, just as you did when editing in Quick Mask mode. This time you'll display and edit the mask as a grayscale image.

1 With the Egret channel selected, click the eye icon next to the RGB channel to display only the channel mask and to hide all channels except the Egret channel. Only the Egret channel displays an eye icon. The image window displays a black-and-white mask of the egret selection. (If you left all of the channels selected, then the colored egret image would appear with a red overlay.)

Look for any black or gray flecks within the body of the egret. You'll erase them by painting with white to increase the selected area. Remember these guidelines on editing a channel with a painting or editing tool:

• Painting with white erases the mask and increases the selected area.

• Painting with black adds to the mask and decreases the selected area.

• Painting with gray values adds to or subtracts from the mask in varying opacity, in proportion to the level of gray used to paint. For example, if you paint with a medium gray value, when you use the mask as a selection the pixels will be 50% selected. If you paint with a dark gray and then use the mask as a selection, the pixels will be less than 50% selected (depending on the gray value you choose). And if you paint with a light gray, when you use the mask as a selection, the pixels will be more than 50% selected.

2 Make sure that the Egret channel is the active channel by clicking on the channel in the Channels palette. A selected channel is highlighted in the Channels palette.

3 Now make sure that white is the foreground color. (If necessary, click the Switch Colors icon above the foreground and background color selection boxes in the toolbox.) Then select a small brush in the Brushes palette, and paint out any black or gray flecks.

Selection in channel   *Painting out black or gray*

4 If any white specks appear in the black area of the channel, make black the foreground color, and paint those out as well. Remember that when you paint with black, you increase the masked area and decrease the selection.

5 Choose File > Save to save your work.

You'll start with an image that consists of only one layer. You must be working in a layer to use the Extract command. If your original image has no layers, you can duplicate the image to a new layer.

Extracting an object from its background

You'll use the Extract command on a foxtail image set against a dark background.

1 Choose File > Open, and open the Foxtail.psd image, located in the Lessons/Lesson05 folder on your hard drive.

The Foxtail image has the same resolution as the Egret image, 72 pixels per inch (ppi). To avoid unexpected results when combining elements from other files, you must either use files with the same image resolution or compensate for differing resolutions. If not, results may be unexpected.

For example, if your original image is 72 ppi and you add an element from a 144-ppi image, the additional element will appear twice as large because it contains twice the number of pixels.

⧉ For complete information on differing resolutions, see "About image size and resolution" in Chapter 3 of the Photoshop 5.0 User Guide or in "Getting Images into Photoshop" of Photoshop 5.0 online Help. A similar topic can be found in ImageReady 2.0 online Help.

2 Choose Image > Extract. The Extract dialog box appears with the edge highlighter tool (𝒫) selected.

To extract an object, you use the Extract dialog box to highlight the edges of the object. Then you define the object's interior and preview the extraction. You can refine and preview the extraction as many times as you wish. Applying the extraction erases the background area to transparency, leaving just the extracted object.

If needed, you can resize the dialog box by dragging its bottom right corner. You specify which part of the image to extract by using the tools and previews in this dialog box.

Now you'll choose a brush size for the highlighter. You'll start with a fairly large brush.

3 Set the Brush Size to 20 by entering a value or dragging the slider. It's easiest to start with a large brush to highlight the general selection, and then switch to a finer brush to fine-tune the selection.

Extract highlighter tool selected; setting Brush Size to 20

4 Using the highlighter, drag over the fuzzy ends and tip of the foxtail until you've completely outlined, but not filled, the foxtail. Draw the highlight so that it slightly overlaps both the foreground and background regions around the edge.

It's OK if the highlight overlaps the edge. The Extract command makes its selection by finding the difference in contrast between pixels. The foxtail has a well-defined interior, so make sure that the highlight forms a complete outline. You do not need to highlight areas where the object touches the image boundaries.

Now you'll highlight the fine stem.

5 Decrease the Brush Size to 5.

6 If desired, select the zoom tool, or use the keyboard shortcut of spacebar+Alt (Windows) or spacebar+Option (Mac OS) and click to zoom in on the stem. You can also use the hand tool to reposition the image preview.

7 Using the highligher tool, drag over the stem to select it.

If you make a mistake and highlight more than desired, select the eraser tool ( ) in the dialog box and drag over the highlight in the preview.

8 Click the fill tool () in the dialog box. Then click inside the object to fill its interior. You must define the object's interior before you can preview the extraction.

Highlighting edges of foxtail tip

Highlighting stem and leaves; then filling

The default Fill color (bright blue) contrasts well with the highlight color (green). You can change either color if you need more contrast with the image colors, using the Highlight and Fill menus in the dialog box.

9 Click Preview to view the extraction.

You can control the preview using one of these techniques:

• To magnify the preview, select the zoom tool (⌕) in the dialog box, and click in the preview. To zoom out, hold down Alt (Windows) or Option (Mac OS), and click with the zoom tool in the preview.

• To view a different part of the preview, select the hand tool in the dialog box and drag in the preview.

To toggle quickly between the edge highlighter and eraser tools when one of the tools is selected, press Alt (Windows) or Option (Mac OS).

10 To refine your selection, edit the extraction boundaries using these techniques:

• Switch between the Original and Extracted views using the View menu.

• Click a filled area with the fill tool to remove the fill.

• Click the eraser tool and then drag to remove any undesired highlighting.

• Select the Show Highlight and Show Fill options to view the highlight and fill colors; deselect the options to hide them.

• Zoom in on your selection using the zoom tool in the dialog box. You can then use a smaller brush size as you edit, switching between the highlighter tool and eraser tool as needed for more precise work.

• Switch to a smaller brush by selecting a different size brush in the Brushes palette and continue to refine the selection's border using the edge highlighter or to erase using the eraser tool.

11 When you are satisfied with your selection, click OK to apply the extraction.

Now you'll add the extracted image to the Egret image.

12 With the Foxtail image active, use the move tool to drag the image to the right side of the Egret image. The foxtail is added as a new layer to the Egret image.

13 With the Egret image active, choose Edit > Transform > Scale to scale the foxtail. Drag the resize handles, holding down Shift to constrain the proportions, until the foxtail is about two-thirds the image height. Press Enter or Return to apply the scaling.

Moving foxtail copy   *Scaling foxtail*   *Result*

14 In the Layers palette with the Foxtail layer (Layer 1) selected, decrease its opacity to 70%.

15 Choose File > Save to save your work. Save and close the Foxtail.psd image.

Extracting an intricate image

The Force Foreground option lets you make intricate selections when an object lacks a clear interior.

1 Choose File > Open, and open the Weeds.psd image, located in the Lessons/Lesson05 folder on your hard drive.

2 Choose Image > Extract. In the Extract Image dialog box, select the Force Foreground option.

You'll start by selecting the color on which to base your selection. The Force Foreground technique works best with objects that are monochromatic or fairly uniform in color.

3 Select the eyedropper tool ( ) in the dialog box, and then click a light area of the weeds to sample the color to be treated as the foreground.

Force Foreground
option

Sampling foreground color

4 Select the highlighter tool ( ).

5 For Brush Size, use the slider or enter a value to select a fairly large brush (about 20 or 30).

6 Drag to begin highlighting the wispy ends of the weeds where they overlap the dark background.

7 When you've enclosed the weed tips, drag to highlight the top third of the weeds fully. The highlight should be solid.

Highlighting weed edges

Selecting top third of weeds

8 Choose Black Matte from the Show pop-up menu at the bottom of the dialog box. A black matte provides good contrast for a light-colored selection.

For a dark selection, try the Gray or White Matte option. None previews a selection against a transparent background.

9 Click Preview to preview the extracted object.

 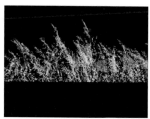

Black Matte option   *Preview*

10 To view and refine the extraction, use one of the following techniques:

• Use the View menu to switch between previews of the original and extracted images.

• Select the Show Highlight or Show Fill option to display the object's extraction boundaries.

• Drag the Smooth slider or enter a value to help remove stray artifacts along the extracted edge.

When you have finished editing, click Preview to view the edited extraction. You can edit and preview the extraction repeatedly until you achieve the desired result.

11 When you are satisfied with the selection, click OK to apply the final extraction. All pixels on the layer outside the extracted object are erased to transparency.

Once you've extracted an image, you can also use the background eraser and history brush tools in the toolbox to clean up any stray edges in the image.

12 Refine the selection as described in step 10 of "Extracting an object from its background."

Now you'll add the extracted weeds to the Egret image.

13 With the Weeds.psd image active, use the move tool to drag the extracted selection to the Egret image. Position the weeds so that they fill the bottom third of the Egret image.

The selection is added to the Egret image as a new layer.

14 In the Layers palette, decrease the opacity of the new layer to 70%.

Moving weed image copy   *Setting new layer opacity to 70%*

15 Choose File > Save to save the Weeds1.psd file, and then close it.

16 If desired, choose File > Save to save your work.

Applying a filter effect to a masked selection

To complete the composite of the marsh grasses and Egret image, you'll isolate the egret as you apply a filter to the image background.

First you'll flatten the image so that the filter is applied only to the active layer.

1 Choose Layer > Flatten Image.

2 In the Channels palette, drag the Egret channel to the Load Selection button ([⬚]) at the bottom of the palette. This loads the channel onto the image.

Now you'll invert the selection so that the egret is protected and you can work on the background.

3 Choose Select > Inverse. Now the previous selection (the egret) is protected, and the background is selected. You can apply changes to the background without worrying about the egret.

4 Choose Filter > Artistic > Colored Pencil. Experiment with the sliders to evaluate the changes before you apply the filter.

Preview different areas of the background by dragging in the preview window of the Colored Pencil filter dialog box. This preview option is available with all filters.

Filter preview   *Filter applied*

5 Click Apply when you're satisfied with the Colored Pencil settings. The filter is applied to the background selection.

You can experiment with other filter effects for the background. Choose Edit > Undo to undo your last performed operation.

6 Choose Select > Deselect to deselect everything.

7 Choose File > Save.

Creating a gradient mask

In addition to using black to indicate what's hidden and white to indicate what's selected, you can paint with shades of gray to indicate partial transparency. For example, if you paint in a channel with a shade of gray that is at least halfway between white and black, the underlying image becomes partially (50% or more) visible.

You'll experiment by adding a gradient (which makes a transition from black to gray to white) to a channel and then filling the selection with a color to see how the transparency levels of the black, gray, and white in the gradient affect the image.

1 In the Channels palette, create a new channel by clicking the New Channel button (▣) at the bottom of the palette.

The new channel labeled Alpha 1 appears at the bottom of the Channels palette, and the other channels are hidden.

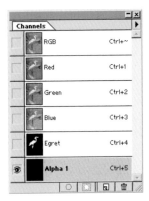

2 Double-click the new channel to open the Channel Options dialog box, and rename the channel **Gradient**. Click OK.

3 Double-click the linear gradient tool (▣) in the toolbox to select the tool and its Options palette.

4 In the Gradient Tool Options palette, choose Black, White from the Gradient menu.

5 Hold down Shift to keep the gradient vertical, and drag the gradient tool from the top of the window to the bottom of the window. The gradient is applied to the channel.

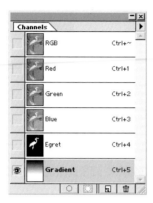

Applying effects using a gradient mask

Now you'll load the gradient as a selection and fill the selection with a color.

When you load a gradient as a selection and then fill the selection with a color, the opacity of the fill color varies over the length of the gradient. Where the gradient is black, no fill color is present; where the gradient is gray, the fill color is partially visible; and where the gradient is white, the fill color is completely visible.

1 In the Channels palette, click the RGB channel to display the full-color preview channel. Next, you'll load the Gradient channel as a selection.

Adjusting the tonal range

The tonal range of an image represents the amount of *contrast*, or detail, in the image and is determined by the image's distribution of pixels, ranging from the darkest pixels (black) to the lightest pixels (white). You'll now correct the photograph's contrast using the Levels command.

1 Choose Image > Adjust > Levels, and make sure that the Preview option is checked.

Notice the histogram in the dialog box. The triangles at the bottom of the histogram represent the shadows (black triangle), highlights (white triangle), and midtones or gamma (gray triangle). If your image had colors across the entire brightness range, the graph would extend across the full width of the histogram, from black triangle to white triangle. Instead, the graph is clumped toward the center, indicating there are no very dark or light colors.

You can adjust the black and white points of the image to extend its tonal range.

2 Drag the left and right triangles inward to where the histogram indicates the darkest and lightest colors begin. Click OK to apply the changes.

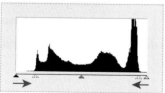
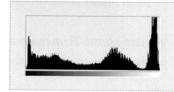

Increasing shadows (black triangle)   *Result*
and adding highlights (white triangle)

3 Choose Image > Histogram to view the new histogram. The tonal range now extends throughout the entire range of the histogram. Click OK.

Note: ImageReady does not have a Histogram command. To adjust and view a histogram, use the Levels command.

4 Choose File > Save.

Using the color correction tools

All Adobe Photoshop color correction tools work essentially the same way: by mapping existing ranges of pixel values to new ranges of values. The difference between the tools is the amount of control you have.

For example, the Brightness/Contrast command makes the same adjustment to every pixel in the selection or image—if you increase the brightness value by 30, 30 is added to the brightness value of every pixel. On the other hand, two of the color adjustment tools are particularly useful because of the control and flexibility they provide. Levels allows you precise adjustments using three variables (highlights, shadows, and midtones). Curves replicates high-end color correction systems and lets you isolate 16 ranges of pixel values between pure highlight and pure shadow.

You can use most color adjustment tools in three ways: applying them to one or more channels, to a regular layer, or to an adjustment layer. When you make color adjustments to a channel or a regular layer, you permanently alter the pixels on that layer.

With an adjustment layer, your color and tonal changes reside only within the adjustment layer and do not alter any pixels. The effect is as if you were viewing the visible layers through the adjustment layer above them. This lets you experiment with color and tonal adjustments without permanently altering pixels in the image. Adjustment layers are also the only way to affect multiple layers at once.

–From the Adobe Photoshop 5.0 User Guide, Chapter 6, "Making Color and Tonal Adjustments."

You can also adjust the contrast (highlights and shadows) and the overall mix of colors in an image automatically using the Image > Adjust > Auto Contrast command. Adjusting contrast maps the darkest and lightest pixels in the image to black and white.

This remapping causes the highlights to appear lighter and the shadows to appear darker and can improve the appearance of many photographic or continuous-tone images. (The Auto Contrast command does not improve flat-color images.)

The Auto Contrast command clips white and black pixels by 0.5%—that is, it ignores the first 0.5% of either extreme when identifying the lightest and darkest pixels in the image. This clipping of color values ensures that white and black values are representative areas of the image's content, rather than extreme pixel values.

Removing a color cast

Some images contain color casts (imbalances of color), which may occur during scanning or which may have existed in the original image. The photograph of the gondolas has a color cast—it's too red.

Note: To see a color cast in an image on your monitor, you need a 24-bit monitor (one that can display millions of colors). On monitors that can display only 256 colors (8 bits), a color cast is difficult, if not impossible, to detect.

Now you'll use a Color Balance adjustment layer to correct the photograph's color cast. An adjustment layer lets you edit an image as many times as you like without permanently changing the original pixel values. Using an adjustment layer to adjust color balance is a particular advantage for images you plan to print. After you see the color proof or printed copy, you can make additional changes to the image, if necessary.

Although ImageReady does not have adjustment layers, you can use the Auto Contrast or Variations command to perform a similar correction. However, the correction affects the entire image, not just a layer. For the greatest control, jump to Photoshop to use an adjustment layer, and then return to ImageReady.

For complete information on color correction tools in ImageReady, see "Adjusting Color and Tone and Sharpening the Image" in ImageReady 2.0 online Help.

1 Choose Layer > New > Adjustment Layer.

2 For Type, choose Color Balance.

3 Click OK to create the adjustment layer and to display the Color Balance Layer dialog box.

4 To adjust the midtones so that they're less red, drag the top slider to the left (we used -15) and the middle slider to the right (we used +8).

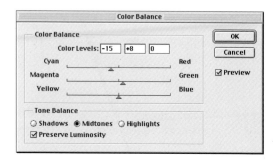

5 Click OK to apply the changes to the Color Balance adjustment layer. Notice that a Color Balance layer has appeared in the Layers palette.

6 In the Layers palette, click the eye icon next to the Color Balance layer to hide and show the layer. You'll see the difference between the adjusted colors and the original colors.

7 Choose File > Save.

Note: *When you double-click an adjustment layer in the Layers palette, the corresponding dialog box appears, where you can edit the values of the adjustment layer.*

Adjusting color balance

Every color adjustment affects the overall color balance in your image. You have numerous ways to achieve similar effects, so determining which adjustment is appropriate depends on the image and on the desired effect.

It helps to keep a diagram of the color wheel on hand if you're new to adjusting color components. You can use the color wheel to predict how a change in one color component affects other colors and also how changes translate between RGB and CMYK color models. For example, you can decrease the amount of any color in an image by increasing the amount of its opposite on the color wheel—and vice versa. Similarly, you can increase and decrease a color by adjusting the two adjacent colors on the wheel, or even by adjusting the two colors adjacent to its opposite.

For example, in a CMYK image you can decrease magenta by decreasing either the amount of magenta or its proportion (by adding cyan and yellow). You can even combine these two corrections, minimizing their effect on overall lightness. In an RGB image, you can decrease magenta by removing red and blue or by adding green. All of these adjustments result in an overall color balance containing less magenta.

–From the Adobe Photoshop 5.0 User Guide, Chapter 6, "Making Color and Tonal Adjustments." A similar topic can be found in ImageReady 2.0 online Help.

Replacing colors in an image

With the Replace Color command, you can create temporary masks based on specific colors and then replace these colors. *Masks* let you isolate an area of an image, so that changes affect just the selected area and not the rest of the image. Options in the Replace Color command's dialog box allow you to adjust the hue, saturation, and lightness components of the selection. *Hue* is color, *saturation* is the purity of the color, and *lightness* is how much white or black is in the image.

You'll use the Replace Color command to change the color of the orange tarp in the gondola at the bottom right corner of the image. The Replace Color command is not available in ImageReady.

1 In the Layers palette, select the Background.

2 Select the zoom tool ( ), and click once on the tarp to zoom in on it.

3 Click the crop tool and drag to select the rectangular marquee tool; then drag a selection around the tarp. Don't worry about making a perfect selection, but be sure to include all the tarp.

4 Choose Image > Adjust > Replace Color to open the Replace Color dialog box. By default, the Selection area of the Replace Color dialog box displays a black rectangle, representing the current selection.

You will now use the eyedropper tool to select the area of color that will be masked and replaced with a new color. Three eyedropper tools are displayed in the Replace Color dialog box.

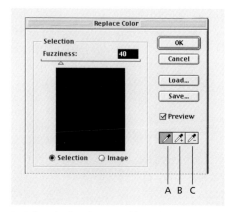

A. Select single color B. Add to selection
C. Subtract from selection

The first eyedropper tool ( ) selects a single color, the eyedropper-plus tool ( ) is used to add colors to a selection, and the eyedropper-minus tool ( ) is used to subtract colors from a selection.

5 Click the eyedropper tool in the dialog box, and click once on the orange tarp to select it.

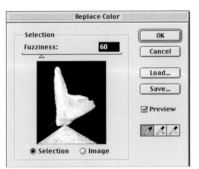

6 Then select the eyedropper-plus tool, and drag over the other areas of the tarp until the entire tarp is highlighted in white in the dialog box.

7 Adjust the tolerance level of the mask by moving the Fuzziness slider to 61. Fuzziness controls the degree to which related colors are included in the mask.

8 In the Transform area of the Replace Color dialog box, drag the Hue slider to 149, the Saturation slider to –17, and the Lightness slider to -39. The color of the tarp is replaced with the new hue, saturation, and lightness.

9 Click OK to apply the changes.

10 Double-click the hand tool (🖐) to fit the image on-screen.

11 Choose Select > Deselect.

12 Choose File > Save.

Adjusting saturation with the sponge tool

Now you'll saturate the color of the gondolas in the foreground using the sponge tool. When you change the saturation of a color, you adjust its strength or purity. The sponge tool is useful in letting you make subtle saturation changes to specific areas of an image. ImageReady also has a sponge tool.

1 Hold down the mouse button on the dodge tool (🔍) in the toolbox, and drag to the sponge tool (◉).

2 Click the Options tab, and choose Saturate from the pop-up menu. To set the intensity of the saturation effect, click the arrow next to the Pressure text box, and drag the Pressure pop-up slider to 90%.

3 Select a large, feathered brush from the second row of the Brushes palette.

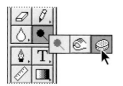  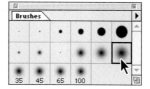

4 Drag the sponge back and forth over the gondolas to saturate their color. The more you drag over an area, the more saturated the color becomes.

Original *Result*

Adjusting lightness with the dodge tool

Next you'll use the dodge tool to lighten the highlights along the gondola's hull and exaggerate the reflection of the water there. The dodge tool is based on the traditional photographer's method of holding back light during an exposure to lighten an area of the image. ImageReady also has a dodge tool.

1 Hold down the mouse button on the sponge tool, and drag to the dodge tool (◉). Then choose Highlights from the menu in the Tool Options palette, and set Exposure to 50%.

2 Select a medium, feathered brush from the second row of the Brushes palette.

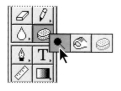 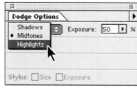 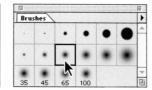

3 Drag the dodge tool back and forth over the gondola's hull to bring out its highlights.

Original   *Result*

Removing unwanted objects

You can remove unwanted objects from a photograph. Using the rubber stamp tool, you can remove an object or area by "cloning" an area of the image over the area you want to eliminate.

You'll eliminate the small boat near the center of the image by painting over it with a copy of the water.

1 Select the zoom tool; then click the small boat to magnify that part of the image.

2 Double-click the rubber stamp tool (🔨) in the toolbox, and make sure that the Aligned option in the Rubber Stamp Options palette is deselected. In the Brushes palette, choose a medium-size brush from the middle row.

3 Center the rubber stamp tool over the water between the large gondola and the post to its right. Then hold down Alt (Windows) or Option (Mac OS), and click to sample or copy that part of the image. Make sure that the area you sample will blend well with the area around the object you are removing.

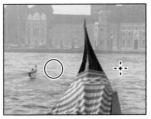

Clicking to sample image   *Dragging to paint over image*

4 Drag the rubber stamp tool over the boat to paint over it with a copy of the water you just sampled. Notice the cross hair that follows your cursor as you paint; it represents the point from which the rubber stamp tool is cloning.

5 Double-click the hand tool in the toolbox to fit the image on-screen.

6 Choose File > Save.

Replacing part of an image

Because the sky is fairly drab and overcast in this photograph, you'll replace it with a more interesting sky from another file. You'll begin by selecting the current sky.

1 Select the magic wand tool ( ). Click to select part of the sky. Hold down Shift, and click the rest of the sky to select it.

2 Open the Clouds.psd file located in the Lesson06 folder.

3 Choose Select > All; then choose Edit > Copy. Close the Clouds.psd file.

4 Choose Edit > Paste Into to paste the clouds into the current selection. Notice that a new layer has been added to the Layers palette.

Note: ImageReady does not have a Paste Into command. To replicate the effect, select the sky in step 1, and delete it. Open the Clouds.psd file, and copy it as in steps 2 and 3. Then choose Edit > Paste, and move the cloud layer beneath the boat layer.

5 Select the move tool ( ), and drag the clouds into the position you want.

Sky selected   *Clouds pasted into sky*   *Clouds moved into position*

Now you'll change the clouds' opacity to make them blend better with the rest of the image.

6 Use the keyboard shortcut of typing any number from 01 (1%) to 100 (100%) to set the new cloud layer's opacity (we used 55%).

7 Choose File > Save.

Opacity set to 55%   *Result*

Now you'll flatten the image into a single layer so that you can apply the Unsharp Mask filter, the final step in retouching the photo. Because you may want to return to a version of the file with all its layers intact, you will use the Save As command to save the flattened file with a new name.

8 Choose Layer > Flatten Image.

9 Choose File > Save As. In the dialog box, type a new filename, and click Save.

Applying the Unsharp Mask filter

The last step you take when retouching a photo is to apply the Unsharp Mask filter, which adjusts the contrast of the edge detail and creates the illusion of a more focused image. ImageReady also has an Unsharp Mask filter.

1 Choose Filter > Sharpen > Unsharp Mask. Make sure that the Preview option is selected so that you can view the effect before you apply it. To get a better view, you can place the pointer within the preview window and drag to see different parts of the image. You can also change the magnification of the preview image with the plus and minus buttons located below the window.

2 Drag the Amount slider until the image is as sharp as you want (we used 120%); then click OK to apply the Unsharp Mask filter.

3 Drag the Radius slider to determine the number of pixels surrounding the edge pixels that affects the sharpening. For high-resolution images, a Radius between 1 and 2 is recommended.

The default Threshold value of 0 sharpens all pixels in the image. You can adjust the Threshold slider to determine how different the sharpened pixels must be from the surrounding area before they are considered edge pixels and sharpened by the filter.

For complete information on the Unsharp Mask filter, see "Step 6: Sharpen the Image" in Chapter 6 of the Photoshop 5.0 User Guide or in "Making Color and Tonal Adjustments" of Photoshop 5.0 online Help. A similar topic can be found in ImageReady 2.0 online Help.

Sharpening the image

Unsharp masking, or USM, is a traditional film compositing technique used to sharpen edges in an image. The Unsharp Mask filter corrects blurring introduced during photographing, scanning, resampling, or printing. It is useful for images intended for both print and online.

The Unsharp Mask filter locates pixels that differ from surrounding pixels by the threshold you specify and increases the pixels' contrast by the amount you specify. In addition, you specify the radius of the region to which each pixel is compared.

The effects of the Unsharp Mask filter are far more pronounced on-screen than in high-resolution output. If your final destination is print, experiment to determine what dialog box settings work best for your image.

–From the Adobe Photoshop 5.0 User Guide, Chapter 6, "Making Color and Tonal Adjustments." A similar topic can be found in ImageReady 2.0 online Help.

Saving the image for four-color printing

Before you save a Photoshop file for use in a four-color publication, you must change the image to CMYK color mode so that it will be printed correctly in four-color process inks. You can use the Mode command to change the image's color mode.

For complete information on color modes, see Chapter 4 of the Photoshop 5.0 User Guide or "Choosing a Color Mode" in Photoshop 5.0 online Help.

You can perform these tasks in Photoshop only. ImageReady does not have printing capability. It uses only one color mode, RGB, for on-screen display.

1 Choose Image > Mode > CMYK.

You can now save the file in the correct format required for Adobe PageMaker and your publication. Because PageMaker uses the Tagged-Image File Format (TIFF) for images that will be printed in process or CMYK colors, you will save the photo as a TIFF file.

2 Choose File > Save As.

3 In the dialog box, select TIFF from the Save As menu (Windows) or Format menu (Mac OS).

4 Click Save.

5 In the TIFF Options dialog box, click the correct Byte Order for your system.

The image is now fully retouched, saved, and ready for placement in the PageMaker layout.

On your own: Painting with the art history brush

In Photoshop, you can simulate the texture of painting with different colors and artistic styles using the art history brush tool. The art history brush paints with stylized strokes, using the source data from a specified history state or snapshot. The brush works well with realistic images to let you create painterly, impressionistic effects. Try out different settings to see the variety of effects you can create in the same image. (ImageReady does not have an art history brush.)

1 Choose File > Open, and open the image you want to paint.

2 Choose File > Save As, rename the file, and save it, to retain a copy of your original image for future use.

3 For a variety of visual effects, experiment with applying filters or filling the image with a solid color before painting with the art history brush tool. For example, add a layer to the image, fill it with white, and then use the art history brush tool to paint.

4 In the History palette, click the icon of the state or snapshot to use as the source for the art history brush tool. A brush icon appears next to the source history state.

 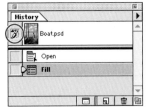

You can select any history state to be your source by clicking in the left column, and if you're not satisfied with an effect, you can return to a previous state or the snapshot by clicking the state thumbnail.

5 Select and double-click the art history brush tool ( ) to display its Options palette. The art history brush tool is grouped with the history brush tool in the toolbox.

6 In the Brushes palette, select a brush. For interesting effects, try using a texture, noncircular, or custom brush. The brush corresponds to the size of individual paint strokes, not the total area covered by the paint.

7 Drag in the image to paint.

When you've practiced painting with the brush to see how it works, experiment with the settings to create various effects:

• Control the shape of the paint stroke by choosing an option from the paint style menu, located below the blending mode menu in the Options palette.

• Try out different blending modes, and vary the opacity.

For information on setting tool options, see "Using the Options palette for painting and editing tools", in Chapter 9 of the Photoshop 5.0 User Guide or in "Painting" of Photoshop 5.0 online Help. A similar topic can be found in ImageReady 2.0 help.

• Vary how much the paint color changes from the color in the source state or snapshot by adjusting the Fidelity. The lower the fidelity, the more the color will vary from the source.

• Set the area covered by the paint strokes using the Area option. Try increasing the size to enlarge the covered area and increase the number of the strokes.

• Limit the regions where paint strokes will be applied to only those areas that differ considerably from the color in the source state or snapshot using a high tolerance. To paint anywhere in the image, use a low tolerance.

• Select a small brush to maintain the image integrity and reveal the brush stroke. The larger the brush you use, the greater the distortion will be to the image.

If you are using a pressure-sensitive tablet, select any of the following stylus options:

• Size to have increased pressure result in a larger area covered by the paint. Note that Size refers to the area of coverage, not the brush size.

• Opacity to have increased pressure result in more opaque paint.

For an illustration of the artwork for this section, see the gallery at the end of the color section.

Review questions

1 What is resolution?

2 How can you use the crop tool in photo retouching?

3 How can you adjust the tonal range of an image?

4 How can you correct a color cast in a photograph?

5 What is saturation, and how can you adjust it?

6 Why would you use the Unsharp Mask filter on a photo?

Review answers

1 The term *resolution* refers to the number of pixels that describe an image and establish its detail. The three different types of resolution include image resolution, measured in pixels per inch (ppi); monitor resolution, measured in dots per inch (dpi); and printer or output resolution, measured in ink dots per inch.

2 You can use the crop tool to scale and straighten an image.

3 You can use the black and white triangles below the Levels command histogram to control where the darkest and lightest points in the image begin and thus extend its tonal range.

4 In Photoshop, you can correct a color cast with a Color Balance adjustment layer. The adjustment layer lets you change the color of the image as many times as you like without permanently affecting the original pixel values.

5 Saturation is the strength or purity of color in an image. You can increase the saturation in a specific area of an image with the sponge tool.

6 The Unsharp Mask filter adjusts the contrast of the edge detail and creates the illusion of a more focused image.

Lesson 7

7 | Basic Pen Tool Techniques

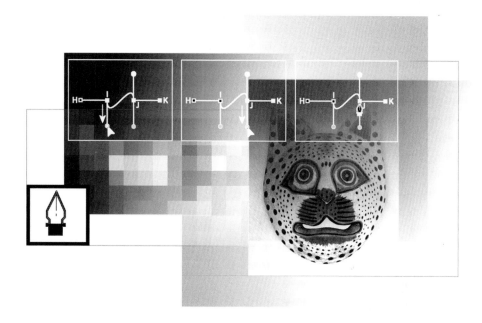

The pen tool draws precise straight or curved lines called paths. You can use the pen tool as a drawing tool or as a selection tool. When used as a selection tool, the pen tool always draws smooth, anti-aliased outlines. These paths are an excellent alternative to using the standard selection tools for creating intricate selections.

In this lesson, you'll learn how to do the following:

- Practice drawing straight and curved paths using the pen tool.
- Save paths.
- Fill and stroke paths.
- Edit paths using the path editing tools.
- Convert a path to a selection.
- Convert a selection to a path.

This lesson will take about 50 minutes to complete. The lesson is designed to be done in Adobe Photoshop. ImageReady does not have a pen tool and does not support paths.

If needed, remove the previous lesson folder from your hard drive, and copy the Lesson07 folder onto it.

Getting started

Before beginning this lesson, restore the default application settings for Adobe Photoshop. See "Restoring default preferences" on page 4.

Now you'll open the start file and begin the lesson by working with templates that guide you through the process of creating straight paths, curved paths, and paths that are a combination of both. In addition, you'll learn how to add points to a path, how to subtract points from a path, and how to convert a straight line to a curve and vice versa. After you've practiced drawing and editing paths using the templates, you'll open an image and practice drawing a path.

1 Restart Adobe Photoshop.

2 Click Cancel to exit the color management dialog box that appears.

3 Choose File > Open, and open the Straight.psd file, located in the Lessons/Lesson07 folder on your hard drive.

An image containing a template of straight lines appears. You'll practice drawing straight paths using a template, so that you can practice drawing the paths as many times as you like.

For an illustration of the finished artwork for this lesson, see the gallery at the beginning of the color section.

4 If desired, select the zoom tool ( ), and drag over the image to magnify the view.

Drawing paths with the pen tool

The pen tool draws straight and curved lines called *paths*. A path is any line or shape you draw using the pen, magnetic pen, or freeform pen tool. Of these tools, the pen tool draws paths with the greatest precision; the magnetic pen and freeform pen tool let you draw paths as if you were drawing with a pencil on paper.

Paths can be open or closed. Open paths have two distinct endpoints. Closed paths are continuous; for example, a circle is a closed path. The type of path you draw affects how it can be selected and adjusted. Paths do not print when you print your artwork. (That is because paths are vector objects that contain no pixels, unlike the bitmap shapes drawn by the pencil and other painting tools.)

1 Click the pen tool ( ) in the toolbox.

 Press Shift+P on the keyboard to select the pen tool. Continue to press Shift+P to scroll through the pen tools.

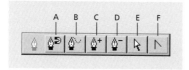

A. *Magnetic pen*
B. *Freeform pen*
C. *Add-anchor-point (+)*
D. *Delete-anchor-point (–)*
E. *Direct-selection (A)*
F. *Convert-anchor-point*

2 Click the Paths palette tab to bring the palette to the front of its group. The Paths palette displays thumbnail previews of the paths you draw.

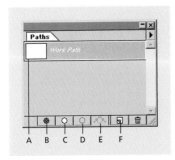

A. Thumbnail preview B. Fill Path
C. Stroke Path D. Make Selection
E. Make Path F. New Path

Drawing straight paths

Straight paths are created by clicking the mouse button. The first time you click, you set a starting point for a path. Each time thereafter that you click, a straight line is drawn between the previous point and the current point.

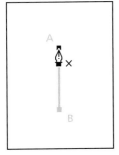
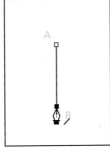

Click to set a starting point...   *click again to draw a straight line.*

1 Position the pen tool on point A, and click the pen tool; then click point B to create a straight line path.

As you draw paths, a temporary storage area named Work Path appears in the Paths palette to keep track of the paths you draw.

2 End the path by clicking the pen tool in the toolbox.

The points that connect paths are called *anchor points*. You can drag individual anchor points to edit segments of a path, or you can select all the anchor points to select the entire path.

You'll learn more about anchor points later in this lesson.

3 Double-click the Work Path in the Paths palette to open the Save Path dialog box. Type the name **Straight lines**, and click OK to rename the path. The path is renamed, and remains selected in the Paths palette.

You must save a work path to avoid losing its contents. If you deselect the work path without saving and then start drawing again, a new work path will replace the first one.

About anchor points, direction lines, and direction points

A path consists of one or more straight or curved segments. Anchor points mark the endpoints of the path segments. On curved segments, each selected anchor point displays one or two direction lines, ending in direction points. The positions of direction lines and points determine the size and shape of a curved segment. Moving these elements reshapes the curves in a path.

A path can be closed, with no beginning or end (for example, a circle), or open, with distinct endpoints (for example, a wavy line).

Smooth curves are connected by anchor points called smooth points. Sharply curved paths are connected by corner points.

When you move a direction line on a smooth point, the curved segments on both sides of the point adjust simultaneously. In comparison, when you move a direction line on a corner point, only the curve on the same side of the point as the direction line is adjusted.

–From the Adobe Photoshop 5.0 User Guide, Chapter 7, "Selecting."

Moving and adjusting paths

You use the direct-selection tool to select and adjust an anchor point, a path segment, or an entire path.

1 Select the direct-selection tool ( ) from the hidden tools palette under the pen tool. A small triangle to the right of the pen tool icon indicates a pull-out menu of hidden tools.

To select the direct-selection tool, press A. You can also select the direct-selection tool when the pen tool is active by holding down Ctrl (Windows) or Command (Mac OS).

2 Click the path in the window to select it, and then move the path by dragging anywhere on the path using the direct-selection tool.

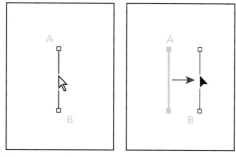

Selecting a path   *Moving a path*

3 To adjust the angle or length of the path, drag one of the anchor points with the direct-selection tool.

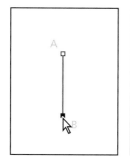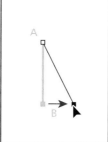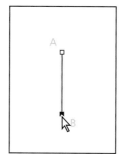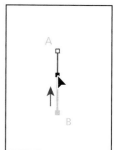

Adjusting the path angle   *Adjusting the path length*

4 Select the pen tool in the hidden tools palette in the toolbox (right now it's under the direct-selection tool).

5 To begin the next path, click point C with the pen tool. Notice that an *x* appears in the Paths palette to indicate that you are starting a new path.

If desired, practice drawing another closed path using the star shape on the template as a guide.

At this point, all of the paths you've drawn appear in the Straight Lines path in the Paths palette. Each individual path on the Straight Lines path is called a *subpath*.

You can convert any path you have drawn into a selection and combine this selection with others. (You'll try this later.) You can also convert selection borders into paths and fine-tune them.

Painting paths

Painting paths adds pixels that appear when you print an image. Filling paints a closed path with color, an image, or a pattern. Stroking paints color along the path. To fill or stroke a path, you must first select it.

1 Click the Swatches palette tab to bring the palette forward. Click a swatch to select a foreground color to use to paint the path.

2 Select the direct-selection tool (↖) in the hidden tools palette under the pen tool.

3 In the image window, click the zigzag line with the direct-selection tool to select it. Then choose Stroke Subpath from the Paths palette menu.

4 For Tool, choose Airbrush, and click OK. The path is stroked with the current airbrush settings.

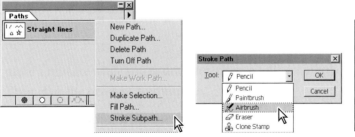

Using the Stroke Path command   *Airbrush tool*   *Result*

Note: You can select a painting tool and set attributes before you select the tool in the Stroke Subpath dialog box.

Now try filling one of the paths.

5 In the Swatches palette, click a swatch to select a different foreground color for the fill.

6 Click the triangular closed path with the direct-selection tool. Then choose Fill Subpath from the Paths palette menu. The Fill dialog box appears.

7 Click OK to accept the defaults. The triangular path is filled with the foreground color.

Using the Fill command to fill a   *Result*
closed path

8 To hide the paths, click below the pathnames in the blank area of the Paths palette.

9 Choose File > Close, and do not save changes.

Drawing curved paths

Curved paths are created by clicking and dragging. The first time you click and drag, you set a starting point for the curved path and also determine the direction of the curve. As you continue to drag, a curved path is drawn between the previous point and the current point.

As you drag the pen tool, Photoshop draws *direction lines* and *direction points* from the anchor point. Direction lines and points are used to edit the shape of curves and to change the direction of curves. You'll edit paths using the direction lines and direction points in a few minutes.

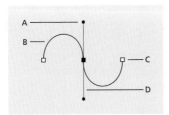

Direction lines and points setting the curve direction
A. *Direction point* **B.** *Curved segment*
C. *Anchor point* **D.** *Direction line*

Like paths, direction lines and points do not print when you print your artwork because they are vector objects that contain no pixels.

1 Choose File > Open, and open the Curves.psd file,

2 located in the Lessons/Lesson07 folder on your hard drive.

3 Select the pen tool from the hidden tools palette in the toolbox.

4 Click on point A of the first curve. Hold down the mouse button, and drag toward the red dot.

5 To complete the first curve of the path, drag from point B to the red dot. If you make a mistake while you're drawing, choose Edit > Undo to undo the last point you drew. Then continue drawing the path.

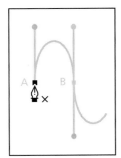 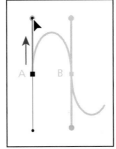 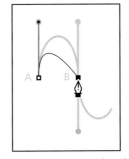 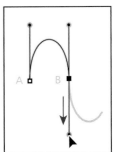

Position pointer on point A and drag to draw a curve.   *Drag again to complete the curve.*

6 Complete the curved path by dragging from point C to the red dot and from point D to the red dot. End the path using one of the methods you learned.

7 Now you'll save the temporary work path so that you don't lose its contents.

8 Double-click the Work Path in the Paths palette to open the Save Path dialog box. Type the name **Curve1,** and click OK to rename the path. The named path is selected in the Paths palette.

You must save the work path before you deselect it to prevent a new work path from replacing the first one as you start drawing again.

Creating separate paths

Now that you've created a new path in the Paths palette, as you continue to draw the path, you create a connected series of segments, or subpaths. Subpaths are saved automatically.

But sometimes you'll want to create separate named paths for each path you draw. To start a new Work Path, you click away from the current path in the Paths palette.

1 In the Paths palette, click in the blank area below the Curve1 path to deselect the path.

When you deselect a path in the Paths palette, any paths on the named path are deselected (hidden). To make them reappear, you click the desired path in the Paths palette (don't click the path now, because you're going to create a new one in a moment).

2 Drag up from point E to the red dot; then drag up from point F to the red dot. You'll notice that as soon as you begin drawing, a new Work Path appears in the Paths palette.

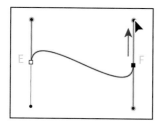 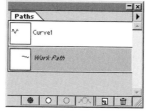

3 End the path using one of the methods you learned.

4 Double-click the Work Path in the Paths palette, name the path **Curve2,** and then click OK.

5 Click away from the path in the Paths palette to deselect it.

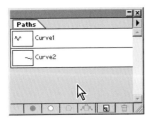

Now you'll create a closed curved path.

6 Drag up from point G to the red dot; then drag down from point H to the red dot. To close the path, position the pointer over point G, and click.

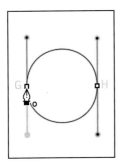

7 In the Paths palette, double-click the Work Path, save the path as **Closed Path**, and then click away from the path to deselect it.

Now you'll have a chance to edit the curved paths you've drawn.

8 Select the direct-selection tool (⬚) from the hidden tools under the pen tool.

 Hold down Ctrl (Windows) or Command (Mac OS) when the pen tool is active to select the direct-selection tool from the keyboard.

9 In the Paths palette, click the Curve2 path to select it; then click the path in the window to select it.

5 Now drag fr
the next curve.

*Alt-clicking (Windo
point; then dragging*

6 Drag from pc
the methods yoı

7 To start the sé
tool; then hold c

8 Position the µ
the direction of

9 Drag from po
point F to set a c

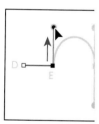

*Dragging in the direc
the opposite direction*

10 Hold down S
one of the methc

11 To create the
click point I.

12 To set a curve

13 Drag from pc

10 Click one of the anchor points in the curve; then drag a direction point at the end of the direction line emanating from the anchor point.

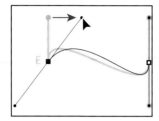

Dragging a direction point…   *to change the direction of a curve*

11 Now drag an anchor point to change the location of the curve.

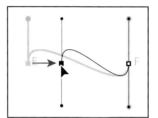

Dragging an anchor point…   *to change the location of the curve*

Stroking and filling paths

In addition to using the Stroke Subpath command, you can stroke paths by dragging a named path onto the Stroke Path button at the bottom of the Paths palette. To determine which painting option you want to stroke the path with, select the desired painting tool in the toolbox before you drag the path onto the Stroke Path button.

1 Click the paintbrush tool (✎) in the toolbox.

2 Drag the
stroke it wi

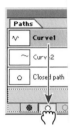

Note: *You ca*
bottom of th
the button.

3 Drag the
it with the c

When you fi
starting poi

4 Choose F

Combinir

Now that yo
them togeth

To create a p
indicate the

1 Choose Fi
folder on you

2 Select the

3 Drag up fi

4 At point E
Alt-click (Wi

10 Still on point H, Alt-drag (Windows) or Option-drag (Mac OS) to the yellow dot to set the direction of the final curve.

11 To end the path, Alt-drag (Windows) or Option-drag (Mac OS) point A to the yellow dot. (This adds a slight curve to the line between the ears.)

12 In the Paths palette, double-click the Work Path, name the path **Face**, and click OK to save it.

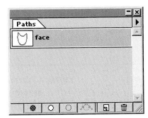

13 Choose File > Save to save your work.

Converting selections to paths

Now you'll create a second path using a different method. First, you'll use a selection tool to select a similarly colored area, and then you'll convert the selection to a path.

1 Click the Layers palette tab to display the palette, and then drag the Template layer to the Trash button at the bottom of the palette. You won't need this layer any longer. Only the background should remain.

2 Double-click the magic wand tool ( ) in the toolbox. In the Magic Wand Options palette, enter **60** in the Tolerance text box.

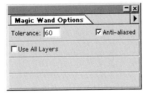

3 Click the gray background where it shows through the cat's mouth.

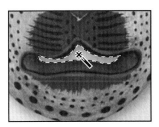

4 If you don't select the entire area the first time, Shift-click again on the mouth with the magic wand to add to the selection.

5 Click the Paths palette tab to bring the Paths palette to the front. Then click the Make Path button at the bottom of the palette. The selection is converted to a path, and a new Work Path is created. You can convert any selection made with a selection tool into a path.

Note: If desired, use the tools you've learned to adjust the points on the path.

6 Double-click the Work Path, and name it **Mouth**; then click OK to save the path.

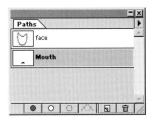

7 Choose File > Save to save your work.

Converting paths to selections

Just as you can convert selection borders to paths, you can convert paths to selections. With their smooth outlines, paths let you make precise selections. Now that you've drawn paths for the cat's face and mouth, you'll convert them to selections and apply a filter to the selection.

1 In the Paths palette, click the Face path to make it active.

2 Convert the Face path to a selection using either of the following methods:

• Choose Make Selection from the Paths palette menu, and click OK.

• Drag the Face path to the Make Selection button at the bottom of the Paths palette.

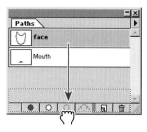

Next, you'll subtract the mouth selection from the face selection so that you can apply a filter without affecting the gray area of the background, which shows through the cat's mouth.

3 In the Paths palette, click the Mouth path; then choose Make Selection from the Paths palette menu.

4 In the Make Selection dialog box, select Subtract from Selection in the Operation section; then click OK.

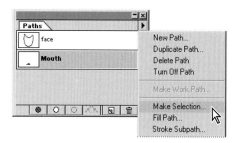

The Mouth path is simultaneously converted to a selection and subtracted from the Face selection.

Subtracting the mouth selection   *Result*
from the face selection

5 Before adding a filter to the mask, make sure that the foreground is set to white and the background is set to black (if necessary, click the Default Colors icon in the toolbox, and then click the Switch Colors icon).

6 Choose Filter > Artistic > Neon Glow. Accept the defaults, and click OK to apply the filter.

Neon Glow filter   *Result*

The filter has been applied to only the mask area. As a final step, you'll apply a textured filter to the entire image.

7 Choose Select > Deselect to deselect everything.

8 Choose Filter > Texture > Texturizer. Select the Sandstone option from the Texture menu; then click OK to apply the settings.

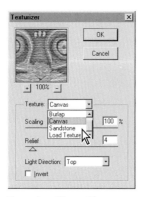

Texturizer filter with Sandstone option   *Result*

9 Choose File > Save to save your work; then close the file.

You've completed the Basic Pen Tool lesson. Try drawing paths around different objects in your artwork to practice using the pen tool. With practice, you'll find that the pen tool can be invaluable for creating intricate outlines and selections.

For the Web: Creating perfect transparency edges

Adding artwork to a Web page often involves outlining an object and defining a transparent background area so that the object displays properly on the Web page. The process of making a selection and deleting the unwanted portions of an image is a fairly simple one, but one that all too often results in an unsightly *halo* or *matte line* effect around the object. This halo occurs when dark or light shading of the pixels near or at the edge of the object don't match the new background that the object is placed against. With ImageReady, you can change the edge shading to match any background color, eliminating halos completely.

1 Open the file you want to work with in Photoshop or ImageReady.

2 Select the portion of the image that you want to keep.

Note: Although you can use any of the selection tools to select your object (or even use the magic eraser tool to delete the area around the object), the pen tools may be a better choice if you need to isolate the object from a very busy background or a background with colors similar to your object. Unless the shape of the object is very complex, you can use the pen tools to create very precise boundaries, which can then be converted to a selection (using the Make Selection command in the Paths palette menu).

3 If your image does not already have a transparent background, copy the selection, create a new file with a transparent background, and paste the selection into the new file.

You now have a smaller file with the desired image isolated against a transparent background.

4 If you have been working in Photoshop, jump to ImageReady.

5 Create a new layer below the object layer and fill it with the predominant background color of the Web page where the object will be placed.

This gives you an idea how the object will look when placed on the Web page. It is usually at this point that the undesirable color cast or halo at the edge of the object becomes obvious.

In this lesson, you'll learn how to do the following:

- Add guides to an image to help you make selections and align artwork.

- Create and edit layer masks to selectively hide and reveal portions of artwork on a layer.

- Align images and layers.

- Create clipping groups, which let you use an image on one layer as a mask for artwork on other layers.

- Add adjustment layers to an image, and use them to apply color and tonal adjustments without permanently changing pixel data.

- Add layer effects to a type layer, and apply the effects to multiple layers.

- Delete a layer mask.

- Save layered files.

This lesson will take about 40 minutes to complete. The lesson is designed to be done in Adobe Photoshop, but information on using similar functionality in Adobe ImageReady is included where appropriate.

If needed, remove the previous lesson folder from your hard drive, and copy the Lesson08 folder onto it.

Getting started

Before beginning this lesson, restore the default application settings for Adobe Photoshop. See "Restoring default preferences" on page 4.

You'll start the lesson by viewing the final Lesson file to see what you'll accomplish.

1 Restart Adobe Photoshop.

2 Click Cancel to exit the color management dialog box that appears.

3 Choose File > Open, and open the 08End.psd file, located in the Lessons/Lesson08 folder.

4 When you have finished viewing the file, either leave the End file open on your desktop for reference, or close it without saving changes.

For an illustration of the finished artwork for this lesson, see the gallery at the beginning of the color section.

Now you'll open the start file, which contains an image that has two layers, and you'll work with various layering and masking techniques to complete the image.

5 Choose File > Open, and open the 08Start.psd file, located in the Lessons/Lesson08 folder on your hard drive.

The Layers palette shows that there are two layers in the file—the Tulips layer and the background. At this point, you can see only the Tulips layer, because the background is positioned under the tulips.

6 In the Layers palette, click the eye icon next to the Tulips layer to hide it. The winter scene on the background beneath the Tulips layer is revealed. Make the Tulips layer visible before continuing to the next step.

Adding guides to align artwork

Guides help you align artwork in an image. To create a guide, you turn on the rulers and then drag from the horizontal or vertical ruler. Here you'll add guides to divide the image into four equal quadrants; later you'll make a selection based on one of these quadrants. ImageReady also includes rulers and guides for working with images.

1 Choose View > Show Rulers. This image is 8 inches by 5 inches.

Note: To change the unit of measurement for the rulers, choose File > Preferences > Units and Rulers, and select the desired unit of measurement from the Units menu. The ImageReady rulers show only pixels, as befits a Web application.

2 Click anywhere within the horizontal ruler at the top of the image, and drag downward to align a guide at the 2.5-inch mark on the vertical ruler. Release the mouse button to place the guide.

3 Click anywhere within the vertical ruler at the left side of the image, and drag to the right to align a guide at the 4-inch mark on the horizontal ruler. Release the mouse button to place the guide.

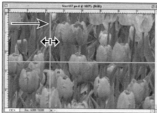

Dragging guide

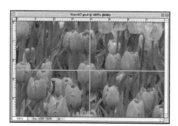

Setting guide at 4 in. horizontally, 2.5 in. vertically

💡 *If you need to reposition a guide, click the move tool in the toolbox, position the move tool on the guide, and drag to reposition the guide.*

4 Choose File > Save.

Using guides and the grid

Guides appear as lines that float over the entire image and do not print. You can move, remove, or lock a guide to avoid accidentally moving it. The grid appears by default as nonprinting lines but can also be displayed as dots. The grid is useful for laying out elements symmetrically.

Guides and grids behave in similar ways:

• *Selections, selection borders, and tools snap to a guide or the grid when dragged within 8 screen (not image) pixels. Guides also snap to the grid when moved. You can turn this feature on and off.*

• *Guide spacing, along with guide and grid visibility and snapping, is specific to an image.*

• *Grid spacing, along with guide and grid color and style, is the same for all images.*

–From the Adobe Photoshop 5.0 User Guide, Chapter 8, "Editing and Retouching."

Note: *Although ImageReady does have ruler guides, it does not have a grid feature.*

Working with layer masks

Layer masks let you hide or reveal portions of the artwork on an individual layer. When you hide artwork, that part of the layer becomes transparent, and underlying layers show through. You can control how much artwork on a layer is hidden or revealed by making selections for the mask and by painting on the mask using black, white, or shades of gray. ImageReady also uses layer masks to conceal artwork.

Using a selection with a layer mask

You'll start by selecting one of the quadrants on the Tulips layer, and then you'll use a layer mask to hide all but the selected quadrant.

1 In the Layers palette, make sure that the Tulips layer is active.

2 Select the rectangular marquee tool (⌷) in the toolbox. Then drag a selection around the bottom left quadrant of the image.

3 Choose Layer > Add Layer Mask > Reveal Selection. The Reveal Selection command displays the selected quadrant of the tulips and hides the rest of the Tulips layer. The winter scene now shows through in the other three quadrants of the image.

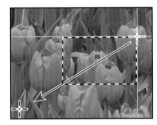  

Selecting bottom left quadrant   *Selection made*   *Selection revealed through layer mask*

In the Layers palette, several changes take place when you add a layer mask. A layer mask thumbnail appears to the right of the Tulips layer thumbnail, indicating that a layer mask has been added. A link icon (⅄) appears between the layer thumbnail and the layer mask thumbnail, indicating that the layer and the mask are linked, and a layer mask icon (▣) appears in the column next to the eye icon, indicating that the layer mask is active.

You can make either the layer or the layer mask active by clicking the corresponding thumbnail.

4 Click the Tulips layer thumbnail. The mask icon changes to a paintbrush icon, indicating that the Tulips layer is active. Then click the layer mask thumbnail to make the layer mask active.

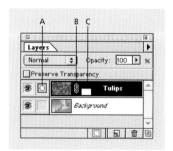

A. *Layer mask icon (indicating layer mask is selected)* **B.** *Link icon* **C.** *Layer mask thumbnail*

5 Choose File > Save.

Painting on a layer mask

Painting with white on a layer mask erases some of the mask, revealing artwork on that layer. Painting with black adds to the layer mask, hiding artwork so that the image beneath shows through. Painting with shades of gray on a layer mask partially hides artwork, making it semitransparent. ImageReady does not allow you to edit a layer mask directly. To edit a layer mask in ImageReady, convert the mask to a selection, use the selection tools to edit the selection, then convert the selection back to a layer mask. You can also jump to Photoshop to edit the mask directly, then save it as a selection.

Now you'll paint on the layer mask with white to reveal the tulip heads that were cut off by the rectangular selection. Don't worry if you bring in some tulip leaves along with the heads. You can paint with black later to remove the leaves.

1 Make sure that white is the foreground color and black is the background color in the toolbox color selection box.

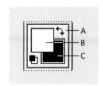

A. Switch Colors icon
B. Foreground color
C. Background color

Note: When you paint a layer mask, the default foreground color is white and the default background color is black.

2 Select the paintbrush tool ( ) in the toolbox. Then click the Brushes palette tab, and select a large, soft-edged brush.

3 Begin painting above the horizontal guide where the layer mask has cropped the tops of the tulips. (Don't be too careful here.)

As you paint with white, you erase some of the layer mask, and the tulip heads appear. In the Layers palette, notice how the layer mask changes as you paint.

Now you'll paint with black to hide the green leaf areas that came in accidentally when you painted in the tulip heads.

4 Click the Switch Colors icon to make black the foreground color.

Pressing the x key switches the foreground and background colors.

5 Select a small, soft-edged brush from the Brushes palette.

6 Paint with black to extend the mask and hide the extra leaf areas. Again notice how the layer mask thumbnail changes as you paint.

Painting with white to show tulips and leaves *Painting with black to remove leaves* *Result*

Viewing layer masks

There are several different ways to view and hide layer masks in an image. For instance, you can use the Layers palette to view just the layer mask without the layer's artwork.

1 To display the layer mask, hold down Alt (Windows) or Option (Mac OS), and click the layer mask thumbnail. The artwork in the 08Start window disappears, and the black-and-white layer mask takes its place.

Note: ImageReady cannot replace the image with the layer mask.

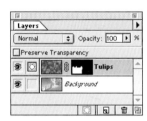 

2 To hide the layer mask and redisplay the artwork, hold down Alt (Windows) or Option (Mac OS), and click the layer mask thumbnail again.

You can also view the tulips artwork without its layer mask simply by turning off the mask.

3 To turn off the layer mask, hold down Shift, and click the layer mask thumbnail on the Tulips layer. A large red *x* appears on the layer mask thumbnail.

4 To turn the layer mask back on, click the layer mask thumbnail in the Layers palette. The *x* disappears, and the tulips are again masked.

5 Choose File > Save.

Unlinking layer masks

By default, layer masks are linked to the artwork on the layer. When you move a mask or the artwork, both the mask and the artwork are repositioned. You can unlink the layer mask and the artwork on the layer if you want to move them independently.

1 In the Layers palette, click the link icon between the layer thumbnail and the layer mask thumbnail to turn off linking.

2 Click the layer thumbnail for the Tulips layer to make the layer active.

3 Select the move tool () in the toolbox, and drag in the image window to move the artwork. Notice that the layer mask does not move with the artwork.

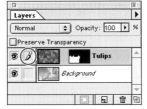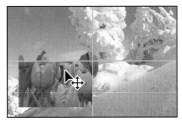

Turning linking off *Making thumbnail layer active* *Moving artwork without mask linked*

4 Choose Edit > Undo to undo the move.

5 Close the Sunflowr.psd and Leaves.psd files.

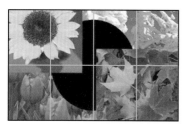

You can center the two new images over the circle image by using the Align Linked command. The command allows you to align the contents of linked layers to the contents of the active layer.

6 Click the Circle layer to make it active.

7 Click the link column to the right of the eye icon for Layer 1 and Layer 2 to link them to the Circle layer.

8 Choose Layer > Align Linked > Vertical Center. The sunflower and leaves images shift into vertical alignment with the circle image.

9 Choose Layer > Align Linked > Horizontal Center. The sunflower and leaves images shift again into horizontal alignment with the circle.

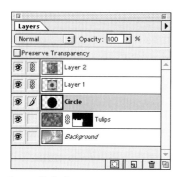
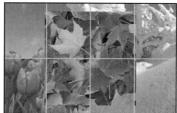

Layers linked   *Layers aligned*

All three images are now centered on top of each other. To see how they are aligned, you can turn off some layers by clicking their eye icons in the Layers palette.

10 Click the eye icon for Layer 2 to hide the layer. Then click the eye icon for Layer 1 to hide that layer. Notice how the layers align with the circle image.

11 Click the link icon for Layer 1 and Layer 2 to unlink them from the Circle layer.

12 Choose File > Save.

Creating a clipping group

You can mask artwork on one layer using an image from another layer by creating a *clipping group.* In a clipping group, artwork on the *base layer* of the group masks or controls the shape of any successive layers. (ImageReady does support grouping layers to form clipping groups.)

You'll now use the circle you drew as the base layer of a clipping group for the Sunflower and Leaves layers.

1 Click Layer 1 to display it and make it active.

2 Choose Layer > Group with Previous. The sunflower is now clipped to the Circle layer and is masked by the shape of the circle.

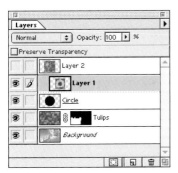 

When you add layers to a clipping group, some changes take place in the Layers palette. The base layer of the clipping group (in this lesson, the circle) is underlined, and any layers above the base layer that are part of the clipping group (in this case, the Sunflower layer) are indented. In addition, the solid lines separating the grouped layers change to dotted lines.

Now you'll redisplay the Leaves layer and use a keyboard shortcut to add the layer to the clipping group.

3 Click Layer 2 to display it and make it active.

4 In the Layers palette, position the pointer on the line between Layer 2 and Layer 1, hold down Alt (Windows) or Option (Mac OS), and click to add the leaves to the clipping group.

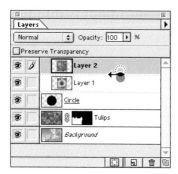
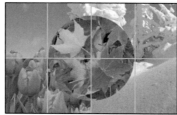

Layer 2 now completely covers Layer 1. You'll adjust the position of the leaves so that the sunflower is partially displayed.

5 Select the move tool in the toolbox, and drag Layer 2 toward the bottom of the circle. Continue dragging until the top of the leaves image aligns with the horizontal guide. The sunflower now appears in the top half of the circle and the leaves in the bottom half.

Moving leaves   *Result*

6 Choose View > Hide Guides to turn off the guides while you continue to work.

7 Choose File > Save.

About Photoshop adjustment layers

An adjustment layer lets you experiment with color and tonal adjustments to an image without permanently modifying the pixels in the image. The color and tonal changes reside within the adjustment layer, which acts as a veil through which the underlying image layers appear.

When you create an adjustment layer, its effect appears on all the layers below it. This lets you correct multiple layers by making a single adjustment, rather than making the adjustment to each layer separately. To confine the effects of an adjustment layer to the layers immediately below it, create a clipping group consisting of these layers.

Adjustment layers have the same opacity and blending mode options as image layers and can be rearranged in order, deleted, hidden, and duplicated in the same manner as well. However, you also specify a color adjustment type for an adjustment layer. Depending on your choice, the dialog box for the selected adjustment command may appear. The adjustment layer takes the name of the adjustment type and is indicated in the Layers palette by a partially filled circle to the right of the name.

Adjustment layers are also layer masks, as indicated by the mask icon to the left of the layer thumbnail. When an adjustment layer is active, the foreground and background colors default to grayscale values. By painting the adjustment layer, you can apply the adjustment to just portions of the underlying layers.

–From the Adobe Photoshop 5.0 User Guide, Chapter 11, "Using Layers."

Adding adjustment layers

Adjustment layers can be added to an image to apply color and tonal adjustments without permanently changing the pixel values in the image. For example, if you add a Color Balance adjustment layer to an image, you can experiment with different colors repeatedly, because the change occurs only on the adjustment layer. If you decide to return to the original pixel values, you can hide or delete the adjustment layer.

Here you'll add a Levels adjustment layer to correct the contrast in part of the image. An adjustment layer affects all layers below it in the image's stacking order. Because you'll place the Levels adjustment layer just above the Tulips layer, the adjustment will affect both the Tulips layer and the background winter scene.

ImageReady recognizes and preserves adjustment layers but cannot create or modify them.

1 In the Layers palette, click the Tulips layer to make it active. Then choose Layer > New > Adjustment Layer.

Holding down Ctrl (Windows) or Command (Mac OS) and clicking the New Layer button in the Layers palette creates a new adjustment layer.

2 In the New Adjustment Layer dialog box, choose Levels for Type, and click OK.

3 In the Levels dialog box, drag the histogram's left triangle to the right, and position it where the darkest colors begin. Notice how the tonal range improves in both the tulips and the winter scene.

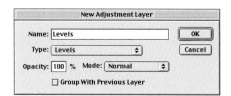
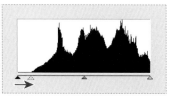

4 Click OK to apply the changes. An adjustment layer named Levels appears in the Layers palette. The new layer does not include a layer thumbnail; only layer mask thumbnails are displayed for adjustment layers.

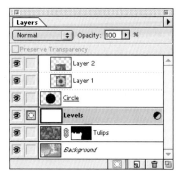

Next you'll apply a Color Balance adjustment layer to the 08Start image and add the adjustment layer to the circle clipping group.

5 In the Layers palette, click Layer 2 to make it active. Then choose Layer > New > Adjustment Layer.

6 In the New Adjustment Layer dialog box, choose Color Balance for Type, and click OK.

7 In the Color Balance dialog box, make sure the Preview option is selected. Then, by using the sliders or by typing in the text boxes, set the color levels to 47, 22, -41. Click OK.

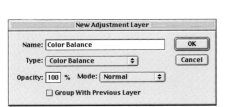
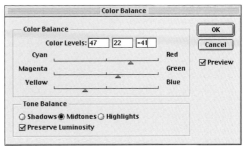

A Color Balance adjustment layer now appears above the Leaves layer in the Layers palette. Notice how the adjustment layer improves the color of the Sunflower and Leaves layers directly below it. But because it is at the top of the image's stacking order, the adjustment layer also affects the tulips and background and distorts their colors.

To contain the color balance to just the Sunflower and Leaves layers, you will add the adjustment layer to the circle clipping group. An adjustment layer that is part of a clipping group affects just the layers in the group.

8 In the Layers palette, position the pointer on the line that separates the Color Balance layer and Layer 2. Hold down Alt (Windows) or Option (Mac OS), and click the line. The adjustment layer is now part of the clipping group and no longer affects colors in the Tulips layer or background winter scene.

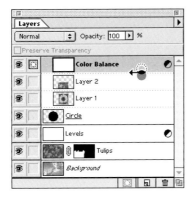

9 Choose File > Save.

Adding text

Text is added to images with the type tool. Each use of the type tool adds a new type layer to the image. Each of these type layers can be moved, edited, or modified independently, giving you virtually unlimited typographic flexibility. ImageReady and Photoshop have comparable type features, although each application handles type somewhat differently.

Now you'll add the names of the seasons to the image. Because each name is on a different type layer, you'll have the flexibility to position the text exactly where you want it.

1 Make sure that the Color Balance adjustment layer is active in the Layers palette.

2 Select the type tool (**T**), and click somewhere in the upper left quadrant of the image.

3 In the Type Tool dialog box, select a font from the Font menu, and enter a point size in the Size text box. (We chose 50-point Helvetica Inserat Regular.)

Note: ImageReady uses the Type palette, rather than a dialog box, to display type options. This palette is in the Color/Swatches/Type/Brushes palette group.

4 To select a color for the type, click the color box at the left of the Type Tool dialog box, and move the pointer into the image area. The pointer temporarily changes to the eyedropper tool ( ), which you can use to sample a color from the image.

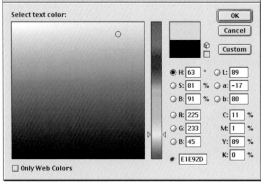

5 Click on a part of the image that is appropriate to the type's season. (We sampled a yellow from the sunflower.) Then click OK to close the Color Picker dialog box.

6 Type **summer** in the large text box at the bottom of the dialog box, and click OK. The text is automatically placed on a new layer in the upper left quadrant of the image where you clicked.

Note: In ImageReady you can type directly on the image, rather than in a dialog box. When a text layer is selected in the Layers palette, changes in the Text palette affect all text on the selected layer. The text color is changed by simply changing the foreground color of the active text layer.

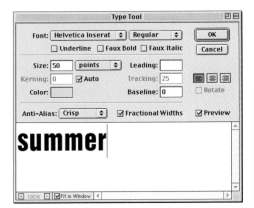 

7 Create a new type layer in the same way for the word "fall," but sample a color from the leaves. Then create two similar type layers for the words "spring" and "winter," but this time position the type in the lower right quadrant of the image and sample colors from the tulips and the winter scene.

You can now use the move tool to reposition the layers.

8 Select the move tool, make different type layers active, and experiment moving the layers around until you are satisfied with the placement of the text.

Adding multiple layer effects

Once you have the text arranged on the image, you can add some layer effects to enhance the look of the type. Layer effects are automated special effects that you can apply to a layer with the Effects command. For more information on layer effects, see Lesson 3, "Layer Basics."

In addition to having a different way of working with layer effects, ImageReady supports styles—collections of layer effects that you can apply to layers.

Now you'll add two different layer effects to the winter type layer.

1 In the Layers palette, click the winter type layer to make it active. Then choose Layer > Effects > Bevel and Emboss.

2 In the Effects dialog box, change Style to Inner Bevel, Depth to 3 pixels, and Blur to 3 pixels.

3 Now choose Drop Shadow from the menu at the top of the dialog box.

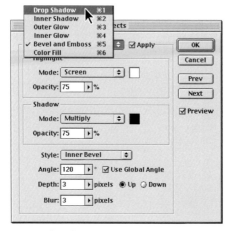

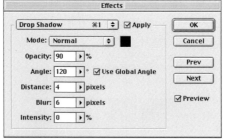

Bevel and Emboss settings   *Drop Shadow settings*

4 In the new dialog box, click Apply. Then change Mode to Normal, Opacity to 90%, Distance to 4 pixels, and Blur to 6 pixels.

5 Click OK to apply the layer effects. The type for "winter" appears with a combination drop shadow and inner bevel.

You can copy the modified layer effects you just created for the winter type layer and paste them into the other three type layers, so that all the type appears with exactly the same look. By linking the type layers, you can paste the effects in just one step.

6 With the winter type layer still active, choose Layer > Effects > Copy Effects.

7 Click the link column for the spring, fall, and summer type layers to link them to the winter type layer.

8 Choose Layer > Effects > Paste Effects to Linked. All four type layers now have the same layer effects applied.

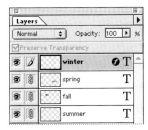

Layers linked for Paste Effects *Result*
to Linked command

9 Choose File > Save.

Defining styles in ImageReady

Styles are sets of one or more layer effects that you can apply to any layer in an ImageReady document. You can apply predefined styles included with ImageReady. You can also define new styles by adding the effects you apply to a layer to the Styles palette. You can define a new style using a single effect or a group of effects.

To define a new style:

1 *Apply effects to a layer in an ImageReady document.*

2 *Select a single effect or a group of effects:*

- *Click an individual effect name or icon (●) to select it.*

- *Click in the gray Effects bar or on the style icon (⑤) to select all effects on a layer.*

3 *Create a new style:*

- *Drag the selected effect or style into the list in the Styles palette or onto the New Item button (▣) in the Styles palette. The effect or style is added as a new style (with a default name) in the Styles palette list.*

- *Click the New Item button at the bottom of the Styles palette, and give the style a name.*

- *Choose New Style from the Styles palette menu, and give the style a name.*

If you create a new style using the New Item button or the New Style menu command, all effects on the current layer are included in the new style.

4 *To rename a style you created by dragging, select the new style (highlighted in the Styles palette), choose Style Options from the Styles palette menu, enter a name for the style, and then click OK.*

–From the Adobe Photoshop 5.5 User Guide Supplement, Chapter 3, "Using Photoshop and ImageReady Together." A similar topic can be found in ImageReady 2.0 online Help.

Removing layer masks

Each layer mask in a file increases the file's size. To minimize the size of your files, it's important to remove or merge layer masks after you've made final design decisions.

You'll use the Remove Layer Mask command to merge the layer mask on the Tulips layer with the artwork on the layer. ImageReady layer masks can also be removed to reduce file size.

1 In the Layers palette, select the Tulips layer.

2 Choose Layer > Remove Layer Mask.

3 When the prompt appears, click Apply to merge the layer mask with the artwork on the layer.

4 Choose File > Save.

Flattening a layered image

If you plan to send a file out for proofs, it's also a good idea to save two versions of the file—one containing all the layers so that you can edit the file if necessary and one flattened version to send to the print shop. When you flatten a file, all layers are merged into a single background, drastically reducing the size of the file.

ImageReady does not support backgrounds, but it does support image flattening. If you flatten an image in ImageReady, all layers are merged into the currently selected layer.

1 First, note the file size in the lower left corner of the 08Start.psd image.

2 Choose Image > Duplicate, name the duplicate file **08Final.psd**, and click OK.

3 Choose Flatten Image from the Layers palette menu. The 08Final.psd file is combined onto a single background.

4 Now check the file size of the 08Final.psd image. You'll notice that it is significantly smaller than the 08Start.psd image, because it has been flattened onto the background.

5 Choose File > Save.

You've completed the Advanced Layers lesson. If you like, you can also experiment using layer masks, clipping groups, and adjustment layers with your own work.

For the Web: Animated layer masks

You can use the advanced layer techniques you apply in Photoshop to create interesting animation effects in ImageReady. You can create animations in ImageReady by varying layer attributes across animation frames.

Now that you've worked with layer masks, try adding a layer mask to an image in Photoshop and animating the image in ImageReady. In this example, you'll use a gradient layer mask to make an image appear to fade in from left to right.

1 In Photoshop, start with an image in RGB mode, in appropriate size and resolution for use on the Web. Position the image in the center of a transparent background.

2 Increase the canvas size so that the canvas is about four times wider than the image.

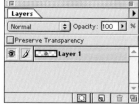

3 Choose Layer > Add Layer Mask > Reveal All.

4 Double-click the gradient tool (▨) to select the tool and view the Gradient Options palette. In the Options palette, choose Black, White for Gradient and select Reverse. Then drag across the document window from left to right to create a gradient on the layer mask.

5 Save the file and click the Jump To button (📷🖼) in the toolbox to open the file in ImageReady.

6 In the ImageReady Layers palette, click the link icon (⅜) between the image thumbnail and the layer mask thumbnail to unlink the image and the mask. Unlinking the image and the mask allows you to move them independently.

7 In the Animation palette, click the New Frame button (🔲).

8 Select frame 1. In the Layers palette, click the layer mask thumbnail to select the mask. Select the move tool (▸₊) and drag in the image window to move the mask to the left. The gradient disappears from the image when you move the mask.

Drag layer mask to the left.   *Mask conceals image.*

9 Select frame 2 and click the layer mask thumbnail to select the mask. Use the move tool to drag the layer mask to the right in the image window.

Drag layer mask to the right.

Image is revealed.

10 In the Animation palette, select Tween from the palette menu. For Parameters, select Position. For Tween With, select Previous Frame. Enter a number for Frames to Add. We entered 6. Click OK.

11 In the Animation palette, click the Play button (▷) to preview the animation. Click the Stop button (□) to end the preview.

Note: *For clearer previewing, choose File > Preferences > Transparency, and choose None for Grid Size.*

12 Double-click the crop tool (**⌶**) to select the tool and view the Crop Options palette. In the Options palette, select Hide for Cropped Area. Drag with the crop tool to select the image and crop the transparent background. Press Return (Windows) or Enter (Mac OS).

13 Click the Play button to preview the animation again.

14 Choose Optimize Animation from the Animation palette menu. In the Optimize Animation palette, select Bounding Box and Redundant Pixel Removal. Click OK.

You can add, delete, or modify frames in the animation and set playback options as needed.

For complete information on animation in ImageReady, see Chapter 5 in the Photoshop 5.5 User Guide Supplement or "Animation" in Photoshop 5.5 online Help. A similar topic can be found in ImageReady 2.0 online Help.

15 In the Optimize palette, select GIF from the file format menu and choose other options to optimize the file for display on the Web.

16 Choose Save Optimized to save the animation.

You can use layer masks to create animations with logos or text. Simply place the logo or text on a transparent background in step 1. When using text, render the text layer before applying the layer mask.

For an illustration of the artwork for this section, see the gallery at the end of the color section.

Review questions

1 Why would you paint with black on a layer mask? With white? With gray?

2 How do you turn off a layer mask to view only the artwork on the layer?

3 What is a clipping group? How could you use it in your work?

4 How do adjustment layers work, and what is the benefit of using an adjustment layer?

5 What does an adjustment layer affect when it is added to a clipping group?

Review answers

1 To hide part of the artwork on a layer, you paint with black on the layer mask. To reveal more of the artwork on a layer, you paint with white on the layer mask. To partially reveal artwork on a layer, you paint with shades of gray on the layer mask.

2 Hold down Shift, and click the layer mask thumbnail in the Layers palette.

3 A clipping group consists of at least two layers, where the artwork on the base layer is used as a mask for artwork on the layer or layers above.

4 Adjustment layers are a special type of Photoshop layer that work specifically with color and tonal adjustments. When you apply an adjustment layer, you can edit an image repeatedly without making a permanent change to the colors or tonal range in the image. You can view adjustment layers in ImageReady, but you can create or edit them only in Photoshop.

5 When an adjustment layer is added to a clipping group, only the layers in the clipping group are affected.

Finished lesson artwork gallery

A Web Tour of Photoshop 5.5

A Tour of Photoshop 5.5 Basics

Lesson 2

Lesson 3

Finished lesson artwork gallery

Lesson 4

Lesson 5

Lesson 6

Lesson 7

Finished lesson artwork gallery

Lesson 8

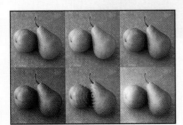

Lesson 9

Lesson 10

Lesson 11

Finished lesson artwork gallery

Lesson 13

Lesson 15

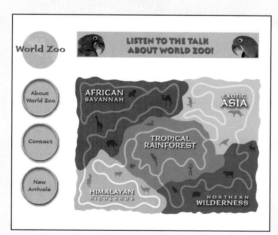

Lesson 16

1-1: Toolbox Overview

The rectangular marquee tool *makes rectangular selections.*

The rounded rectangles marquee tool *makes rectangular selections with rounded corners.*

The elliptical marquee tool *makes elliptical selections.*

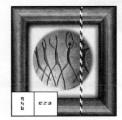

The single row and single column marquee tools *make 1-pixel-wide selections.*

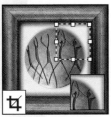

The crop tool *trims images.*

The move tool *moves selections, layers, and guides.*

The lasso tool *makes freehand selections.*

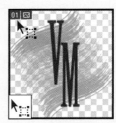

The polygon lasso tool *makes freehand and straight-edged selections.*

The magnetic lasso tool *draws selection borders that cling to the edges of objects.*

The magic wand tool *selects similarly colored areas.*

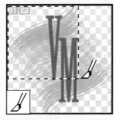

The slice tool *creates slices.*

The slice selection tool *selects slices.*

The airbrush tool *paints soft-edged strokes.*

The paintbrush tool *paints brush strokes.*

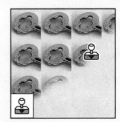

The clone stamp tool *paints with a copy of an image.*

The pattern stamp tool *paints with the selection as a pattern.*

1-1: Toolbox Overview

The history brush tool paints with the selected state or snapshot.

The art history brush tool paints with stylized strokes that simulate the look of different paint styles.

The pencil tool draws hard-edged strokes.

The line tool draws straight lines.

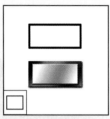

The rectangle tool draws squares and rectangles.

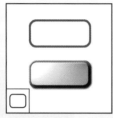

The rounded rectangle tool draws squares and rectangles with rounded corners.

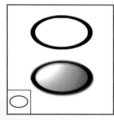

The ellipse tool draws circles and ovals.

The eraser tool erases pixels and restores parts of an image to a previously saved state.

The background eraser tool erases areas to transparency by dragging.

The magic eraser tool erases solid-colored areas to transparency with a single click.

The blur tool blurs hard edges in an image.

The sharpen tool sharpens soft edges.

The smudge tool smudges data in an image.

The dodge tool lightens areas in an image.

The burn tool darkens areas in an image.

The sponge tool changes the color saturation of an area.

1-1: Toolbox Overview

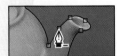

The pen tool *lets you draw smooth-edged paths.*

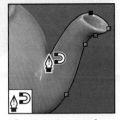

The magnetic pen tool *draws paths that cling to the edges of objects.*

The freeform pen tool *draws paths directly as you drag.*

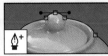

The add-anchor-point tool *adds anchor points to a path.*

The delete-anchor-point tool *deletes anchor points from a path.*

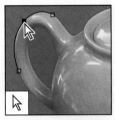

The direct-selection tool *selects and moves paths and parts of paths.*

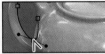
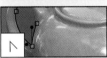

The convert-anchor-point tool *converts straight-line segments to curved segments, and vice versa.*

The measure tool *measures distances, locations, and angles.*

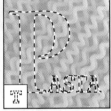

The type tool *creates type on an image.*

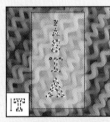

The type mask tool *creates selection borders in the shape of type.*

The vertical type tool *creates vertical type on an image.*

The vertical type mask tool *creates selection borders in the shape of the vertical type.*

1-1: Toolbox Overview

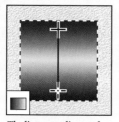

The linear gradient tool *creates a straight-line blend between colors.*

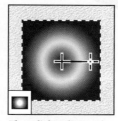

The radial gradient tool *creates a circular blend between colors.*

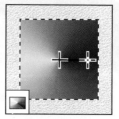

The angle gradient tool *creates an angular blend between colors.*

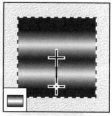

The reflected gradient tool *creates symmetric straight-line blends between colors.*

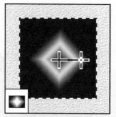

The diamond gradient tool *creates diamond-shaped blends between colors.*

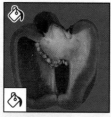

The paint bucket tool *fills similarly colored areas with the foreground color.*

The eyedropper tool *samples colors in an image.*

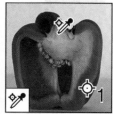

The color sampler tool *samples up to four locations simultaneously.*

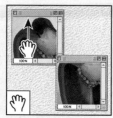

The hand tool *moves an image within its window.*

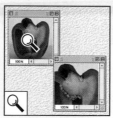

The zoom tool *magnifies and reduces the view of an image.*

3-1: Layer mode samples

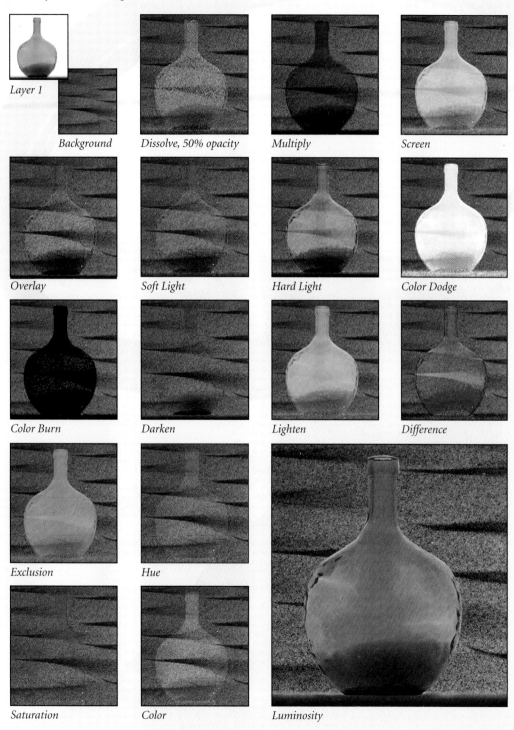

Layer 1

Background

Dissolve, 50% opacity

Multiply

Screen

Overlay

Soft Light

Hard Light

Color Dodge

Color Burn

Darken

Lighten

Difference

Exclusion

Hue

Saturation

Color

Luminosity

4-1: Application of brush stroke to background using blending modes

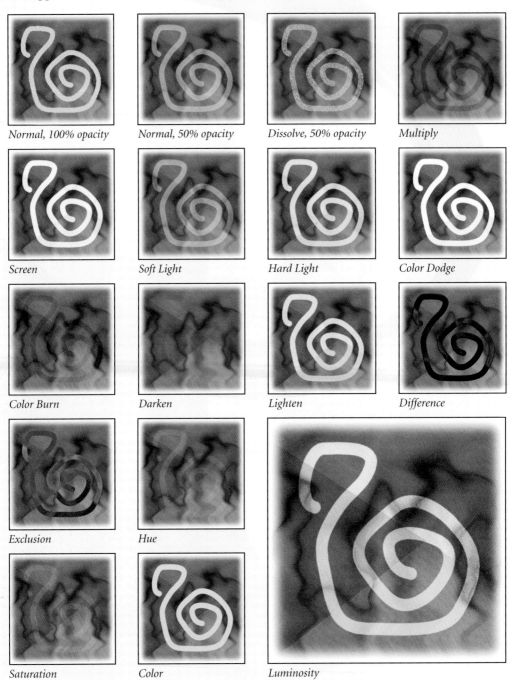

Normal, 100% opacity

Normal, 50% opacity

Dissolve, 50% opacity

Multiply

Screen

Soft Light

Hard Light

Color Dodge

Color Burn

Darken

Lighten

Difference

Exclusion

Hue

Saturation

Color

Luminosity

Lesson 9

For the Web: Lesson 15 —
Animating color changes

*Use an adjustment layer to
create animated effects.*

For the Web: Lesson 16 — Creating a tiled
border stripe

Tile single rows of pixels to form multicolored backgrounds.

For the Web: Lesson 9 — Animated rollover button

 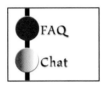

For the Web: Lesson 11 — Creating two-color Web graphics

Adjust levels to give more or less color saturation to the image.

For the Web: Lesson 7 — Creating perfect transparent edges

Original helmet image

Helmet isolated on a transparent background

Helmet with halo when placed against a contrasting color

Helmet after halo removed

For the Web: Lesson 8 — Animated layer masks

Move a layer mask over a graphic to apply a Web effect.

For the Web: Lesson 4 — Painting with Web-safe colors

Original image

Painted with Web-safe colors

On your own: Lesson 6 — Painting with the art history brush

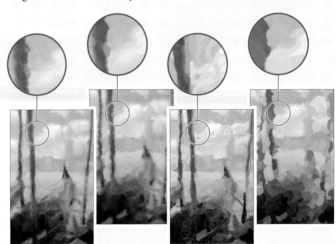

Original image

Painted with varying brush strokes

14-2: Optimized solid graphics

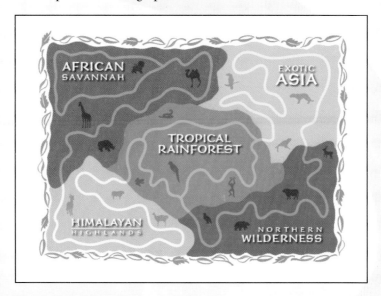

GIF, 128 colors,
88% dither

GIF, 128 colors,
No dither

GIF, 32 colors,
88% dither

GIF, 32 colors,
No dither

GIF, 64 colors,
88% dither

GIF, 64 colors,
No dither

GIF, Web palette,
auto colors

JPEG, Quality 60

JPEG, Quality 10

14-1: Optimized continuous-tone images

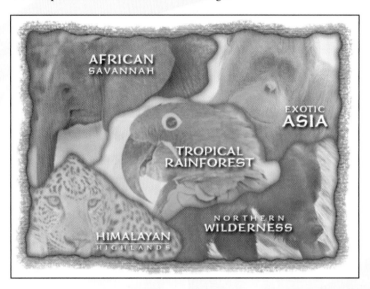

GIF, 128 colors,
88% dither

GIF, 128 colors,
No dither

GIF, 32 colors,
88% dither

GIF, 32 colors,
No dither

GIF, 64 colors,
88% dither

GIF, 64 colors,
No dither

GIF, Web palette,
auto colors

JPEG, Quality 60

JPEG, Quality 10

13-2: CMYK image with cyan, magenta, yellow, and black channels

13-3: Color gamuts

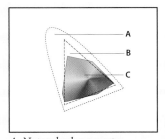

A. *Natural color gamut*
B. *RGB color gamut*
C. *CMYK color gamut*

13-4: RGB color model

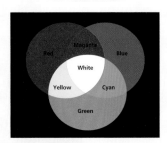

13-5: CMYK color model

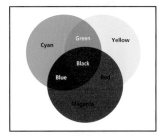

12-3 Setting the monitor's white point

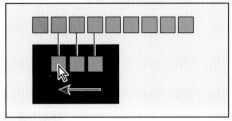

A shade cooler

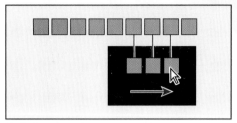

A shade warmer

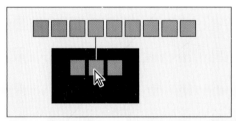

A neutral gray

13-1: RGB image with red, green, and blue channels

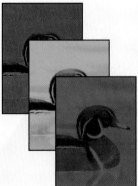

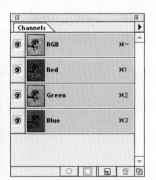

12-1

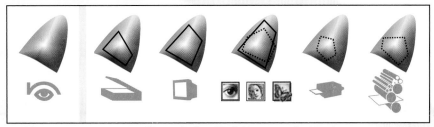

Visible spectrum containing millions of colors (far left) compared with color gamuts of various devices and documents.

12-2

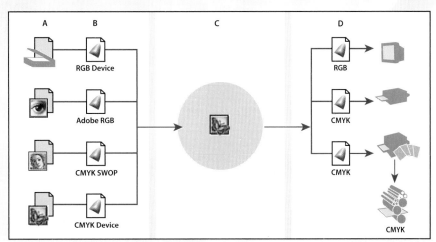

A. *Scanners and software applications create color documents. Users choose document's working color space.* **B.** *ICC source profiles describe document color spaces.* **C.** *A color management engine uses ICC source profiles to map document colors to a device-independent color space through supporting applications.* **D.** *The color management engine maps document colors from the device-independent color space to output device color spaces using destination profiles.*

Lesson 5 start file

5-1: Original selection in Standard mode and Quick Mask mode

A. Selected Areas
B. Hidden Areas

5-2: Painting in Quick Mask mode

Quick Mask mode

Painting with white

Resulting selection

Painting with black

Resulting selection

9 Creating Special Effects

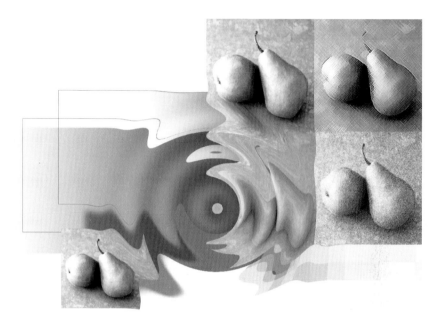

The huge assortment of filters available for Adobe Photoshop lets you transform ordinary images into extraordinary digital artwork. You can select filters that simulate a traditional artistic medium— a watercolor, pastel, or sketched effect— or you can choose from filters that blur, bend, wrap, sharpen, or fragment images. In addition to using filters to alter images, you can use adjustment layers and painting modes to vary the look of your artwork.

In this lesson, you'll learn how to do the following:

- Add a grid to an image to help you make precise selections.

- Desaturate a selection without affecting the color in other parts of the image.

- Paint on a layer above the artwork to color the underlying artwork without changing it permanently.

- Choose colors that are safe to use on the Web.

- Add an adjustment layer to make a color correction to a selection.

- Apply filters to selections to create various effects.

This lesson will take about 30 minutes to complete. The lesson is designed to be done in Adobe Photoshop, but information on using similar functionality in Adobe ImageReady is included where appropriate.

If needed, remove the previous lesson folder from your hard drive, and copy the Lesson09 folder onto it.

Getting started

Before beginning this lesson, restore the default application settings for Adobe Photoshop. See "Restoring default preferences" on page 4.

You'll start the lesson by viewing the final lesson file, to see what you'll accomplish.

1 Restart Adobe Photoshop.

2 Click Cancel to exit the color management dialog box that appears.

3 Choose File > Open, and open the 09End.psd file, located in the Lessons/Lesson09 folder.

An image containing six sets of pears appears. Some of the pears have been painted, and some have had filters applied to them.

4 When you have finished viewing the file, either leave the End file open on your desktop for reference, or close it without saving changes.

For an illustration of the finished artwork for this lesson, see the gallery at the beginning of the color section.

Now you'll open the start file and begin working.

5 Choose File > Open, and open the 09Start.psd file, located in the Lessons/Lesson09/ folder on your hard drive.

Saving and loading a selection

You'll start by making a selection of a set of pears and then saving it. That way you can reuse the selection by reloading it as needed. ImageReady includes the basic marquee selection tools, the lasso and polygon lasso tools, and the magic wand tool familiar to users of Photoshop.

1 Use the zoom tool (⌕), and drag over the set of pears in the upper left corner to magnify your view.

2 Position the pointer on the lasso tool (⟁) in the toolbox, and drag to the right to select the magnetic lasso tool (⟁).

Note: *ImageReady does not include the magnetic lasso tool.*

3 To draw a freehand segment, drag the pointer along the edge you want to trace. Notice that the pointer doesn't have to be exactly on the edge for the segment to snap to it.

As you move the pointer, the active segment snaps to the strongest edge in the image. Periodically, the magnetic lasso tool adds fastening points to the selection border to anchor previous sections. As you move the pointer over the starting point, a hollow circle appears next to the pointer, indicating that you are about to close the segment.

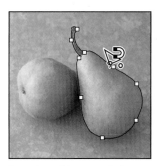 

Dragging with magnetic lasso pointer   *Result*

4 When a circle appears next to the magnetic lasso pointer, release the mouse button to close the segment.

Note: For best results when tracing the pear stem with the magnetic lasso tool, zoom in on your work and decrease the tool's lasso width and frequency values. For example, try tracing the pear using a Lasso Width of 1 or 2 pixels and a Frequency of 40.

5 Save the selection of the right pear by choosing Select > Save Selection. Enter **Alpha 1** in the Name text box, and click OK to save the selection in a new channel. You'll use the selection again for another set of pears. (To learn more about using channels in Photoshop, see Lesson 5, "Masks and Channels.")

6 Choose Select > Deselect to deselect the right pear.

7 Now select the left pear using the magnetic lasso tool.

8 Choose Select > Save Selection, enter **Alpha 2** in the Name text box, and click OK to save the selection of the right pear in a new channel.

9 Choose Select > Deselect to deselect the pear. You'll use this selection again for other sets of pears.

You'll begin this lesson by hand-coloring a set of the pears. You'll begin with the right pear, so you'll need to load the selection you created.

10 Choose Select > Load Selection, and select Alpha 1. Click OK. A selection border appears around the right pear in your image.

Note: If you load a channel in ImageReady using the Select > Load Selection command, the channels appear under the names Channel 1, Channel 2, and so on, regardless of the name that has been designated in Photoshop.

Hand-coloring selections on a layer

First you'll remove the color from the selection so that you can color it by hand. Then you'll add a layer above the pears and apply any new color on the layer. This way, if you don't like the results, you can simply erase the layer and start over.

Desaturating a selection

You'll use the Desaturate command to *desaturate*, or remove the color, from the pear selection. Saturation is the presence or absence of color in a selection. When you desaturate a selection within an image, you create a grayscale-like effect without affecting the colors in other parts of the image. ImageReady has many of the same color correction tools available in Photoshop, including Desaturation.

1 Choose Image > Adjust > Desaturate. The color is removed from the selection.

2 Choose Select > Deselect.

3 Choose File > Save to save your work.

Creating a layer and choosing a blending mode

Now you'll add a layer and specify a layer blending mode. By painting on a layer, you won't permanently alter the image. This makes it easy to change your mind and start again.

You use layer blending modes to determine how the pixels in a layer are blended with underlying pixels on other layers. By applying modes to individual layers, you can create myriad special effects. Blending modes can also be used in ImageReady to blend layers.

1 In the Layers palette, click the New Layer button to add Layer 1 to the image. To rename the layer, double-click Layer 1, rename the layer **Paint**, and click OK.

Next to the New Layer button, you'll see the Trash button. Any time you want to throw your Painting layer away, you can drag the layer to the trash in the Layers palette.

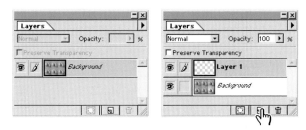

Original

Clicking New Layer button to add layer

Now you'll choose a layer blending mode to determine how the pixels in this layer are blended with underlying pixels on the Background layer.

2 In the Layers palette, choose Color from the pop-up mode menu to the left of the Opacity slider.

The Color mode lets you change the hue of a selection without affecting the highlights and shadows. This means you can apply a variety of color tints without changing the original highlights and shadows of the pears.

Applying painting effects

To begin painting, you must again load the selection that you created earlier. You will open the Alpha 1 channel. Photoshop and ImageReady share a common set of tools for applying and tracking color.

1 Choose Select > Load Selection > Alpha 1. (Notice in the Load Selection dialog box that the color mode change you just made also was saved as a selection, called "Paint Transparency.")

2 In the toolbox, double-click the paintbrush tool ( ) to display its Options palette. Set the Opacity to about 50%.

Change the paintbrush opacity by pressing a number on the keypad from 0 to 9 (where 1 is 10%, 9 is 90%, and 0 is 100%).

3 In the Brushes palette, select a large, soft-edged brush. (To display the Brushes palette, choose Window > Show Brushes.)

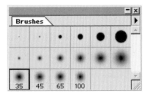

4 In the Swatches palette, click a yellow-green color that appeals to you for the foreground color. Paint the entire pear with the light yellow-green color. As you paint, you'll notice that the color of the pear changes to the color you selected. (If you want your colors to be appropriate for use on the Web, first choose Web Color Sliders from the Colors palette menu and then choose a color for the pear.)

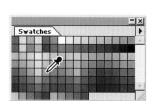

Selecting yellow-green swatch   Result

5 Next, select a darker green from the Swatches palette. In the Paintbrush Options palette, set the brush opacity to about 30%. Paint around the edges in the pear selection, avoiding the highlight area.

6 To add additional highlights to the pear, select a rose color from the Swatches palette, and select a smaller brush from the Brushes palette. In the Paintbrush Options palette, decrease the paint opacity to about 20%, and paint more highlights on the pear.

7 Choose Select > Deselect.

8 Choose File > Save to save your work.

Adding a gradient

Now you'll use the gradient tool to add a gradient to the other pear for a highlight effect. (ImageReady does not have a gradient tool. Instead, gradients are created as ImageReady layer effects.)

First you'll need to load the selection of the left pear you made earlier.

1 Choose Select > Load Selection, and select Alpha 2. Click OK. A selection border appears around the left pear in your image

2 Select red as the foreground color.

3 Click the background color swatch, and select yellow as the background color.

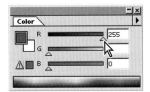 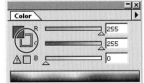

Selecting red as the foreground   *Yellow selected as the background*
color   *color*

4 Select the radial gradient tool (▢) in the toolbox. (To select a hidden tool, position the pointer on the visible tool, and drag to highlight the tool you want.)

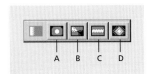

A. *Radial gradient*
B. *Angle gradient*
C. *Diamond gradient*
D. *Reflected gradient*

5 In the Radial Gradient Options palette, for Gradient, make sure that Foreground to Background is selected, so that the color blends from the foreground color (red) to the background color (yellow). Set the opacity to 40%.

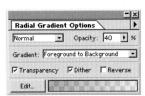

6 Position the gradient tool near the pear's highlight, and drag toward the stem. (You can select other gradient tools and then drag to try out different effects.)

Applying radial gradient from pear's highlight to stem   *Result*

7 Choose Select > Deselect.

8 When you've finished painting the set of pears, choose Layer > Merge Visible to merge the painting layer with the pear image and to keep the file size small. You'll continue the project by applying effects to the other pears in the image.

9 Choose File > Save to save your work.

Combining and moving selections

Before you begin to apply special effects to the next set of pears, you'll combine the earlier selections you made. You'll also move the new combined selection so that you can use it with a different set of pears. Although the process is slightly different, you can combine selections in ImageReady as well.

1 Select the zoom tool from the toolbox. Then hold down Alt (Windows) or Option (Mac OS) to select the zoom-out tool ( ).

2 Click the zoom-out tool as many times as necessary until both the top left pears and top middle pears are visible.

3 Choose Select > Load Selection, and select Alpha 1. Click OK.

4 Choose Select > Load Selection. Select Alpha 2. Click Add to Selection. Click OK.

Both pears are now selected.

When using the Select > Load Selection command in ImageReady, the channels appear in the dialog box as Channel 1, Channel 2, and so on, regardless of the name that has been designated in Photoshop. To add to a channel to an existing selection in ImageReady, hold down the Shift key and keep using the Select > Load Selection command (picking a different channel each time) until all of the channels you want to use have been loaded as one combined selection.

5 Using the rectangular marquee tool ([⬚]), drag the selection border to the right to position it over the middle pears in the top row.

Alpha 1 and Alpha 2 selections combined and then moved using marquee tool

Colorizing a selection

Now you will colorize the selected set of pears. A colorized image has only one hue of color. You colorize a selection or image with the Colorize option in the Hue/Saturation dialog box. You can use the Colorize option to add color to a grayscale image or to reduce the color values in an image to one hue. ImageReady also includes Hue/Saturation.

1 Double-click the hand tool ([🖐]) in the toolbox to fit the image in the window. The top middle pears should still be selected.

2 Choose Image > Adjust > Hue/Saturation.

The Hue/Saturation command lets you adjust the hue, saturation, and lightness of individual color components in an image.

3 Make sure that Preview is selected. Then select the Colorize option.

The upper color bar shows the color before the adjustment; the lower bar shows how the adjustment affects all of the hues at full saturation. The image takes on a reddish tint.

4 Experiment with values in the Hue and Saturation text boxes until you get a desirable color. You can use the sliders to adjust the Hue, Saturation, and Lightness, or you can type in numbers in the text boxes. We used a Hue of 83 and a Saturation of 28 for a greenish color.

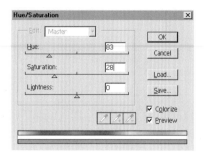

Decreasing the saturation lowers the intensity of the color.

5 Click OK to apply the changes.

6 To preview the changes without the selection border, choose View > Hide Edges.

7 Choose View > Show Edges, and then choose Select > Deselect to deselect everything.

8 Choose File > Save to save your work.

Using a grid

Before you adjust the next set of pears, you'll display a grid and use it to make a precise rectangular selection that you can repeat on the remaining sets of pears. A grid helps you lay out images or elements symmetrically. Selections, selection borders, and tools snap to the grid when they are dragged within 8 screen pixels of it. (Grids are not available in ImageReady.)

1 In Photoshop, choose View > Show Grid. The grid with the default settings appears in the image window.

2 Choose File > Preferences > Guides & Grid.

You adjust the grid settings using the Preferences dialog box. You can set the grid to display as lines or as points, and you can change its spacing or color.

Tips for creating special effects

Try the following techniques to create special effects with filters. For illustrations of these techniques, see online Help.

Create edge effects. *You can use various techniques to treat the edges of an effect applied to only part of an image. To leave a distinct edge, simply apply the filter. For a soft edge, feather the edge, and then apply the filter. For a transparent effect, apply the filter, and then use the Fade command to adjust the selection's blending mode and opacity.*

Apply filters to layers. You can apply filters to individual layers or to several layers in succession to build up an effect. For a filter to affect a layer, the layer must be visible and must contain pixels—for example, a neutral fill color.

Apply filters to individual channels. You can apply a filter to an individual channel, apply a different effect to each color channel, or apply the same filter but with different settings.

Create backgrounds. *By applying effects to solid-color or grayscale shapes, you can generate a variety of backgrounds and textures. You might then blur these textures. Although some filters have little or no visible effect when applied to solid colors (for example, Glass), others produce interesting effects. You might try Add Noise, Chalk & Charcoal, Clouds, Conté Crayon, Craquelure, Difference Clouds, Glass, Grain, Graphic Pen, Halftone Pattern, Mezzotint, Mosaic Tiles, Note Paper, Patchwork, Pointillize, Reticulation, Rough Pastels, Sponge, Stained Glass, Texture Fill, Texturizer, and Underpainting.*

Combine multiple effects with masks or with duplicate images. *Using masks to create selection areas gives you more control over transitions from one effect to another. For example, you can filter the selection created with a mask. You can also use the history brush tool to paint a filter effect onto part of the image. First, apply the filter to an entire image. Next, step back in the History palette to the image state before applying the filter, and set the history brush source to the filtered state. Then, paint the image.*

Improve image quality and consistency. You can disguise faults, alter or enhance, or make a series of images look related by applying the same effect to each. Use the Actions palette to record the process of modifying one image, and then use this action on the other images.

–From the Adobe Photoshop 5.0 User Guide, Chapter 13, "Using Filters."

Improving performance with filters

Some filter effects can be memory intensive, especially when applied to a high-resolution image. You can use these techniques to improve performance:

• Try out filters and settings on a small portion of an image.

• Apply the effect to individual channels—for example, to each RGB channel—if the image is large and you're having problems with insufficient memory. (With some filters, effects vary if applied to the individual channel rather than the composite channel, especially if the filter randomly modifies pixels.)

• Experiment on a low-resolution copy of your file and note the filters and settings used. Then apply the filters and settings to the high-resolution original.

• Free up memory before running the filter by using the Purge command.

• Allocate more RAM to Photoshop or ImageReady. If necessary, exit from other applications to make more memory available to Photoshop or ImageReady.

• Try changing settings to improve the speed of memory-intensive filters such as Lighting Effects, Cutout, Stained Glass, Chrome, Ripple, Spatter, Sprayed Strokes, and Glass filters. (For example, with the Stained Glass filter, increase cell size. With the Cutout filter, increase Edge Simplicity, or decrease Edge Fidelity, or both.)

• If you plan to print to a grayscale printer, convert a copy of the image to grayscale before applying filters. However, applying a filter to a color image and then converting to grayscale may not have the same effect as applying the filter to a grayscale version of the image.

This concludes this lesson. Try out other filters to see how you can add different effects to your images.

For detailed information on individual filters and a gallery of examples, see "Using Filters" in Photoshop 5.0 online Help. A gallery can also be found in ImageReady 2.0 online Help.

For the Web: Animated rollover button

Here's a way to quickly create an eye-catching button for your Web pages from an animated rollover that uses layer effects. In this technique, you'll create a button graphic with text that starts animating when the pointer is over it and that changes to a different color when the mouse button is clicked.

This technique requires that you work in ImageReady because you're working with rollovers.

1 In ImageReady, start with a button with type or a contrasting graphic element that will lend itself to an eye-catching gradient. The type or graphic should be on a separate layer from the button. (For the button to work realistically, it should be in a slice of its own, and the slice should be selected.)

Boldfaced fonts with contrasting colors increase legibility. Light or serif fonts with minimal contrast are more difficult to read. For the button background, use simple photos or textures that don't conflict with the text or icon on the button.

2 Click the Rollover palette tab. (If the palette isn't visible, choose Window > Show Rollover.) The palette contains one state, Normal.

3 Choose New State from the Rollover palette pop-up menu to create the Over state.

4 With the Over state selected, in the Layers palette, click the Type layer to select it. Then click the Layer Effect button (🕜) at the bottom of the palette. Choose Gradient/Pattern from the Layer Effect pop-up menu.

5 In the Gradient/Pattern palette, choose Linear.

6 Choose a gradient from the pop-up menu to the right of the color ramp, or double-click the color stops beneath the color ramp and use the color picker to select your own gradient combinations.

7 Click the Animation palette tab. The button and the type gradient appear as the first frame. From the Delay Frame pop-up menu beneath the frame, choose 0.1 seconds to delay playing the frame.

8 Click the New Frame button (🖫) at the bottom of the Animation palette to create a new frame that duplicates the original frame's settings.

Make sure that the second frame is selected in the Animation palette and the Gradient/Pattern effect under the Type layer is still selected in the Layers palette.

9 In the Gradient/Pattern palette tab, click the double-triangle (♦) to expand the palette, or choose Show Options from the Gradient/Pattern palette menu. Select Reverse to reverse the direction of the linear gradient.

10 Return to the Rollover palette, and choose New State from the Rollover palette menu to create the Down state.

If desired, you can adjust the type in the Down frame. For example, you can change the type color or remove the gradient to create a different animation when the button is pressed.

11 Choose File > Preview In, and choose a browser to preview the effect.

12 Click the Optimize palette tab. In the Optimize palette. Choose GIF, and set other optimization options as desired.

13 Choose File > Save Optimized or File > Save Optimized As to save the file as a GIF.

You can repeat this technique to create other eye-catching buttons, using other layer effects applied to graphics or type.

⬤ For an illustration of the artwork for this section, see the gallery at the end of the color section.

Review questions

1 What is the purpose of saving selections?

2 Name a benefit of using a grid in your image.

3 Describe one way to isolate color adjustments to an image.

4 Describe one way to remove color from a selection or image for a grayscale effect.

Review answers

1 By saving a selection, you can create and reuse time-consuming selections and uniformly select artwork in an image. You can also combine selections or create new selections by adding to or subtracting from existing selections.

2 A grid helps you make precise, rectangular selections and lay out images symmetrically. Selections, selection borders, and tools snap to the grid when they are dragged within 8 screen pixels of it.

3 You can use adjustment layers to try out color changes before applying them permanently to a layer.

4 You can use the Desaturate command to desaturate, or remove the color, from a selection. Or you can use the Hue/Saturation command and adjust only the Saturation component. Photoshop also includes the sponge tool for removing color.

Lesson 10

10 | Combining Illustrator Graphics and Photoshop Images

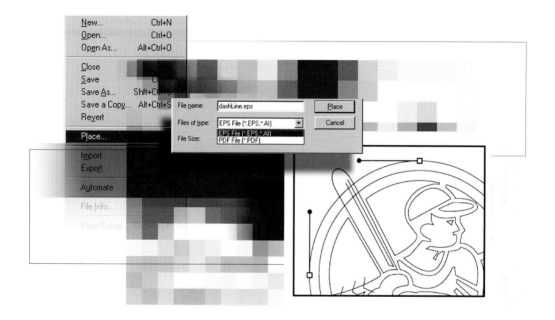

You can easily add a graphic created in a drawing program to an Adobe Photoshop or Adobe ImageReady file. This is an effective method for seeing how a line drawing looks applied to a photograph or for trying out Photoshop special effects on vector art. You can also export the resulting artwork for use in other graphics programs.

In this lesson, you'll learn how to do the following:

• Differentiate between bitmap and vector graphics.

• Place an Adobe Illustrator graphic in an Adobe Photoshop file.

• Scale the placed graphic.

• Distort a graphic to match the perspective of a photograph.

• Apply different blending modes to a graphic.

• Use the Export Transparent Image wizard to prepare a Photoshop image for use in an Illustrator file.

This lesson will take about 60 minutes to complete. The lesson is designed to be done in Adobe Photoshop, but information on using similar functionality in Adobe ImageReady is included where appropriate.

If needed, remove the previous lesson folder from your hard drive and copy the Lesson10 folder onto it.

Combining artwork

You can combine Adobe Photoshop and Adobe ImageReady images with artwork from other graphics applications in a variety of ways for a wide range of creative results. Sharing artwork between applications lets you combine line art with continuous-tone paintings and photographs. It also lets you move between two types of computer graphics—bitmap images and vector graphics.

Bitmap versus vector graphics

Photoshop and ImageReady use *bitmap images*, also called raster images, which are based on a grid of pixels. In working with bitmap images, you edit groups of pixels rather than objects or shapes. Because bitmap graphics can represent subtle gradations of shade and color, they are appropriate for continuous-tone images such as photographs or artwork created in painting programs. A disadvantage of bitmap graphics is that they lose definition and appear jagged when scaled up.

Vector graphics, also called draw graphics, are made up of shapes based on mathematical expressions and are created in drawing applications. These graphics consist of clear, smooth lines that retain their crispness when scaled. They are appropriate for illustrations, type, and graphics such as logos that may be scaled to different sizes.

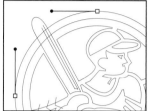

Logo drawn as vector art

Logo rasterized as bitmap art

In deciding whether to use a bitmap graphics program such as Photoshop or ImageReady, or a vector graphics program such as Illustrator for creating and combining graphics, consider both the elements of the image and how the image will be used. In general, use Photoshop or ImageReady for images that have the soft lines of painted or photographic art and for applying special effects to line art. Use Illustrator if you need to create art or type with clean lines that will look good at any magnification. In most cases, you will also want to use Illustrator for laying out a design, because Illustrator gives you more flexibility in working with type and with reselecting, moving, and altering images.

Project overview

To illustrate how you can combine vector art with bitmap images and work between applications, this lesson steps you through the process of creating a composite image. In this lesson, you will add a logo created in Adobe Illustrator to a photographic image in Adobe Photoshop and adjust the logo so that it blends with the photo. You will then save the resulting image so that it can be brought back into Illustrator for final layout as a print advertisement.

Logo drawn in Illustrator

Logo applied to image in Photoshop

Final layout in Illustrator

Getting started

Before beginning this lesson, restore the default application settings for Adobe Photoshop. See "Restoring default preferences" on page 4.

You'll start the lesson by viewing the final image for this project to see how the adjustments you'll make will affect the final artwork.

1 Restart Adobe Photoshop.

2 Click Cancel to exit the color management dialog box that appears.

3 Choose File > Open, and open the 10End.psd file, located in the Lessons/Lesson10 folder.

4 When you have finished viewing the file, either leave the End file open on your desktop for reference, or close it without saving changes.

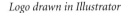 For an illustration of the finished artwork for this lesson, see the gallery at the beginning of the color section.

Now you'll open the start file and begin the lesson by adding a logo to a photographic image.

5 Choose File > Open, and open 10Start.psd file, located in the Lessons/Lesson10 folder on your hard drive.

Placing an Adobe Illustrator file

You can open an Adobe Illustrator file as a new file in Adobe Photoshop or Adobe ImageReady, or you can use the Place or Paste commands to add an Illustrator file to an existing Photoshop or ImageReady file. When you open, place, or paste an Illustrator image, both Photoshop and ImageReady *rasterize* it so that it becomes a bitmap (raster) image.

In this lesson, you will use the Place command to add an Illustrator file to an existing Photoshop image. The Photoshop Place command offers the advantage of letting you scale the image while it is still vector art, so that the scaling does not sacrifice image quality. The graphic is not rasterized until you press Enter or Return. However, when you cut or paste a graphic from Illustrator into Photoshop or when you place a file in ImageReady, the image is rasterized at the size it was in the Illustrator file. Subsequent scaling of the graphic then degrades the image quality. Placing a file in Photoshop and then scaling and rotating the graphic requires fewer steps than performing the same tasks in ImageReady.

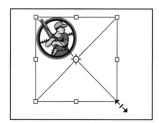 

Scaling placed Illustrator graphic   *Result*

Scaling pasted Illustrator graphic   *Result*

1 With the photo of the gift box open, choose File > Place to place the image. Select the file Logo.ai located in the Lessons/Lesson10 folder, and click Place.

💡 *In ImageReady, choose File > Place. Click Choose, and select the file Logo.ai located in the Lessons/Lesson10 folder; click Open. In the Rasterize Options dialog box, accept the defaults and click OK.*

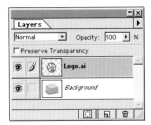

The logo appears with a bounding box around it, and the new layer Logo.ai now appears in the Layers palette.

Now you'll transform the logo to fit the gift box.

2 Hold down Shift, and drag a corner handle of the bounding box to scale the logo to fit the gift box. (Holding down Shift constrains the proportions of the logo.) Position the pointer outside the bounding box (the pointer turns into a curved arrow), and drag to rotate the logo slightly counterclockwise.

💡 *In ImageReady, choose Edit > Free Transform. Drag a corner handle of the bounding box to scale the logo to fit the gift box. Then position the pointer outside the bounding box (the pointer turns into a curved arrow), and drag to rotate the logo slightly counterclockwise.*

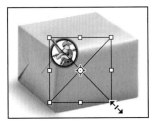

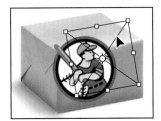

Scaling logo   *Rotating logo*   *Repositioning logo*

3 If necessary, position the pointer inside the bounding box so that you see a move pointer (▶), and drag to reposition the logo so that it fits within the borders of the box. Fine-tune with other rotation or scaling adjustments; then press Enter or Return to apply the changes and rasterize the logo.

Distorting the graphic to match the photograph

Your next step is to distort the logo so that it appears to wrap around the top and front of the box. To create this effect, you'll cut the logo in half, place each half on its own layer, and then apply the distortion to the logo's top half.

1 With the Logo.ai layer active, select the polygon lasso tool (▽), and click the right front corner of the box top. Drag to the next corner, click, and then continue dragging around the box top, clicking at each corner. Complete the selection by crossing over the starting point.

Top half of box selected   *Selection placed on new layer*

2 Choose Layer > New > Layer Via Cut to cut the top half of the logo from the Logo.ai layer and place it on its own layer. Notice that a new layer, Layer 1, has appeared in the Layers palette. To see the artwork on the layer, turn off the other two layers by clicking the eye icon (👁) to the left of the layers in the Layers palette. Click again to turn all layers back on.

Now you're ready to distort the top of the logo.

3 Make sure that Layer 1 is active, and then choose Edit > Transform > Skew. A transformation bounding box appears around the top half of the logo.

4 Experiment by dragging the handles of the bounding box to distort the logo so that it matches the perspective of the box. In particular, try dragging the upper left handle in the direction of the back left corner of the box top.

Top half of logo distorted via   *Result*
Skew command

💡 *To undo the last handle adjustment, choose Edit > Undo. To cancel the transformation, press Esc.*

5 When the logo appears to wrap around the top of the box, apply the transformation by pressing Enter or Return.

Transforming objects in two dimensions in Photoshop

You can scale, rotate, skew, distort, and apply perspective to selected parts of an image, entire layers, paths, and selection borders. You can also rotate and flip part or all of a layer, an entire image, path, or selection border. Use the following guidelines when applying transformations:

• *You can transform a linked layer. The transformation affects all the layers in the linking group.*

• *You cannot apply transformations to the background as a layer, or on 16-bit-per-channel images. You can, however, transform selections on the background.*

• *You can apply transformations to an alpha channel by first selecting it in the Channels palette.*

• *You can apply transformations to a layer mask by first selecting its thumbnail in the Layers palette.*

Pixels are added or deleted during transformations. To calculate the color values of these pixels, Adobe Photoshop uses the interpolation method selected in the General Preferences dialog box. This option directly affects the speed and quality of the transformation. Bicubic interpolation, the default, is slowest but yields the best results.

–From the Adobe Photoshop 5.0 User Guide, Chapter 8, "Editing and Retouching."

Using blending modes on the graphic

Now you'll make the logo appear more integrated with the box by using different blending modes on each half of the logo. First you'll lighten the top half of the logo so that it matches the box top.

1 With Layer 1 still active in the Layers palette, change the opacity of the layer to 60%, and make sure that Normal is selected for the blending mode. Changing the opacity of the layer lightens the top of the logo and makes it blend better with the highlights on the top of the box.

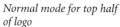

Normal mode for top half of logo   *Multiply mode for bottom half of logo*   *Result*

Next you'll darken the bottom half of the logo so that it blends with the shadow on the box front.

2 Click the Logo.ai layer in the Layers palette to make it active, change the opacity to 70%, and select Multiply from the blending mode menu. Using the Multiply blending mode on the layer darkens the bottom of the logo and makes it appear to be in shadow.

3 Choose File > Save.

About clipping paths and transparency

By default, when you export a Photoshop file to another program such as Illustrator, the entire image becomes opaque, including the background. In Photoshop, you can use a clipping path to create transparent areas in an image that can be placed in page-layout applications. A *clipping path* isolates part of a Photoshop image and makes everything outside the isolated area transparent when the image is printed or placed in another application. This lets you place an image into another file without obscuring the other file's background. (ImageReady does not have clipping paths.)

You can create clipping paths using the Paths palette or from the Paths to Illustrator command. You can also have the Export Transparent Image wizard create a clipping path automatically for you. The Export Transparent Image wizard identifies the desired portion of the photograph and makes everything outside it appear transparent when the image is exported.

Placed Photoshop file, exported with background

Placed Photoshop file, exported via Export Transparent Image

Exporting the image

You'll now prepare the new composite image so that it can be placed back into Illustrator for its final layout. In this project, the gift box in the Photoshop file is targeted for an Illustrator file with a colored background. If you export the file without any adjustment, the white background around the box will appear as an opaque white area against the colored Illustrator background.

Using the Export Transparent Image wizard, you can export a Photoshop image to Illustrator with a hidden, or clipped, background. Wizards are assistants available through the Help menu that guide you through common tasks in Photoshop.

Before running the Export Transparent Image wizard, you must select the part of the image you want to make transparent. In the Work10.psd file, you will select the white background around the box.

1 In the Layers palette, click Background to make it active.

2 Select the polygon lasso tool, and draw a selection around the box. Then choose Select >Inverse to select the background around the box.

Selecting box with polygon lasso tool   *Box selected*   *Background selected via Select > Inverse*

You're now ready to run the wizard, which uses dialog boxes to step you through the process of exporting the file.

3 Choose Help > Export Transparent Image.

4 In the first dialog box, choose the second option, indicating that you have already selected the area of the image you want to make transparent. Then click Next.

5 In the next dialog box, choose Print and click Next.

6 In the third dialog box, accept the Photoshop EPS default file format and the default filename, and click Save.

7 In the EPS Options dialog box, choose a Preview option:

• For Windows, choose TIFF (8 bits/pixel), and click OK.

• For Mac OS, choose Macintosh (8 bits/pixel), and click OK.

Note: *If you place an EPS file with a TIFF preview into Adobe Illustrator, the transparency created by the wizard won't display properly. This display affects the on-screen preview only; when the image prints to a PostScript® printer, the areas designated for transparency in the wizard will in fact be transparent.*

8 In the final dialog box, click Finish.

Note that you now have two files open on your desktop: 10Start.psd and Export Wizard-1.eps (Windows) or Export Assistant-1 (Mac OS). Because you have finished with the 10Start.psd file, you can close it. Be careful not to save the file, however, because the Export Transparent Image wizard flattened the file's layers as one of the steps in preparing the file for export. If you save this version of the file, you will lose the original file's separate layers.

9 With the 10Start.psd file active, choose File > Close.

10 In the dialog box, click the Don't Save option.

The final step in preparing the Photoshop file for export to a print color publication is to change the image to CMYK color mode so that it will be printed correctly in four-color process inks. You can use the Mode command to change the image's color mode.

For complete information on color modes, see Chapter 4 in the Photoshop 5.0 User Guide or "Choosing a Color Mode" in Photoshop 5.0 online Help.

11 With the Export Wizard-1.eps (Windows) or Export Assistant-1 (Mac OS) window active, choose Image > Mode > CMYK Color.

12 Choose File > Save.

The box-and-logo image is now fully composed and ready for placement in the Adobe Illustrator layout.

If you have a copy of Illustrator, you can either jump to Illustrator to continue to edit the image, or start Illustrator and use the Place command to place the logo image (Mailer.ai, located in the Lessons/Lesson10 folder).

Which technique you use determines whether you can continue to edit the image. If you jump to Illustrator, the image comes into Illustrator as an editable mask (with anchor points in addition to those created in Photoshop) and the embedded image, and you can continue to edit the image. If you place the image, the art comes into Illustrator as a linked image within a mask that can't be edited.

Jumping between applications

You can jump between Photoshop and ImageReady to transfer an image between the two applications for editing, without closing or exiting the originating application. In addition, you can jump to other graphics-editing applications from Photoshop or ImageReady, and jump to HTML editing applications from ImageReady.

When you jump to another application, the file remains open in Photoshop or ImageReady while you work in the destination application. You can set Photoshop or ImageReady to automatically update an image that is modified in a jumped-to application.

Each time an image in Photoshop or ImageReady is updated with changes made in a jumped-to application, a single history state is added to the Photoshop or ImageReady History palette. You can undo the update in Photoshop or ImageReady as you do other states in the History palette.

Jumping between Photoshop and ImageReady

You can easily jump between Photoshop and ImageReady to use features in both applications when preparing graphics for the Web or other purposes. Jumping between the applications allows you to use the full feature sets of both applications while maintaining a streamlined workflow.

Jumping from Photoshop or ImageReady to other applications

You can jump to graphics-editing applications from within Photoshop and ImageReady, and HTML editing applications from within ImageReady.

When you install Photoshop and ImageReady, Adobe graphics-editing applications currently on your system such as Adobe Illustrator, are added to the Jump To submenu in both programs. In addition, Adobe HTML editing applications such as Adobe GoLive™, are added to the Jump To submenu in ImageReady.

You can add additional applications, including non-Adobe applications, to the Jump To submenu. You can also specify which application will be launched when using a keyboard shortcut.

When you jump to a graphics-editing application, the original file is opened in the destination application. When you jump to an HTML editing application from ImageReady, the optimized file and the HTML file are opened in the destination application. If the document contains slices, all files for the full document are included.

–From the Adobe Photoshop 5.5 User Guide Supplement, Chapter 3, "Using Photoshop and ImageReady Together." A similar topic can be found in ImageReady 2.0 online Help.

On your own: Transforming a placed image

Now that you've learned the basic steps involved in combining an Illustrator graphic with a Photoshop image, you can try applying the logo to a new Photoshop image.

1 Locate and open the Lesson10 folder. Then select Cap.psd or Cup.psd, and click Open.

2 Choose File > Place. Select the Logo.ai file, and click Place.

Now try out transformation techniques presented here to blend the graphic with the Photoshop image.

For the Web: Animating Illustrator layers

You can create an animation from a multilayer Illustrator file by making the layers into animation frames in ImageReady. When you use Illustrator to create graphics for an animation, you can resize the artwork while you work without changing the artwork's detail or clarity.

Now that you've combined an Illustrator graphic with a Photoshop image, try exporting an Illustrator file into ImageReady and using the animation features in ImageReady to create an animation.

Note: You must use Illustrator 8.0 or later in order to preserve Illustrator layers when opening the file in ImageReady.

1 In Illustrator, open a multilayer document that you want to use as an animation. Make sure the layers are in the order in which you want to display them as animation frames. (The bottom layer becomes the first frame in the animation when you convert the layers to frames in ImageReady. You can also rearrange the layers after opening the file in ImageReady if necessary.)

2 Choose File > Export. Choose Photoshop 5 for format. Choose a location where the file will be saved, and click Save.

3 In the Photoshop Options dialog box, select RGB for Color Model and Screen (72 dpi) for Resolution. Select Anti-Alias to smooth edges in the exported image, and select Write Layers to preserve layers. Click OK and exit Illustrator.

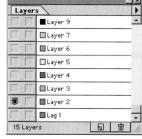

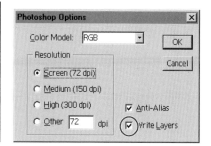

Single layer of multilayer   Illustrator Layers palette   Export the file with Write Layers selected.
file in Illustrator 8.0

4 Launch ImageReady and open the file you saved in step 3. Notice that the layers are preserved in the ImageReady layers palette.

Multilayer file in ImageReady   ImageReady Layers palette

Note: *Exporting a multilayer file from Illustrator in Photoshop format may cause an additional background layer to be added to the file. If an empty layer labeled "background" appears as the bottom layer in the ImageReady Layers palette, select the layer and click the Trash button in the Layers palette to delete the layer.*

5 In the ImageReady Animation palette, choose Make Frames From Layers from the palette menu.

6 Click the Play button (▷) in the Animation palette to preview the animation. Click the Stop button (□) to end previewing.

You can add, delete, or modify frames in the animation and set playback options as needed.

[?] For complete information see Chapter 5 in the Photoshop 5.5 User Guide Supplement or "Animation" in Photoshop 5.5 online Help. A similar topic can be found in ImageReady 2.0 online Help.

7 Choose Optimize Animation from the Animation palette menu. In the Optimize Animation palette, select Bounding Box and Redundant Pixel Removal. Click OK.

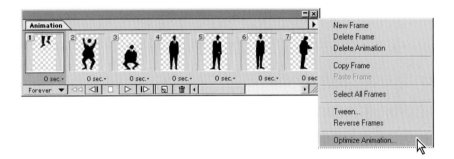

Note: If you choose the Redundant Pixel Removal optimization option, also choose the Automatic disposal option to enable ImageReady to preserve frames that include transparency.

8 Save the animation as an optimized GIF for Web display, choosing one of the following options:

• In Photoshop, choose File > Save for Web, and optimize and save the file.

• In ImageReady, choose File > Save Optimized As, and optimize and save the file.

For an illustration of the artwork for this section, see the gallery at the end of the color section.

Review questions

1 What is the difference between bitmap images and vector graphics?

2 What is the advantage of using the Place command to add an Illustrator file to an image in Photoshop?

3 How can you export an image from Photoshop into Illustrator without also exporting its opaque background?

Review answers

1 Bitmap or raster images are based on a grid of pixels and are appropriate for continuous-tone images such as photographs or artwork created in painting programs. Vector graphics are made up of shapes based on mathematical expressions and are appropriate for illustrations, type, and drawings that require clear, smooth lines.

2 The Photoshop Place command lets you scale the image while it is still vector art, so that the scaling does not sacrifice image quality.

3 You can use a clipping path to create transparent areas in an image that can be placed in page-layout applications. You can create a clipping path several ways: using the Paths palette, the Paths to Illustrator command, or the Export Transparent Image wizard. ImageReady does not have clipping paths, and you cannot export an image with a transparent, or hidden background from ImageReady.

Lesson 11

11 Preparing Images for Two-Color Printing

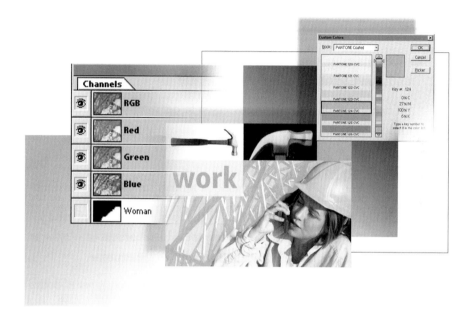

Not every commercially printed publication requires four-color reproduction. Printing in two colors using a grayscale image and spot color can be an effective and inexpensive alternative. In this lesson, you'll learn how to use Adobe Photoshop to prepare full-color images for two-color printing.

Mixing color channels

Sometimes it's possible to improve the quality of an image by blending two or more color channels. For instance, one channel in an image may look particularly strong but would look even better if you could add some detail from another channel. In Photoshop, you can blend color channels with the Channel Mixer command in either RGB mode (for on-screen display) or CMYK mode (for printing). For more information on color modes, see Lesson 13, "Producing and Printing Consistent Color."

In this lesson, you'll use the Channel Mixer command to improve the quality of an RGB image that you'll then convert to grayscale mode. But first, you'll use the Channels palette to view the different channels in the image.

1 Choose Window > Show Channels, click the Channels tab, and drag the palette from the Layers and Paths palette group. Place the Channels palette on your screen where you can easily access it.

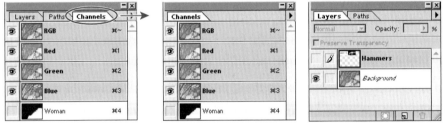

Drag the Channel palette from the Layers palette to make both palettes visible at the same time.

Because the image is in RGB mode, the Channels palette displays the image's red, green, and blue channels. Notice that all the color channels are currently visible, including the RGB channel, which is a composite of the separate red, green, and blue channels. To see the individual channels, you can use the palette's eye icons.

2 Click the eye icons to turn off all color channels in the Channels palette except the red channel. The colors in the 11Start image change to shades of gray.

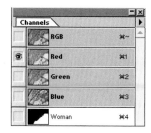 

Red channel

3 Drag the eye icon from the red channel to the green channel and then to the blue channel. Notice how the monochrome image in the 11Start window changes with each channel. The green channel shows the best overall contrast and the best detail in the woman's face, while the blue channel shows good contrast in the framework behind the woman.

Green channel   *Blue channel*

4 In the Channels palette, click the eye icon column for the composite RGB channel to display all the color channels in the image.

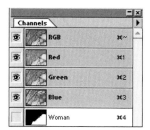 

All channels displayed   *RGB image*

Now you'll use the Channel Mixer command to improve the image in this lesson. Specifically, you'll divide the image into two areas, the woman and the framework, and mix different amounts of source channels in each selection.

Mixing the woman's image

First you'll select the woman's image by loading a premade selection.

1 In the Layers palette, make sure that the background is selected.

2 Choose Select > Load Selection. In the dialog box, select Woman from the Channel menu to load a selection that outlines the image of the woman. Click OK.

Now you'll mix the green and blue channels to improve the selection's contrast. You'll use green as the base channel because it has the best overall contrast for the image.

3 Choose Image > Adjust > Channel Mixer.

4 In the Channel Mixer dialog box, choose Green for the Output Channel. The Source Channel for Green changes to 100%.

5 Select Monochrome to change the image to shades of gray. This option gives you an idea of how the selection will look in Grayscale mode, so that you can more accurately adjust the selection's tonal range.

The resulting image is a little flat. You can bring out the contrast and improve the highlights by blending in some of the blue channel.

6 Drag the slider for the Blue Source Channel to 10%. Click OK.

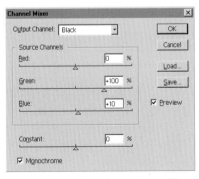

Selection loaded   *Channel Mixer dialog box with 10% blue*

Mixing the framework's image

Next you'll select the framework, convert this part of the image to monochrome, and again mix channels to improve the contrast and detail.

1 Choose Select > Inverse to select the framework behind the woman.

2 Choose Image > Adjust > Channel Mixer.

3 In the Channel Mixer dialog box, choose Green for the Output Channel, and select Monochrome.

This time the resulting image is dark and lacks contrast. You can improve the image again by blending in some of the blue channel to increase the contrast.

4 Drag the slider for the Blue Source Channel to 27%. Click OK.

 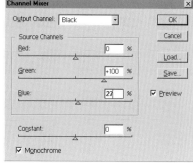

Inverse of selection   *Channel Mixer dialog box with 27% blue*

5 Choose Select > Deselect.

Both the woman and the framework now show better contrast and detail. But the image is still an RGB color image (one that contains only gray values). To convert the image to Grayscale mode, you will use the Grayscale command.

6 Choose Image > Mode > Grayscale. When prompted, select Don't Flatten to keep the image's two layers intact. (You'll use the second layer later in this lesson.) The image converts to Grayscale mode, and the color channels in the Channels palette are replaced by a single Black channel.

7 Choose File > Save.

Assigning values to the black and white points

You can further improve the quality of the image by adjusting the black and white limits of its tonal range. In Lesson 6, "Photo Retouching," you learn to use the sliders on the Levels command histogram to adjust the range. In this lesson, you'll control the range more accurately by using the Levels command eyedropper to assign specific values to the darkest and lightest points.

1 Choose Image > Adjust > Levels.

2 In the Levels dialog box, double-click the white eyedropper tool to open the color picker for the white point.

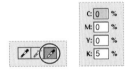

3 Enter **0, 0, 0,** and **5** in the CMYK text boxes, and click OK. These values generally produce the best results when printing the white points (highlights) of a grayscale image onto white paper.

4 Next double-click the black eyedropper tool in the Levels dialog box to open the color picker for the black point.

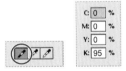

5 Enter **0, 0, 0,** and **95** in the CMYK text boxes, and click OK. These values generally produce the best results when printing the black points (shadows) of a grayscale image onto white paper.

Now that you've defined the values for the black and white points, you'll use the Levels command eyedropper to assign the values to the darkest and lightest areas in the image.

6 Reselect the black eyedropper tool, and position it in the darkest area of the framework behind the woman's elbow. Click to assign this area the values you set in step 5.

7 Next click the white eyedropper tool in the Levels dialog box, position the tool in the lightest area of the woman's collar, and click to assign this area the values you set in step 3.

Black eyedropper selecting
darkest area behind elbow

White eyedropper selecting
lightest area in collar

8 Click OK to close the dialog box and apply the changes.

Assigning the black and white points shifts the image's histogram to produce a more evenly distributed tonal range.

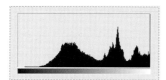

Original

Result

9 Choose File > Save.

Sharpening the image

By applying the Unsharp Mask filter to the image, you can create the illusion of a more focused image.

1 Choose Filter > Sharpen > Unsharp Mask. Make sure that the Preview option is selected so that you can view the effect before you apply it. To get a better view, you can place the pointer within the preview window and drag to see different parts of the image (we focused on the woman's face). You can also change the magnification of the preview image with the plus and minus buttons located below the window.

2 Drag the Amount slider until the image is as sharp as you want (we used 57%), and make sure that the Radius is set to 1 pixel.

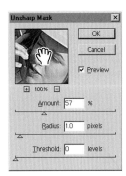

3 Click OK to apply the Unsharp Mask filter to the image.

Setting up for spot color

Spot colors, also called *custom colors*, are premixed inks that are used instead of, or in addition to, the cyan, magenta, yellow, and black process color inks. Each spot color requires its own color separation or printing plate. Graphic designers use spot colors to specify colors that would be difficult or impossible to achieve by combining the four process inks.

You'll now add spot color to the image in this lesson by creating a spot color channel.

1 In the Channels palette, choose New Spot Channel from the palette menu.

2 In the New Spot Channel dialog box, click the color box, and select Custom in the color picker.

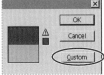

3 In the Custom Colors dialog box, type **124** for the Pantone custom color 124. (Because there is no text box for the number, you must type it quickly.) Then click OK.

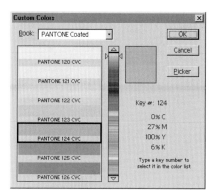

4 In the New Spot Channel dialog box, enter **100**% for Solidity. The solidity setting lets you simulate on-screen the ink solidity of the printed spot color. Inks range from transparent (0% solidity) to opaque (100% solidity). The Solidity option affects the on-screen preview only and has no effect on the printed output.

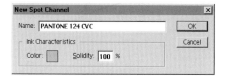

5 Click OK to create the spot color channel. A new spot color channel named PANTONE 124 CVC is added to the Channels palette.

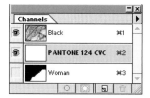

6 Choose File > Save.

Using spot channels

Spot channels let you add and preview spot colors in an image. The following guidelines can help you in using spot channels:

- *If you need spot color graphics that have crisp edges and knock out the underlying image, consider creating the additional artwork in a page-layout or illustration application.*
- *You can create new spot channels or convert an existing alpha channel to a spot channel.*
- *Like alpha channels, spot channels can be edited or deleted at any time.*
- *Spot colors can't be applied to individual layers.*
- *Spot colors are overprinted on top of the fully composited image.*
- *If you print an image that includes spot color channels to a composite printer, the spot colors print out as extra pages.*
- *You can merge spot channels with color channels, splitting the spot color into its color channel components. Merging spot channels lets you print a single-page proof of your spot color image on a desktop printer.*
- *The names of the spot colors print on the separations.*
- *Each spot channel is overprinted in the order in which it appears in the Channels palette.*
- *You cannot move spot colors above a default channel in the Channels palette except in Multichannel mode.*

–From the Adobe Photoshop 5.0 User Guide, Chapter 10, "Using Channels and Masks."

Adding spot color

You can add spot color to selected areas of an image in different ways with varying effects. For instance, you can apply spot color to part of a grayscale image so that the selection prints in the spot color rather than in the base ink. Because spot colors in Photoshop print over the top of a fully composited image, you may also need to remove the base color in an image when adding spot color to it. If you do not remove the base color, it may show through the semitransparent spot color ink used in the printing process.

You can also use spot color to add solid and screened blocks of color to an image. By screening the spot color, you can create the illusion of adding an extra, lighter color to the printed piece.

Removing a grayscale area and adding spot color

You'll begin your work in spot color by changing the framework behind the woman to the color. You must first select the framework, remove it from the grayscale image, and then add the selection to the spot color channel.

1 In the Channels palette, select the Black channel.

2 Choose Select > Load Selection. In the dialog box, choose Woman from the Channel menu and select Invert. Click OK to load a selection of the framework behind the woman.

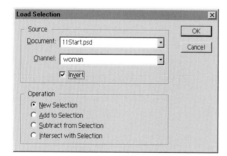

3 Choose Edit > Cut to cut the selection from the image.

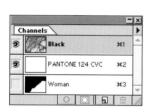
Black channel active

Selection made in Black channel

Selection cut from Black channel

4 In the Channels palette, select the PANTONE 124 CVC channel.

5 Choose Edit > Paste to paste the framework selection into the spot color channel. In the 11Start window, the framework reappears in the Pantone color.

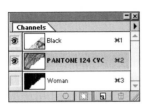 

Selection pasted into spot color channel

6 Choose Select > Deselect.

7 Choose File > Save.

Removing spot color from a grayscale area

Now you'll remove some spot color where it overlaps the grayscale area of a second layer of the image.

1 In the Layers palette, click the eye icon column next to the Hammers layer to make it visible. (Click just the eye icon column. Do not select the layer.)

Notice that the spot color of the framework overlaps part of the Hammers layer. You'll remove this overlap by making a new selection and cutting it from the spot color channel.

2 Choose View > Show Guides.

3 Select the rectangular marquee tool ([⬚]), and drag a selection from the top left edge of the image to the right horizontal guide and top vertical guide.

4 Make sure that the spot channel in the Channels palette is still active, and press Delete to remove the rectangular selection from the channel. In the 11Start window, the spot color disappears from the hammers image.

Making selection   *Selection cut from spot color channel*

5 Choose Select > Deselect.

6 Choose File > Save.

Adding solid and screened areas of spot color

Next you'll vary the effect of adding spot color by adding a solid block of the color and then a block of the color screened to 50%. The two areas will appear to be different colors even though you have used the same Pantone custom color on the same color separation.

First you'll make a selection for the solid block of color and fill the selection using a keyboard shortcut.

1 With the rectangular marquee tool still selected, make a selection in the upper right corner of the image bounded by the two guides.

2 Hold down Alt (Windows) or Option (Mac OS), and press Delete to fill the selection with the foreground color. Because you are in the PANTONE 124 CVC channel, the foreground color is PANTONE 124 and fills the square with solid color.

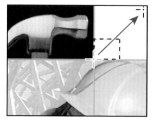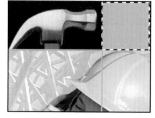

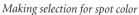

Making selection for spot color   *Selection filled with solid color*

Now you can add a lighter block of spot color to the image.

3 Make a rectangular selection directly below the left hammer and bounded by the guides.

4 In the Color palette, drag the color slider to 20% to set the value for the new block of color.

5 Hold down Alt/Option and press Delete to fill the selection with a 20% screen of PANTONE 124.

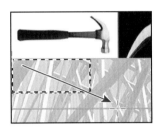
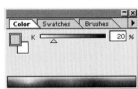
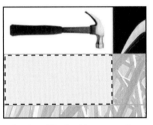

Making selection   *Color value set to 20%*   *Selection filled with 20% color*

6 Choose Select > Deselect.

7 Choose View > Hide Guides.

8 Choose File > Save.

Adding spot color to text

Text in an image can also appear in spot color. There are different methods for creating this effect, but the most straightforward is to add the text directly to the spot color channel. Note that text in a spot channel behaves differently from text created on a type layer. Spot channel text is uneditable. Once you create the type, you cannot change its specifications, and once you deselect the type, you cannot reposition it.

Now you'll add text to the spot color channel and place the text in the light block of spot color.

1 In the Color palette, return the color slider to 100%.

2 Select the type tool (**T**) in the toolbox, and click the image in the light block of color.

3 In the Type Tool dialog box, choose a type face from the Font menus, and enter **66** for the point size in the Size text box.

4 Type **work** in the large text box at the bottom of the dialog box.

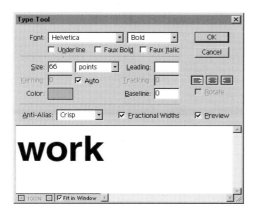

5 Click OK. The text appears in solid PANTONE 124 where you first clicked the image.

6 Select the move tool () in the toolbox, and drag the text so that it is centered in the light block of color.

7 Choose Select > Deselect.

8 Choose File > Save.

You have finished preparing the image for two-color printing. To see how the color separations for the printed piece will look, try alternately hiding and displaying the two color channels in the Channels palette.

9 Click the eye icon for the Black channel in the Channels palette. The Black channel is hidden, and the image window changes to just the areas of the image that will print in the spot color.

10 Redisplay the Black channel by clicking its eye icon column. Then hide the PANTONE 124 CVC channel by clicking its eye icon. Just the grayscale areas of the image appear in the image window.

11 Click the eye icon column for the PANTONE 124 CVC channel to display both channels.

Final image   *Black channel*   *PANTONE 124 CVC channel*

If you have a printer available, you can also try printing the image. You'll find it prints on two sheets of paper—one representing the color separation for the spot color and one representing the grayscale areas of the image.

For the Web: Creating two-color Web graphics

Two-color images are used in print to keep costs down and expand the tonal range of grayscale images. Even when printing costs aren't an issue, you can use two-color images for effect. Try this technique in ImageReady for creating small yet punchy two-color graphics for the Web that give maximum impact without increasing the file size. You can start with an image in Photoshop, or work exclusively in ImageReady.

1 For a duotone effect, start by creating a grayscale image in Photoshop or by desaturating an ImageReady image. To convert your color Photoshop image to grayscale, choose Image > Modes > Grayscale.

In ImageReady, it's not possible to create a grayscale image. But you can use the Image > Adjust > Desaturate command. ImageReady only supports RGB files. Even an image that may appear to be a grayscale in ImageReady is actually an RGB file.

2 In Photoshop, to convert your grayscale image to RGB mode, choose Image > Mode > RGB Color.

3 Create a new layer and position it beneath the grayscale image in the Layers palette.

In Photoshop, if the grayscale image is the Background, you must convert the Background to a layer by double-clicking the Background in the Layers palette and naming it in the Make Layer window.

4 In the image, fill the new layer with the second color of choice.

5 Select the top layer of the image and choose Multiply from the Layers palette mode menu.

Multiply mode looks at the color information in each layer and multiplies the base color by the blend color. The result color is always a darker color. Multiplying any color with a color produces progressively darker colors.

6 Duplicate the top layer by dragging it to the New Layer button at the bottom of the Layers palette.

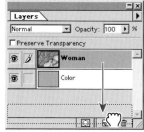

Grayscale image with color layer beneath

Duplicating the top layer

7 With the new layer selected, choose Hard Light from the Layers palette mode menu. This mode brings out the color underneath.

Hard Light filter applied

This technique works most effectively on the top layer of an image with the Hard Light mode applied. Hard Light mode multiplies or screens the colors, depending on the blend color. The effect is similar to shining a harsh spotlight on the image. If the blend color (light source) is lighter than 50% gray, the image is lightened, as if it were screened. This is useful for adding highlights to an image. If the blend color is darker than 50% gray, the image is darkened as if it were multiplied. This is useful for adding shadows to an image.

8 Select the middle layer. Choose Image > Adjust > Levels and adjust the histogram using the sliders to let more or less color from the bottom layer show through.

9 If desired, decrease the opacity of the different layers and note the effect.

10 Save the file in the GIF file format for the Web, optimizing the file as needed.

As a variation, select the dodge or burn tool and adjust one detail or object in your image at a time.

For an illustration of the artwork for this section, see the gallery at the end of the color section.

Review questions

1 What are the three types of channels in Photoshop, and how are they used?

2 How can you improve the quality of a color image that has been converted to grayscale?

3 How do you assign specific values to the black and white points in an image?

4 How do you set up a spot color channel?

5 How do you add spot color to a specific area in a grayscale image?

6 How can you apply spot color to text?

Review answers

1 Channels in Photoshop are used for storing information. Color channels store the color information for an image; alpha channels store selections or masks for editing specific parts of an image; and spot color channels create color separations for printing an image with spot color inks.

2 You can use the Color Mixer command to blend color channels to bring out the contrast and detail in an image. You can extend the tonal range of the image by adjusting its black and white points. You can also sharpen the image by applying the Unsharp Mask filter.

3 You assign specific values with the Levels command black and white eyedropper tools.

4 You set up a spot color channel by choosing New Spot Channel from the pop-up menu on the Channels palette and by specifying a color from the Custom color picker in the New Spot Channel dialog box.

5 With the Black channel active, you select the area, cut it from the Black channel, and paste it into the spot color channel.

6 You can add the text to the spot color channel. However, text created in this way is not editable and cannot be repositioned once it is deselected.

Lesson 12

12 | Setting Up Your Monitor for Color Management

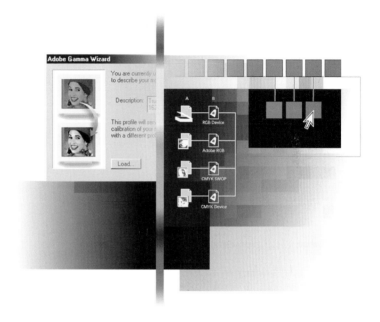

The most basic requirement for color management is to calibrate your monitor and create an ICC profile for it. Applications that support color management will use your monitor's ICC profile to display color graphics consistently. If you don't have a hardware-based calibration and profiling utility, you can get reasonably accurate results using Adobe Gamma.

In this lesson, you'll learn how to do the following:

- Examine the principles associated with color management.
- Calibrate your monitor using Adobe Gamma.
- Create an ICC profile for your monitor using Adobe Gamma.

This lesson will take about 40 minutes to complete.

Note: You can skip this lesson if you have already calibrated your monitor using a hardware-based tool or an ICC-compliant calibration tool such as the Adobe Gamma utility included with Photoshop 5.0 and later, Illustrator 8.0 and later, and InDesign™ 1.0 and later, and if you haven't changed your video card or monitor settings.

Getting started

In this lesson, you'll learn some basic color management concepts and terminology. In addition, you'll calibrate your monitor to a known color condition, and then create an ICC profile that describes your monitor's specific color characteristics. For information about setting up RGB and CMYK color spaces in Photoshop, see Lesson 13, "Producing and Printing Consistent Color."

Before beginning this lesson, restore the default application settings for Adobe Photoshop. See "Restoring default preferences" on page 4.

Color management: An overview

Although all color gamuts overlap, they don't match exactly, which is why some colors on your monitor can't be reproduced in print. The colors that can't be reproduced in print are called *out-of-gamut* colors, because they are outside the spectrum of printable colors. For example, you can create a large percentage of colors in the visible spectrum using programs such as Photoshop, Illustrator, and InDesign, but you can reproduce only a subset of those colors on a desktop printer. The printer has a smaller *color space* or *gamut* (the range of colors that can be displayed or printed) from the application that created the color.

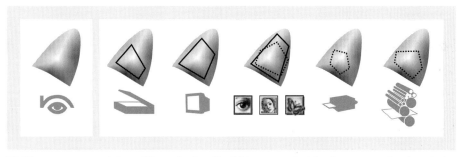

Visible spectrum containing millions of colors (far left) compared with color gamuts of various devices and documents.

To compensate for these differences and to ensure the closest match between on-screen colors and printed colors, applications use a color management system (CMS). Using a color management engine, the CMS translates colors from the color space of one device into a device-independent color space, such as CIE (Commission Internationale d'Eclairage) LAB. From the device-independent color space, the CMS fits that color information to another device's color space by a process called *color mapping*, or *gamut mapping*. The CMS makes any adjustments necessary to represent the color consistently among devices.

For an illustration of the color gamuts of various devices, see figure 12-1 in the color signature.

A CMS uses three components to map colors across devices:

• A device-independent (or reference) color space.

• ICC profiles that define the color characteristics of particular devices and documents.

• A color management engine that translates colors from one device's color space to another according to a *rendering intent*, or translation method.

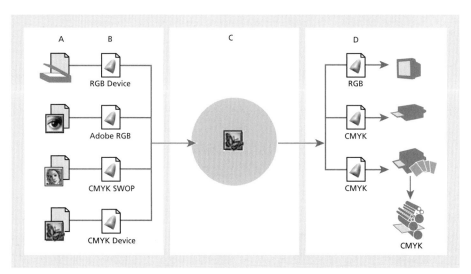

A. *Scanners and software applications create color documents. Users choose document's working color space.* **B.** *ICC source profiles describe document color spaces.* **C.** *A color management engine uses ICC source profiles to map document colors to a device-independent color space through supporting applications.* **D.** *The color management engine maps document colors from the device-independent color space to output device color spaces using destination profiles.*

For a color illustration, see figure 12-2 of the color signature.

About the device-independent color space

To successfully compare gamuts and make adjustments, a color management system must use a reference color space—an objective way of defining color. Most CMSs use the CIE LAB color model, which exists independently of any device and is big enough to reproduce any color visible to the human eye. For this reason, CIE LAB is considered *device-independent.*

About ICC profiles

An *ICC profile* describes how a particular device or standard reproduces color using a cross-platform standard defined by the International Color Consortium (ICC). ICC profiles ensure that images appear correctly in any ICC-compliant applications and on color devices. This is accomplished by embedding the profile information in the original file or assigning the profile in your application.

At a minimum, you must have one *source profile* for the device (scanner or digital camera, for example) or standard (SWOP or Adobe RGB, for example) used to create the color, and one *destination profile* for the device (monitor or contract proofing, for example) or standard (SWOP or TOYO, for example) that you will use to reproduce the color.

About color management engines

Sometimes called the color matching module (CMM), the color management engine interprets ICC profiles. Acting as a translator, the color management engine converts the out-of-gamut colors from the source device to the range of colors that can be produced by the destination device. The color management engine may be included with the CMS or may be a separate part of the operating system.

Translating to a gamut—particularly a smaller gamut—usually involves a compromise, so multiple translation methods are available. For example, a color translation method that preserves correct relationships among colors in a photograph will usually alter the colors in a logo. Color management engines provide a choice of translation methods, known as *rendering intents*, so that you can apply a method appropriate to the intended use of a color graphic. Examples of common rendering intents include *Perceptual (Images)* for preserving color relationships the way the eye does, *Saturation (Graphics)* for preserving vivid colors at the expense of color accuracy, *Relative* and *Absolute Colorimetric* for preserving color accuracy at the expense of color relationships.

Color management resources

You can find additional information on color management on the Web and in print. Here are a few resources:

• On the Adobe Web site (www.adobe.com), search for **color management**.

• On the Apple Web site (www.apple.com), search for **ColorSync**.

• On the LinoColor Web site (www.linocolor.com), open the *Color Manager Manual*.

• On the Agfa Web site (www.agfa.com), search for the publication, *The Secrets of Color Management*.

• On the ColorBlind Web site (www.color.com), click Resources.

• At your local library or bookstore, look for *GATF Practical Guide to Color Management*, by Richard Adams and Joshua Weisberg (May 1998); ISBN 0883622025.

▣ For information about setting up color management in Photoshop, see Chapter 5 in the Photoshop 5.0 User Guide or "Reproducing Color Accurately" in Photoshop 5.0 online Help.

Calibrating and characterizing your monitor using Adobe Gamma

The first requirement for color management is to calibrate your monitor and create an accurate ICC profile for it. Although this doesn't address your entire workflow, at least it ensures that your monitor displays colors as precisely as it can. *Calibration* is the process of setting your monitor, or any device, to known color conditions. *Characterization*, or profiling, is the process of creating an ICC profile that describes the unique color characteristics of your device or standard. Always calibrate your monitor, or any device, before creating a profile for it; otherwise, the profile is only valid for the current state of the device.

Although monitor calibration and characterization are best done with specialized software and hardware, you can get reasonably accurate results with the Adobe Gamma utility included with Photoshop 5.0 and later, Illustrator 8.0 and later, and InDesign 1.0 and later. If you have used other calibration utilities to calibrate and characterize your monitor, such as Apple ColorSync, Adobe Gamma will overwrite those settings.

💡 *You may find it helpful to have your monitor's user guide convenient while using Adobe Gamma.*

1 If you have the Mac OS Gamma control panel (included with Adobe Photoshop 4.0 and earlier) or the Monitor Setup utility (included with PageMaker 6.0) for Windows, remove it because it is obsolete. Use the latest Adobe Gamma utility instead.

2 Make sure your monitor has been turned on for at least a half hour. This gives it sufficient time to warm up for a more accurate color reading.

3 Make sure your monitor is displaying thousands of colors or more.

4 Set the room lighting to the level you plan to maintain consistently.

5 Remove colorful background patterns on your monitor desktop. Busy or bright patterns surrounding a document interfere with accurate color perception. Set your desktop to display neutral grays only, using RGB values of 128. For more information, see the manual for your operating system.

6 If your monitor has digital controls for choosing the white point of your monitor from a range of preset values, set those controls before starting Adobe Gamma. Later, in Adobe Gamma, you'll set the white point to match your monitor's current setting. Be sure to set the digital controls before you start Adobe Gamma. If you set them after you begin the calibration process in Adobe Gamma, you'll need to begin the process again.

Starting Adobe Gamma

You'll use the Adobe Gamma utility to calibrate and characterize your monitor. The resulting ICC profile uses the calibration settings to precisely describe how your monitor reproduces color. Depending on your workflow scenario, an ICC monitor profile can be either a source or destination profile. In this section, you'll load an existing monitor profile as a starting point for calibrating your monitor.

Note: Adobe Gamma can characterize, but not calibrate, monitors used with Windows NT®. Its ability to calibrate settings in Windows 98 depends on the video card and video driver software. In such cases, some calibration options documented here may not be available. For example, if you're only characterizing your monitor, you'll choose the default white point and gamma, but not the target calibration settings.

1 Do one of the following to start Adobe Gamma:

• In Windows, choose Start > Settings > Control Panel, and double-click Adobe Gamma.

• In Mac OS, from the Apple menu choose Control Panels > Adobe Gamma.

You can use either the control panel or a step-by-step wizard to make all the adjustments necessary for calibrating your monitor. In this lesson, you will use the Adobe Gamma control panel. Any time while working in the Adobe Gamma control panel, you can click the Wizard (Windows) or Assistant (Mac OS) button to switch to the wizard for instructions that guide you through the same settings as in the control panel, one option at a time.

2 Select Control Panel, and click Next.

The next step is to load an ICC monitor profile that describes your monitor. This profile serves as a starting point for the calibration process by supplying some preset values. You'll adjust these values in Adobe Gamma to characterize the profile to match your monitor's particular characteristics.

3 Do one of the following:

• If your monitor is listed in the Description area at the top of the control panel, select it.

• Click the Load button for a list of other available profiles, and then locate and open the monitor ICC profile that most closely matches your monitor. To see an ICC profile's full name at the bottom of the Open Monitor Profile dialog box, select a file. (Windows profile filenames have the .icm extension, which you may not see if the extension display is off.) Make your choice, and click Open.

• Leave the generic Adobe monitor profile selected in the Description area.

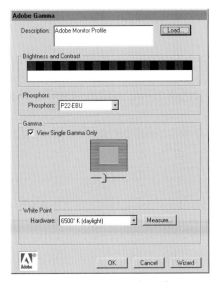

Adobe Gamma utility control panel

Setting the optimum brightness and contrast

Now you'll adjust the monitor's overall level and range of display intensity. These controls work just as they do on a television. Adjusting the monitor's brightness and contrast enables the most accurate screen representation for the gamma adjustment that follows.

1 With Adobe Gamma running, set the contrast control on your monitor to its highest setting.

2 Adjust the brightness control on your monitor as you watch the alternating pattern of black and gray squares across the top half of the Brightness and Contrast rectangle in Adobe Gamma. Make the gray squares in the top bar as dark as possible without matching the black squares, while keeping the bottom area a bright white. If you can't see a difference between the black and gray squares while keeping the bottom area white, your monitor's screen phosphors may be fading.

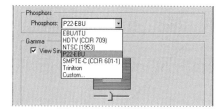

*A. Gray squares too light **B.** Gray squares too dark and white area too gray **C.** Gray squares and white area correctly adjusted*

Do not adjust the brightness and contrast controls on your monitor again unless you are about to update the monitor profile. Adjusting the controls invalidates the monitor profile. You can tape the hardware controls in place if necessary.

Selecting phosphor data

The chemical phosphors in your monitor determine the range of colors you see on your screen.

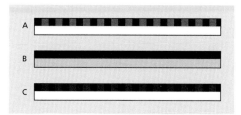

Do one of the following from the Phosphors menu:

• Choose the exact phosphor type used by the monitor you are calibrating. The two most common phosphor types are EBU/ITU and Trinitron.

• If the correct type is not listed but you were provided with chromaticity coordinates with your monitor, choose Custom, and enter the red, green, and blue chromaticity coordinates of the monitor's phosphors.

• If you're not sure which phosphors your monitor uses, see the monitor's documentation; contact the manufacturer; or use a color measuring instrument such as a colorimeter or spectrophotometer to determine them.

Setting the midtones

The gamma setting defines midtone brightness. You can adjust the gamma based on a single combined gamma reading (the View Single Gamma Only option). Or you can individually adjust the midtones for red, green, and blue. The second method produces a more accurate setting, so you will use that method here.

For the Gamma option in the Adobe Gamma utility, deselect the View Single Gamma Only option. Drag the slider under each box until the shape in the center blends in with the background as much as possible. It may help to squint or move back from the monitor.

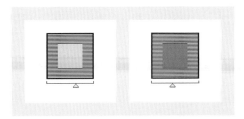

Single gamma not calibrated (left), and calibrated (right)

Make adjustments carefully and in small increments; imprecise adjustments can result in a color cast not visible until you print.

Selecting a target gamma

You may also have an option for specifying a separate gamma for viewing graphics.

Note: This option is not available in Windows NT due to its hardware protection shield that prevents Adobe Gamma from communicating with the computer's video card.

If you have this option, choose one of the following from the Desired menu:

• Windows Default for Windows systems. Leave the setting at 2.2.

• Macintosh Default for Mac OS computers. Leave the setting at 1.8.

Setting the monitor's white point

Now you'll adjust the hardware *white point*, the whitest white that a monitor is capable of displaying. The white point is a measurement of color temperature in Kelvin and determines whether you are using a warm or cool white.

Now you'll make sure that the white point setting matches the white point of your monitor. Do one of the following:

• If you know the white point of your monitor in its current state, you can select it from the Hardware menu in the White Point section. If your monitor is new, select 9300 Kelvin, the default white point of most monitors and televisions.

• If you started from a manufacturer's profile for your monitor, you can use the default value. However, the older your monitor, the less likely it is that its white point still matches the manufacturer's profile.

• If your monitor is equipped with digital controls for setting the white point, and you already set those controls before starting Adobe Gamma, make sure the Hardware menu matches your monitor's current setting. Remember, though, that if you adjust these hardware controls at this point in the calibration process, you'll need to start over, beginning with the procedure in "Setting the optimum brightness and contrast" on page 400.

• If you don't know the white point and don't know the appropriate values, you can use the Measure option to visually estimate it. If you choose this option, continue to step 1.

   To get a precise value, you need to measure the white point with a desktop colorimeter or spectrophotometer and enter that value directly using the Custom option.

If you were unable to choose a hardware setting as described, try the following experiment.

1 For best results, eliminate all ambient light before proceeding.

2 Click Measure, and then click OK (Windows) or Next (Mac OS). Three squares will appear.

The goal here is to make the center square as neutral gray as possible. You'll train your eyes to see the contrasts between the extreme cooler (blue) white and warmer (yellow) white, and then adjust the colors in the squares to find the most neutral gray between them.

3 Click the left square several times until it disappears, leaving the middle and right squares. Study the contrast between the bluish square on the right and the center square.

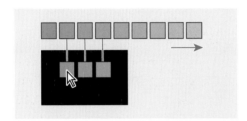

*Clicking on the left square will reset all the squares
a shade cooler.*

4 Click the right square several times until it disappears, and study the contrast between the yellowish square on the left and the center square.

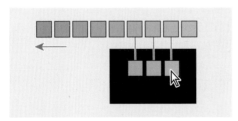

*Clicking on the right square will reset all the squares
a shade warmer.*

5 Click the left or right square until the center square is a neutral gray. When complete, commit the changes by clicking the center square.

For a color illustration of adjusting the white point, see figure 12-3 of the color signature.

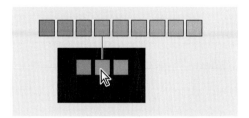

Setting an adjusted white point

This option, when available, sets a working white point for monitor display, if that value differs from the hardware white point. For example, if your hardware white point is 6500 Kelvin (daylight), but you want to edit an image at 5000 Kelvin (warm white) because that most closely represents the environment in which the image will be viewed, you can set your adjusted white point to 5000 Kelvin. Adobe Gamma will change the monitor display accordingly.

Do one of the following to specify a separate white point for viewing graphics:

• To use the current white point of your monitor, choose Same as Hardware from the Adjusted menu.

• To specify your monitor's white point to a target value other than the Hardware value, choose the gamma setting you want from the Adjusted menu.

Saving the monitor profile

Now that you have adjusted all settings for your monitor, you will save the ICC profile you have created. Applications that support color management will use this monitor profile to display color graphics.

1 In Adobe Gamma, rename the monitor profile by editing the text in the Description text box. (We named the profile My Monitor.) When you name the monitor here, it appears by default when you start Adobe Gamma.

2 Click OK (Windows) or click the Close button (Mac OS). In Mac OS, click Save when prompted.

3 In the Save As dialog box, type the filename again, and save the file in the Color folder (Windows) or the ColorSync Profiles folder (Mac OS).

Adobe Gamma makes the new monitor profile the default. You can use this profile in any application that supports ICC-compliant color management. In Mac OS, the profile information will be supplied to Apple ColorSync as the default monitor setting.

Review questions

1 What does the color management engine do?

2 What is calibration?

3 What is characterization?

4 What are the four main monitor settings you adjust when you run the Adobe Gamma utility, and why do you adjust them?

Review answers

1 The color management engine translates colors from the color space of one device to another device's color space by a process called color mapping.

2 Calibration is the process of setting a device to known color conditions.

3 Characterization, or profiling, is the process of creating an ICC profile that describes the unique color characteristics of a particular device. You should always calibrate a device before creating a profile for it.

4 Using Adobe Gamma, you adjust the brightness and contrast, phosphors (color characteristics), gamma (color contrast), and white point (extreme highlight) of the monitor. You adjust these settings to calibrate your monitor. Adobe Gamma uses those settings to create an ICC monitor profile that defines your monitor's color space for working on graphics.

Lesson 13

13 Producing and Printing Consistent Color

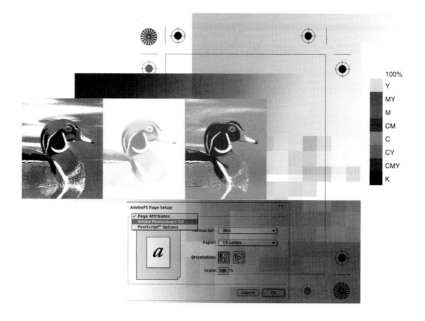

To produce consistent color, you define the color space in which to edit and display RGB images, and in which to edit, display, and print CMYK images. This helps ensure a close match between on-screen and printed colors.

In this lesson, you'll learn how to do the following:

• Define RGB, grayscale, and CMYK color spaces for displaying, editing, and printing images.

• Create a color separation, the process by which the colors in an RGB image are distributed to the four process ink colors: cyan, magenta, yellow, and black.

• Understand how images are prepared for printing on presses.

• Prepare an image for printing on a PostScript CMYK printer.

This lesson will take about 30 minutes to complete. The lesson is designed to be done on Adobe Photoshop.

If needed, remove the previous lesson folder from your hard drive, and copy the Lesson 13 folder onto it.

Reproducing colors

Colors on a monitor are displayed using combinations of red, green, and blue light (called RGB), while printed colors are typically created using a combination of four ink colors—cyan, magenta, yellow, and black (called CMYK). These four inks are called *process colors* because they are the standard inks used in the four-color printing process.

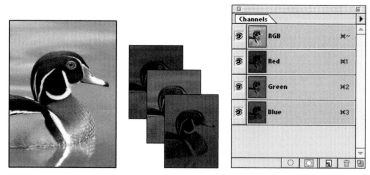

RGB image with red, green, and blue channels

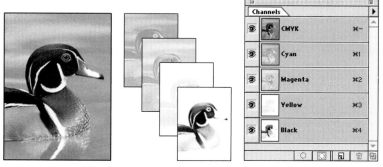

CMYK image with cyan, magenta, yellow, and black channels

For color samples of channels in both RGB and CMYK images, see figures 13-1 and 13–2 in the color signature.

Not surprisingly, because the RGB and CMYK color models use very different methods to display colors, they each reproduce a different *gamut*, or range of colors. For example, because RGB uses light to produce color, its gamut includes neon colors, such as you'd see in a neon sign. In contrast, printing inks excel at reproducing certain colors that can lie outside of the RGB gamut, such as some pastels and pure black. For an illustration of the RGB and CMYK gamuts, see figures 13–3, 13–4, and 13-5 in the color signature.

But not all RGB and CMYK gamuts are alike. Each model of monitor and printer is different, and so each displays a slightly different gamut. For example, one brand of monitor may produce slightly brighter blues than another. The *color space* for a device is defined by the gamut it can reproduce.

RGB model

A large percentage of the visible spectrum can be represented by mixing red, green, and blue (RGB) colored light in various proportions and intensities. Where the colors overlap, they create cyan, magenta, and yellow.

RGB colors are called additive colors because you create white by adding R,G, and B together—that is, all light is reflected back to the eye. Additive colors are used for lighting, television, and computer monitors. Your monitor, for example, creates color by emitting light through red, green, and blue phosphors.

CMYK model

Whereas the RGB model depends on a light source to create color, the CMYK model is based on the light-absorbing quality of ink printed on paper. As white light strikes translucent inks, a portion of the spectrum is absorbed. Color that is not absorbed is reflected back to your eye.

Combining pure cyan (C), magenta (M), and yellow (Y) pigments would result in black by absorbing, or subtracting, all colors. For this reason they are called subtractive colors. Black (K) ink is added for better shadow density. (The letter K came into use because black is the "key" color for registering other colors, and because the letter B also stands for blue.) Combining these inks to reproduce color is called four-color process printing.

In this lesson, you'll choose which RGB and CMYK ICC profiles to use. Once you specify the profiles, Photoshop can embed them into your image files. Photoshop (and any other application that can use ICC profiles) can then interpret the ICC profile in the image file to automatically manage color for that image. For general information about color management and about preparing your monitor, see Chapter 12, "Setting Up Your Monitor for Color Management."

For information on embedding ICC profiles, see Chapter 5 in the Adobe Photoshop 5.0 User Guide or "Reproducing Color Accurately" in Photoshop 5.0 online Help.

Getting started

Before beginning this lesson, restore the default application settings for Adobe Photoshop. See "Restoring default preferences" on page 4.

Defining the RGB color space for images

Photoshop lets you define the color space in which you work on RGB images separately from the RGB color space of the monitor that displays them. This is because a monitor can display only a subset of all possible RGB colors. Rather than restrict Photoshop to the range of colors your particular monitor can display, you can choose from a set of more flexible RGB color spaces. For example, CMYK printing presses can reproduce certain colors that RGB monitors cannot. By editing images using a larger RGB color space than your monitor's, you can preserve a more complete range of colors for the press.

Now you'll use the RGB Setup dialog box to define the RGB color space to use for editing RGB images. As with the Adobe Gamma utility you used in Lesson 12, "Setting Up Your Monitor for Color Management," the RGB Setup dialog box saves the settings you specify as an ICC profile.

1 Choose File > Color Settings > RGB Setup. The ICC profile for your monitor is listed at the bottom of the dialog box.

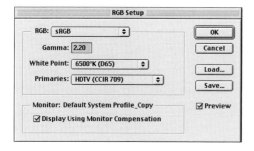

2 Select Display Using Monitor Compensation to display images using the monitor's RGB color space.

This option uses your monitor profile to display the image at maximum color accuracy. When this option is off, Photoshop doesn't adjust the image for your monitor; you'll see a big difference if the RGB editing space is much different from your monitor's. Leave this option on unless you want to approximate what the image will look like on software that doesn't display images using ICC profiles, such as some Web browsers.

3 For RGB, choose different RGB color spaces from the menu.

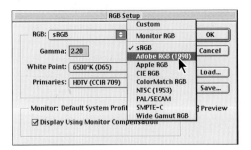

Notice that the Gamma, White Point, and Primaries settings listed in the dialog box change to reflect the different values for each RGB color space you choose.

4 When you are finished experimenting, choose Adobe RGB (1998) as the color space.

This color space more closely matches the printable (CMYK) color gamut. Because this lesson assumes that you will be printing the file, Adobe RGB (1998) is a reasonable choice.

Choose a color space based on the gamut that your final image requires. For example, the default color space, sRGB, represents the gamut that can be displayed by the hypothetical "average" personal computer monitor. The sRGB color space is endorsed by a wide variety of hardware and software manufacturers and is becoming the default color space for many scanners, low-end printers, and software applications. This means it's a good choice if you're creating images to be viewed on the Web.

[?] For information on the individual color spaces available, see Chapter 5 of the Adobe Photoshop 5.0 User Guide or "Reproducing Color Accurately" in Photoshop 5.0 online Help.

5 Click OK.

Defining the CMYK color space for images and printing

Similarly to how you defined the RGB color space for working with RGB images, now you'll define the CMYK color space for editing and printing CMYK images. Photoshop uses the information you enter in the CMYK Setup dialog box when you convert images between RGB and CMYK modes, and to give you an accurate on-screen preview of what an image will look like when printed.

There are several ways to describe the CMYK color space. In this lesson, you'll choose an ICC profile that describes the printer you plan to use. Photoshop can then map the colors in your image to the range of colors the printer can print.

? For information on other methods of describing the CMYK color space, see Chapter 5 in the Photoshop 5.0 User Guide or "Reproducing Color Accurately" in Photoshop 5.0 online Help.

1 Choose File > Color Settings > CMYK Setup.

The CMYK Setup dialog box shows the options you can choose from if you want to describe how a particular ink, printer, and paper work together.

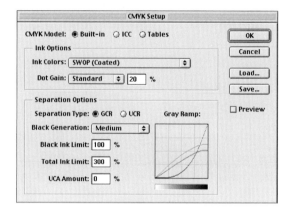

To make the process easier, you'll choose from an existing ICC printer profile.

2 For CMYK Model, select ICC.

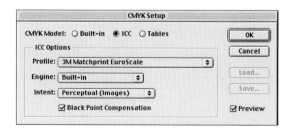

For this exercise, you'll use the default CMYK settings. When you're doing your own work, you'll probably change the values in this dialog box depending on the device you're printing to and the requirements of the individual project.

3 For Profile, choose the printer profile you want to use.

For this lesson, you don't have to print the image, so you can choose any printer profile you want.

Note: For best results, use a CMYK profile generated using professional profiling equipment. Alternatively, your prepress service provider may be able to provide or recommend a profile appropriate for your workflow. You can also create a printer profile using the Olé No Moire CMYK image included with the Adobe Photoshop software. For more information, see the Read Me file that accompanies the Olé No Moire file.

4 For Engine, choose Built-in to use Photoshop's built-in ICC profile interpreter.

5 For Intent, choose Perceptual (Images).

This option maintains the relative color values among the original pixels as they are mapped to the printer's CMYK gamut. This method preserves the relationship between colors, although the color values themselves may change. Unless you are experienced with color and need to select a different option, you should use this option when choosing the Intent.

6 Select Black Point Compensation.

This option makes Photoshop convert the darkest neutral color of the source's color space to the darkest neutral color of the destination's color space rather than to black when converting colors. For example, if you were converting an image from RGB mode to CMYK mode, selecting this option would convert the darkest neutral color in the image's RGB color space to the equivalent in the CMYK color space.

7 Click OK.

Compensating for dot gain in grayscale images

Dot gain is the tendency of the dots of ink to spread and print larger than they should on the press, creating darker tones or color than expected. Different printers and papers have different dot gains.

If your grayscale images will be viewed only on-screen, you don't need to compensate for dot gain. However, for this lesson, we're assuming you're setting up your images for printing, and so you should apply the same dot gain values you used for CMYK output. The Grayscale Setup dialog box lets you specify whether grayscale images behave as RGB images or black ink.

1 Choose File > Color Settings > Grayscale Setup.

2 For Grayscale Behavior, select Black Ink to use the dot gain settings specified as part of the ICC profile you chose in the CMYK Setup dialog box.

3 Click OK.

Preparing images for print

The first step in preparing an image for print is to make any color and tonal adjustments to the image. To try making tonal adjustments on your own, see Lesson 12, "Preparing Images for Two-Color Printing."

For more information, see Chapter 6 in the Photoshop 5.0 User Guide or "Making Color and Tonal Adjustments" in Photoshop 5.0 online Help.

The most common way to output images is to produce a negative image on film, and then transfer the image to a printing plate that will be run on a press.

To print a continuous-tone image, the image must be broken down into a series of dots. These dots are created when you apply a *halftone screen* to the image. The dots in a halftone screen control how much ink is deposited at a specific location. The varying size and density of the dots create the optical illusion of variations of gray or continuous color in the image.

A printed color image consists of four separate halftone screens—one each for cyan, magenta, yellow, and black (the four process ink colors). You can also add extra custom colors, called spot colors. To create a spot color yourself, see Lesson 11, "Preparing Images for Two-Color Printing."

Preparing a color separation in Adobe Photoshop

In Adobe Photoshop, preparing a color separation consists of the following process:

• Entering settings in the CMYK Setup dialog box to specify the properties of the printer you will use and to control how the CMYK plates are generated.

• Converting the image from RGB mode to CMYK mode to apply the CMYK Setup values to the image and to separate the colors in the image onto the four process color plates.

• Setting the line screen at which the image will be printed, either in Photoshop or in the page-layout application from which you're going to print.

Separating an RGB image

You've already calibrated your monitor, and specified the working RGB color space and the CMYK color space. Now you're ready to convert your RGB image to CMYK to separate the colors in the RGB image onto the four process color plates, one each for cyan, magenta, yellow, and black.

When you convert an RGB image to CMYK mode, the settings in the CMYK Setup dialog box are applied to the image.

1 Choose File > Open, and open the 12Start.psd file, located in the Lessons/Lesson13 folder.

A sample RGB image is displayed.

2 With the 13Start.psd image selected, choose Image > Duplicate.

3 Enter the name **CMYK.psd**, and click OK to create a duplicate of the original file.

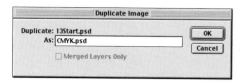

4 Align the images side by side so you can see both of them on your screen.

5 Make sure that the CMYK.psd image is the active window; then choose Image > Mode > CMYK Color.

When you choose the CMYK mode, the image now consists of four channels (cyan, magenta, yellow, and black). You'll notice a difference between the colors in the RGB image and the CMYK image. This is natural when converting RGB colors to CMYK colors, because they have different gamuts.

You have successfully completed the process of preparing a file for color separation and printing.

Strategies for successful printing

The rest of this lesson provides tips and techniques to help you successfully print your images.

Working in RGB mode

One strategy for creating color separations is to work in RGB mode, set the CMYK Setup options to compensate for conditions on press, and then convert the image to CMYK mode. During the conversion, Adobe Photoshop applies the CMYK Setup settings to the image, which alters the pixel values in the image to compensate for the separation preferences.

Working in RGB mode is faster than working in CMYK mode because RGB files are smaller. In addition, some filters and options are available only for RGB images.

Working in CMYK mode

Another strategy for creating color separations is to work in CMYK mode. You can print a color proof to check colors in the image. If you used an ICC printer profile to specify the settings in the CMYK Setup dialog box and if the color proof doesn't match the on-screen preview, you can verify that the printer is calibrated correctly or adjust the image and reprint color proofs until the proof looks the way you want.

For information on making color adjustments to an image, see Chapter 6 in the Photoshop 5.0 User Guide or "Making Color and Tonal Adjustments" in Photoshop 5.0 online Help.

Note: *Keep in mind that even though you may have calibrated your system to create a close match between the on-screen and printed colors, you are still displaying CMYK data on an RGB monitor, and slight discrepancies in color may occur.*

When you work in CMYK mode, the CMYK Setup options affect the way the image is displayed on the monitor. But because you are not converting this CMYK data to RGB mode, any changes affect only the on-screen image—the actual pixel values are not altered. For example, if the ICC profile you chose in the CMYK Setup dialog box specifies an expected dot gain of 30% while your image is in CMYK mode, the image becomes darker on-screen to approximate the dot gain, but the actual pixel values in the image are not changed. (In contrast, setting separation options on the same file while in RGB mode and then converting to CMYK mode *will* affect the actual pixel values in the image.)

Displaying individual channels

Each channel in an image provides information about that image's color values. RGB images are composed of three channels: one each for red, green, and blue. CMYK images are composed of four channels: one each for cyan, magenta, yellow, and black. You can view the individual channels in an image using the Channels palette.

By default, the individual channels are shown in grayscale, to more clearly show the intensity of the RGB phosphors or CMYK inks for that channel. Only the composite image is shown in color. You'll change this temporarily so that you can get an idea of how color in the individual channels blend together to make the final range of colors in the composite channel.

1 Choose File > Preferences > Display & Cursors.

2 In the Display section of the dialog box, select Color Channels in Color; then click OK.

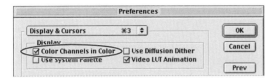

3 Make the 13Start.psd window the active window; then choose Window > Show Channels to display the Channels palette.

Notice that the colors in the RGB image are distributed in the red, green, and blue channels (the composite channel at the top of the palette shows the combined channels).

 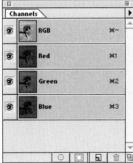

RGB image and channels

For a color illustration of the RGB channels, see figure 13-1 in the color signature.

4 In the Channels palette, click in the far left column of one or more of the individual channels (red, green, or blue) to display and hide the channels and see how they blend to create the composite image.

5 Click the RGB composite channel at the top of the Channels palette to return to the composite view.

6 Now click the CMYK.psd window to make it active.

The Channels palette now shows the distribution of the colors in the image in the cyan, magenta, yellow, and black channels. The color in each channel represents the percentage of ink used on each of the printing plates.

 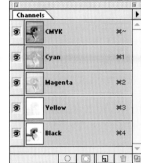

CMYK image and channels

 For a color illustration of the CMYK image and channels, see figure 13-2 in the color signature.

7 To see how each plate contributes to the overall color of the final image, click in the far left column for each of the four process colors in the Channels palette.

Although viewing the individual channels in color is helpful for seeing how the channels blend to make up a range of colors in the image, relying on these color channel previews can be misleading for making color or tonal corrections to the image. For example, yellow in the CMYK image shows up lighter on a monitor than it does in print. So now you'll return the channel previews to grayscale.

8 Choose File > Preferences > Display & Cursors.

9 Deselect Color Channels in Color; then click OK.

10 Close the 13Start.psd file and the CMYK.psd file without saving your changes.

Identifying out-of-gamut colors

Most scanned photographs contain RGB colors within the CMYK gamut, and changing the image to CMYK mode converts all the colors with relatively little substitution. Images that are created or altered digitally, however, often contain RGB colors that are outside the CMYK gamut—for example, neon-colored logos and lights.

Note: Out-of-gamut colors are identified by an exclamation point next to the color swatch in the Colors palette, the Color Picker, and the Info palette. Photoshop determines the gamut using the settings in the Separation Setup and Printing Inks dialog boxes.

Before you convert an image from RGB mode to CMYK mode, you can preview the CMYK color values while still in RGB mode.

1 Choose File > Open, and open the 13Start.psd file, located in the Lessons/Lesson13 folder on your hard drive.

2 Choose Image > Duplicate, enter the name **CMYK.psd**, and click OK to duplicate the image.

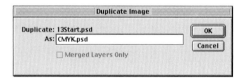

3 Align the images side by side.

4 With the CMYK.psd window active, choose View > Preview > CMYK.

Notice the difference in the two images, particularly in the intensity of the blue areas of the image. At this point, the CMYK.psd image is still in RGB mode, and is just a preview of what it would look like in CMYK mode.

5 With the CMYK.psd window still active, Choose View > Preview > CMYK again to turn off the CMYK preview.

Note: If you plan to continue editing an RGB image, turn off the CMYK preview to improve system performance.

Next you'll identify the out-of-gamut colors in the image.

6 Choose View > Gamut Warning. Adobe Photoshop builds a color conversion table and displays a neutral gray where the colors are out-of-gamut.

Note: *You can change the gamut warning color to distinguish it from the colors in the image by choosing File > Preferences > Transparency & Gamut and then selecting a new color from the Color Picker.*

7 To bring the colors into the CMYK color gamut, choose Image > Mode > CMYK Color.

The gamut warning color is removed, and the out-of-gamut RGB colors are converted to the CMYK gamut (using the Separation Setup and Printing Inks settings you entered).

Note: *You can also adjust the gamut using Photoshop's color-correction tools, such as the Curves command.*

For more information, see Chapter 6 in the Adobe Photoshop 5.0 User Guide or "Making Color and Tonal Adjustments" in Photoshop 5.0 online Help.

8 Choose File > Save to save the CMYK.psd image.

9 Keep both images open on your screen.

Previewing a printed image

Because of the discrepancy between the display resolution and the image resolution, the size of an image on-screen may not accurately represent its printed size. You can preview the print size of a printed image using the Print Size command.

With the image CMYK.psd still active, choose View > Print Size. This preview simulates how the image appears at its printed size.

Important: In Adobe Photoshop, images always print from the center of the page. You cannot change the position of the image on the page to print it in a different location unless you export the file to a page-layout program.

Selecting print options

To select printing options, you make choices in the File Info and Page Setup dialog boxes and then choose Options from the Print dialog box. The next sections introduce you to some of the printing options.

For information on all the print options, see Chapter 15 in the Photoshop 5.0 User Guide or "Printing" in Photoshop 5.0 online Help.

Entering file information

Photoshop supports the information standard developed by the Newspaper Association of America and the International Press Telecommunications Council to identify trans-mitted text and images.

In Windows, you can add file information to files saved in Photoshop, TIFF, and JPEG formats. In Mac OS, you can add file information to files saved in any format.

1 Choose File > File Info.

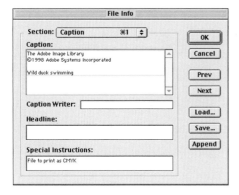

2 In the File Info dialog box, type a description of the file in the Caption text box.

Note: To print a caption when you print an image, choose File > Page Setup, and click the Caption option.

3 Enter your name in the Caption Writer text box.

4 Enter any special instructions you may have for printing the image in the Special Instructions text box.

5 For Section, choose Origin. In the origin section, enter information that you or others can refer to later, including an address, date, and other data.

6 Click the Today button to enter today's date in the date box.

Other types of file information you can record include the following:

• Keywords for use with image browser applications

• Categories for use with the Associated Press regional registry

• Credits for copyrighted images

7 Click OK to attach the information to the file.

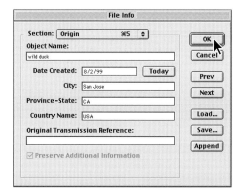

For complete information about all the File Info sections, see Chapter 14 in the Adobe Photoshop 5.0 User Guide or "Saving and Exporting Images" in Photoshop 5.0 online Help.

Specifying settings for different image types

The type of image you're printing and the type of output required by you or your prepress service provider determine the selections you make in the Page Setup and Print dialog boxes.

The Page Setup dialog box lets you set up print labels, crop marks, calibration bars, registration marks, and negatives. You can also print emulsion-side down, and use interpolation (for PostScript LanguageLevel 2 printers).

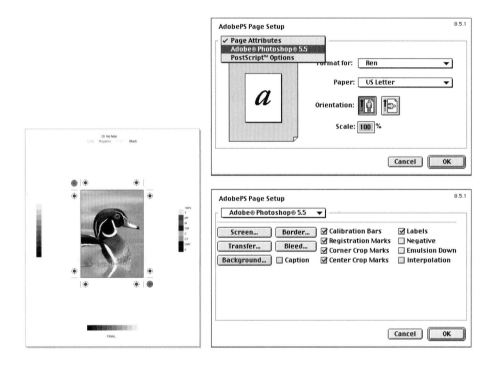

Printing

When you're ready to print your image, use the following guidelines for best results:

• Set the parameters for the halftone screen.

• Print a *color composite*, often called a color *comp*. A color composite is a single print that combines the red, green, and blue channels of an RGB image (or the cyan, magenta, yellow, and black channels of a CMYK image). This indicates what the final printed image will look like.

- Print separations to make sure the image separates correctly.
- Print to film.

Printing a halftone

To specify the halftone screen when you print an image, you use the Halftone Screen option in the Page Setup dialog box. The results of using a halftone screen appear only in the printed copy; you cannot see the halftone screen on-screen.

You use one halftone screen to print a grayscale image. You use four halftone screens (one for each process color) to print color separations. In this example, you'll be adjusting the screen frequency and dot shape to produce a halftone screen for a grayscale image.

The *screen frequency* controls the density of dots on the screen. Since the dots are arranged in lines on the screen, the common measurement for screen frequency is lines per inch (lpi). The higher the screen frequency, the finer the image produced (depending on the line screen capability of the printer). Magazines, for example, tend to use fine screens of 133 lpi and higher because they are usually printed on coated paper stock on high-quality presses. Newspapers, which are usually printed on lower-quality paper stock, tend to use lower screen frequencies, such as 85-lpi screens.

The *screen angle* used to create halftones of grayscale images is generally 45°. For best results with color separations, select the Auto option in the Halftone Screens dialog box (choose Page Setup > Screens > Halftone Screens). You can also specify an angle for each of the color screens. Setting the screens at different angles ensures that the dots placed by the four screens blend to look like continuous color and do not produce moiré patterns.

Diamond-shaped dots are most commonly used in halftone screens. In Adobe Photoshop, however, you can also choose round, elliptical, linear, square, and cross-shaped dots.

Note: By default, an image will use the halftone screen settings of the output device or of the software from which you output the image, such as a page-layout program. You usually don't need to specify halftone screen settings in the following way unless you want to override the default settings.

1 Make sure the 13Start.psd file is open on your desktop.

2 Select 13Start.psd to make it the active window.

3 Choose Image > Mode > Grayscale; then click OK to discard the color information.

4 Choose File > Page Setup, and choose Adobe Photoshop 5.5.

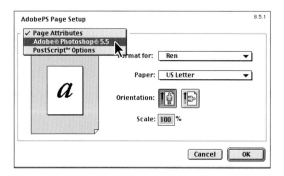

5 Click Screen.

6 In the Halftone Screen dialog box, deselect the Use Printer's Default Screen check box to enter another number.

7 For Frequency, enter **133** in the Frequency text box, and make sure that the unit of measurement is set to lines/inch.

8 Leave the screen angle at the default setting of 45°.

9 For Shape, choose Ellipse.

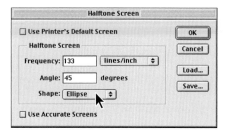

10 Click OK, and click OK again in the Page Setup dialog box.

11 To print the image, choose File > Print. (If you don't have a printer, skip this step.)

12 Look at the printed output to see the shape of the halftone dots (in this case, Ellipse).

13 Choose File > Close, and do not save changes.

For more information about printing halftones, see Chapter 15 in the Photoshop 5.0 User Guide or "Printing" in Photoshop 5.0 online help.

Printing separations

By default, a CMYK image prints as a single document. To print the file as four separations, you need to select the Separations option in the Print dialog box. Otherwise the CMYK image prints as a single, composite image.

In this optional part of the lesson, you can print the file.

1 If the file CMYK.psd is not still open, choose File > Open, and open the CMYK.psd file in the Lessons/Lesson13 folder on your hard drive.

2 Choose File > Print.

3 Do one of the following:

• In Windows, for Space, choose Separations (at the bottom of the dialog box).

• In Mac OS, choose Adobe Photoshop 5.5. For Space, choose Separations.

4 Click Print. (If you don't have a printer, skip this step.)

5 Choose File > Close, and do not save changes.

This completes your introduction to producing color separations and printing using Adobe Photoshop.

For information about all of the color management and printing options, see Chapters 5 and 15 in the Photoshop 5.0 User Guide or "Reproducing Color Accurately" and "Printing" in Photoshop 5.0 online Help.

Review questions

1 What steps should you follow to reproduce color accurately?

2 What is a gamut?

3 What is an ICC profile?

4 What is a color separation? How does a CMYK image differ from an RGB image?

5 What steps should you follow when preparing an image for color separations?

Review answers

1 Calibrate your monitor, and then specify the RGB and CMYK color spaces if you will be working with these types of images. If you will be working with grayscale images, enter settings for the Grayscale Setup dialog box as well.

2 The range of colors that can be reproduced by a color model or device. For example, the RGB and CMYK color models have different gamuts, and so do any two RGB scanners.

3 An ICC profile is a description of a device's color space, such as the CMYK color space of a particular printer. Applications such as Photoshop can interpret ICC profiles in an image to maintain consistent color across different applications, platforms, and devices.

4 A color separation is created when an image is converted to CMYK mode. The colors in the CMYK image are separated in the four process color channels: cyan, magenta, yellow, and black. An RGB image has three color channels: red, green, and blue.

5 You prepare an image for print by following the steps for reproducing color accurately, and then you convert the image from RGB mode to CMYK mode to build a color separation.

Lesson 14

14 Optimizing Images for Web Publication

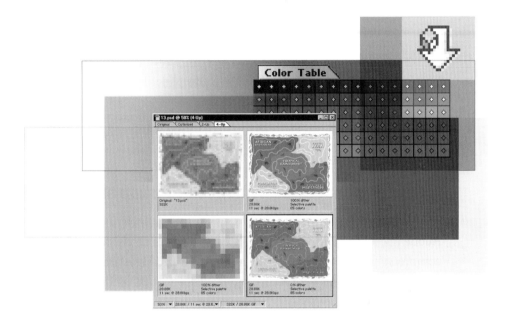

Adobe Photoshop and Adobe ImageReady let you optimize the display and file size of your images for effective Web publishing results. In general, the file size of an image should be small enough to allow reasonable download times from a Web server, but large enough to represent desired colors and details in the image. Adobe ImageReady also lets you turn an image into an image map, creating Web-ready navigation elements from your art.

Getting started

Before beginning this lesson, restore the default application settings for Adobe Photoshop and ImageReady. See "Restoring default preferences" on page 4.

Optimizing a JPEG image

In this lesson you will optimize files in both JPEG and GIF format. You will use Photoshop to perform the JPEG compression and ImageReady for the GIF compression, although either application would work equally well for either type of compression.

Optimizing and saving a file

With the new Save for Web dialog box, Photoshop now has all of the optimization capabilities of ImageReady built right in. You can compare two or more versions of a file as you work, allowing you to adjust optimization settings until you have the optimal combination of file size and image quality.

Now you'll open the start file and begin the lesson by optimizing an image containing photographs in JPEG format and compare the results of different palette and dither settings.

1 Start Photoshop.

2 Click Cancel to exit the color management dialog box that appears.

3 Choose File > Open, and open the 14Start1.psd file, located in the Lessons/Lesson14 folder on your hard drive.

This file is a modified version of the zoo map you will be using later in this lesson. It has been enhanced with scanned photographs of animals, which have been further manipulated in Photoshop. Currently, the file size is far too large for use on a Web site. You'll compare different file compression formats to see which one gives us the most compression without sacrificing too much image quality.

4 Choose File > Save For Web.

5 Click the 4-Up tab above the image window in the Save for Web dialog box.

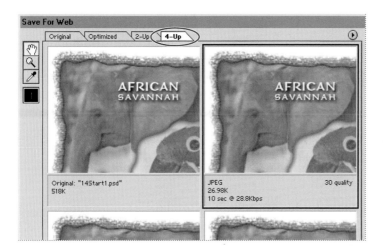

By looking at four different file settings, you can get a good idea of which settings will best suit your purpose. Using either 4-Up or 2-Up view, you can display multiple versions of an image in the same image window. You can then adjust optimization settings for each version of the image to select the best combination of settings.

6 Using the pop-up View menu in the lower left corner of the dialog box, change the magnification to 200% or more so that you can see the details of the image.

7 Place your mouse cursor over the upper right version of the image (which is the active version, as indicated by a dark border). The cursor becomes the hand cursor, indicating that you can drag to move the image. Drag to reposition the image so that the Tropical Rainforest text (in the center of the image, over the green parrot) is visible.

8 From the Settings pop-up menu in the Optimize panel, choose GIF 128 Dithered.

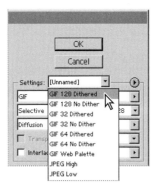

Notice the dark group of pixels around the text and on the parrot's beak. (You may need to scroll to the left to see the beak.) You will use the two bottom panels to see how the image would look as either a JPEG or a PNG file.

9 Click the lower left version of the image to select it.

10 Choose JPEG Low from the Settings pop-up menu.

The image looks pretty choppy and the quality is unacceptably poor around the text. Now you will attempt to increase the image quality without an unacceptable increase in file size.

11 Choose JPEG High from the Settings pop-up menu.

JPEG Low   JPEG High

This improves image quality, but also results in a significant increase in the size of the file.

12 Choose JPEG Medium from the Settings pop-up menu.

The image quality is now acceptable, while file size is still significantly smaller than either the JPEG High version or the GIF version. If you want, experiment with the Quality pop-up slider to compare quality to file size using other settings. (We used a setting of 45.)

13 Click the lower right panel to select it.

14 Choose PNG-8 128 Dithered from the Settings pop-up menu.

Although this gives us a smaller file size than the original image, the image quality is not as good as the JPEG Medium version, which also has a smaller file size. Furthermore, many older browsers cannot read the PNG format. To make this image compatible with older browsers, you will use the JPEG version in the lower left corner.

15 Click the JPEG version.

16 In the Optimize panel (on the right side of the dialog box), make sure the Progressive option is selected (which causes the image to download in several passes, each of which increases the image quality), and click OK.

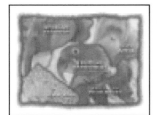 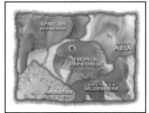 

The Progressive JPEG download

17 In the Save Optimized As dialog box, use the default name (14Start1.jpg), and click Save.

This saves a JPEG version of the 14Start1.psd file in the same folder as the original file.

18 Close the original Photoshop file without saving changes.

Optimizing a GIF image

Now you'll optimize a flat-color image in GIF format in ImageReady and compare the results of different palette and dither settings.

Choosing optimization settings

The Optimize palette lets you specify the file format and compression settings for the optimized image. The optimized image is updated as you edit, letting you interactively preview the effects of different settings.

1 Click the Jump To button at the bottom of the toolbox to jump from Photoshop to ImageReady.

If you do not have enough memory to run both applications simultaneously, you can simply exit Photoshop and then start ImageReady.

2 From within ImageReady, choose File > Open, and open the file 14Start2.psd in the Lessons/Lesson14 folder on your hard drive.

This image was created in Adobe Illustrator, and then rasterized into Photoshop. Notice the many areas of solid color in the image.

3 Click the 2-Up tab in the image window.

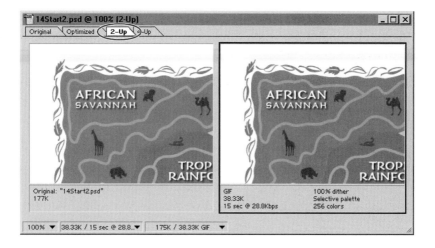

4 In the Optimize palette, choose GIF 128 No Dither from the Settings pop-up menu. (If the Optimize palette is not visible, choose Window > Show Optimize.)

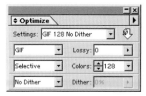

5 Choose Perceptual from the palette pop-up menu.

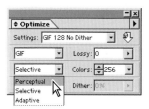

• Perceptual gives priority to colors that appear most commonly in the image and are more sensitive to the human eye. This palette usually produces images with the greatest color integrity.

• Selective creates a color table similar to the Perceptual color table, but favors broad areas of color and the preservation of Web colors.

• Adaptive samples colors from the portion of the RGB spectrum that appears most commonly in the image. For example, an image containing predominantly blue hues produces a palette consisting mostly of shades of blue.

• Web consists of the 216 colors that are shared in common by the Windows and Mac OS system palettes. When displaying images, a browser application will use a 16-bit or 24-bit color table (thousands or millions of colors) if the system display is set to one of these modes; otherwise, the browser will use the default 8-bit system palette. While few Web designers use 8-bit color systems, many Web users do.

• Custom preserves the current perceptual, selective, or adaptive color table as a fixed palette that does not update with changes to the image.

• Mac OS or Windows uses the computer system's default 8-bit (256-color) palette, which is based on a uniform sampling of RGB colors.

The status bar at the bottom of the image window displays the view magnification and other useful information about the original and optimized versions of the image. You can display two sets of file values simultaneously.

In the first image information box, the value on the left represents the file size of the optimized image; the value on the right represents the download time. In the second image information box the two values represent the original and optimized file sizes.

6 Press the triangle in the second box, and choose Image Dimensions.

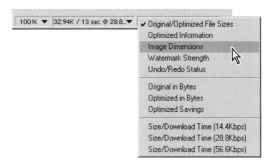

This option displays the size of the image in pixels, which is important when planning how an image will fit into a predesigned Web-page template.

7 If the Color Table palette is not showing, choose Window > Show Color Table.

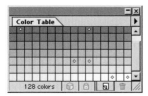

White diamonds indicate
Web-safe colors.

This palette shows the colors that comprise the Perceptual palette for the zoo map image. The white diamonds on certain colors indicate that those colors are Web-safe. The total number of colors appears at the bottom of the palette. You can resize the palette or use the scroll bar to view all the colors. You can also change how the colors are arranged in the palette.

8 Choose Sort By Hue from the Color Table palette menu.

Now you'll observe how a different palette option affects the image.

9 In the Optimize palette, choose Web from the palette menu.

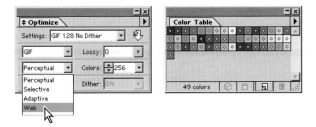

Notice the color changes in the image and in the Color Table palette, which updates to reflect the Web palette.

Experiment with different palette options and notice the effects on the image and on the Color Table palette.

Reducing the color palette

To compress the file size further, you can decrease the total number of colors included in the Color Table palette. A reduced range of colors will often preserve good image quality while dramatically reducing the file space required to store extra colors.

1 In the Optimize palette, choose the Perceptual palette option.

2 In the image window, change the magnification to 200% or more so that you can see details in the image.

3 If necessary, activate the optimized panel and drag (using the Move tool or holding down the spacebar) to place the Tropical Rainforest text at the bottom center of the display.

4 Note the current file size of the optimized image. Change the number of colors in the Optimize palette to 32. Note the new file size.

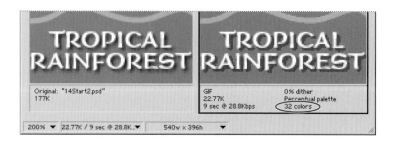

This is a significant reduction in file size, but the quality of the image is less. Specifically, the animal silhouettes have changed colors. For the African Savannah silhouettes, they change to a green-brown, and for the Northern Wilderness, the animal silhouettes change to the background color, making them invisible. (Hold down the spacebar and drag within the active panel to move the image so that you can see the Northern Wilderness area, or simply change the magnification back to 100%.)

5 Change the number of colors back to 128.

This time, before reducing the color palette, you'll lock several colors to ensure that these colors do not drop from the reduced palette.

6 Select the eyedropper tool ( ), and click in the camel silhouette in the African Savannah area to sample its color.

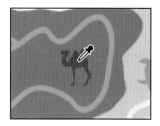
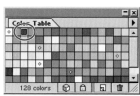

The dark brown color is selected in the Color Table palette. (You may need to scroll through the palette to find it.)

7 Click the Lock button ( ) at the bottom of the Color Table palette to lock the selected color. A small square appears in the lower right corner of the color, indicating that the color is locked. (To unlock a color, select the locked color swatch and click again on the Lock button.)

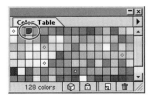

8 Repeat this procedure to lock the dark blue bear silhouette in the Northern Wilderness area.

You may need to move the image down to work in the Northern Wilderness portion of the image.

9 In the Optimize palette, reduce the number of colors to 32.

Notice that the locked colors remain in the palette after the reduction, but you have new color-shift problems.

10 Change the number of colors back to 128.

11 Continue to select and lock colors until the image can be reduced to 32 colors without unacceptable color shifting.

Locking all animal silhouettes and the three shades of blue in the Northern Wilderness area takes care of most of the problems. Don't lock the green background of the Tropical Rainforest area for now, though. You will be working with that color later in this lesson.

Note that significant image degradation can occur when the palette is reduced below 32 colors. In fact, for all but the simplest images, even 32 colors may be too drastic a reduction. For the best file compression of a GIF image, try to use the fewest number of colors that will still display the quality you need.

 For an illustration of the image set to different palette values, see figure 14-1 in the color signature.

12 When you have finished experimenting, set the colors to 32 in the Optimize palette and choose File > Save to save the file.

Controlling dither

You may have noticed that certain areas of the image appear mottled or spotty when optimized with different color palettes and numbers of colors. This spotty appearance results from *dithering,* the technique used to simulate the appearance of colors that are not included in the color palette. For example, a blue color and a yellow color may dither in a mosaic pattern to produce the illusion of a green color that does not appear in the color palette. You can select from three predefined dither patterns.

Note: To fine-tune and improve the appearance of dithered colors, you can create your own dither patterns using the Dither Box filter.

For more information, see Chapter 4 in the Photoshop 5.5 User Guide Supplement or "Optimizing Images for the Web" in Photoshop 5.5 online Help. A similar topic can be found in ImageReady 2.0 online help.

When optimizing images, keep in mind the two kinds of dithering that can occur:

• *Application dither* occurs when Adobe ImageReady attempts to simulate colors that appear in the original image but not in the optimized color palette you specify. You can control the amount of application dither by dragging the Dither slider in the Optimize palette.

• *Browser dither* occurs when a Web browser using an 8-bit (256-color) display simulates colors that appear in the optimized image's color palette but not in the system palette used by the browser. Browser dither can occur in addition to application dither. You can control the amount of browser dither by Web-shifting selected colors in the Color Table palette.

In Adobe ImageReady you can view application dither directly in an optimized image. You can also preview the additional browser dither that will appear in the final image when viewed in a browser using an 8-bit display.

Controlling application dither

The Dither slider lets you control the range of colors that ImageReady simulates by dithering. Dithering creates the appearance of more colors and detail, but can also increase the file size of the image. For optimal compression, use the lowest percentage of application dither that provides the color detail you require.

The 14Start2.psd file should be open. Make sure that the optimized image panel is selected, and that the Optimize palette is set to GIF format, Perceptual palette, and 32 colors.

1 Change the dither from No Dither to Diffusion (using the pop-up menu in the lower left corner of the Optimize palette).

2 Drag the pop-up Dither slider to 100%.

 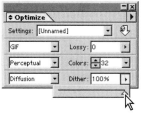

Using a combination of different colors, ImageReady tries to simulate the colors and tonalities that appear in the original image but not in the 32-color palette. Notice the speckled pattern that replaces the blocky drop shadows. While not ideal, this pattern is a vast improvement and is acceptable. The dithered green for the Tropical Rainforest, however, is not acceptable.

3 Drag the Dither slider to 50%. Experiment with different dither amounts.

ImageReady minimizes the amount of dither in the image, but no percentage of dither will preserve the drop shadows without ruining the green background.

For an illustration of the effects of different dither percentages on an image, see figure 14-2 in the color signature.

4 Set the dither back to 100%.

5 Change the number of colors back to 128, lock the Tropical Rainforest green color, and then switch back to 32 colors.

The image is now acceptable.

If it is not already open, the browser application launches and displays the optimized image in the top left corner of the browser window. In addition, the browser displays the pixel dimensions, file size, file format, and optimization settings for the image, along with the HTML code used to create the preview.

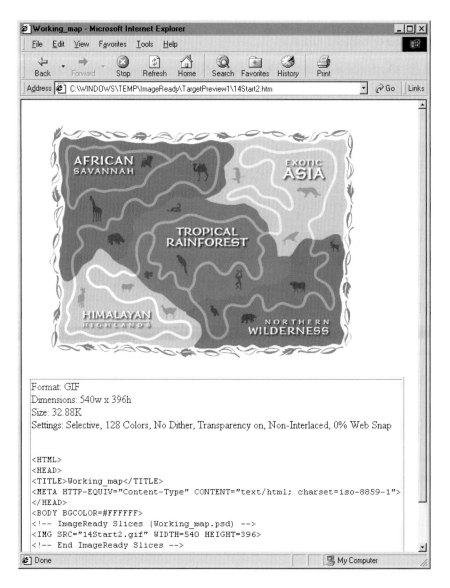

The image displays against the browser background color.

15 Exit your browser to return to ImageReady.

Trimming extra background areas

Although the background of the zoo map image now contains transparent pixels that do not display, these pixels still take up file space, adding to the size of the image. You can trim away unneeded background areas to improve the layout of the image and optimize the file size.

1 Choose Image > Trim.

The Trim command lets you crop your image, according to the transparency or pixel color of the extra border area.

2 Select Transparent Pixels, and click OK.

ImageReady trims the extra transparent areas from the image.

3 Choose File > Save Optimized As. Name the file **14Start2.gif**, and click Save. Then choose File > Close.

You will be prompted to save the 14Start2.psd file before closing. Since you are finished with this file, there is no need to save the last changes.

Creating an image map

An *image map* is an image file that contains multiple hypertext links to other files on the Web. Different areas, or *hotspots,* of the image map link to different files. Adobe ImageReady creates client-side image maps and server-side image maps.

For the Web: Image Maps

Image maps are similar to slices in enabling you to link an area of an image to a URL. However, image maps offer the advantage of enabling you to link circular, polygonal, or rectangular areas in an image, whereas slices enable you to link only rectangular areas. (If you need to link only rectangular areas, using slices may be preferable to using an image map. Using slices enables you to apply different optimization settings to different areas of an image, and to include rollover states.)

You create image maps in ImageReady using layers with layer transparency. You use a different layer for each hotspot in an image map. ImageReady uses the opaque region on the layer to define the hotspot. The image map data is saved in the HTML file for the document. You must save the HTML file with the optimized image in order to create a functioning image map.

You can create a circular, rectangular, or polygonal hotspot. ImageReady places the hotspot to match the layer's opaque region as closely as possible. If you create a polygonal hotspot, ImageReady closely outlines the opaque region's outer edge. If you create a circular or rectangular hotspot, ImageReady uses the smallest shape possible to entirely encompass the opaque region, and includes transparent areas on the layer as necessary to create the shape.

If you overlap hotspots in creating an image map in ImageReady, the topmost layer is the active hotspot in the overlapping areas. To avoid unexpected results, do not create image maps using slices that contain URL links or rollover states. The image map links may cause slice links and rollover states to be ignored in some browsers.

ImageReady can create client-side and server-side image maps. In client-side image maps, the links are interpreted by the browser itself. In server-side image maps, the links are interpreted by the server. (Note that server-side image maps do not work with sliced images.) Because client-side image maps don't need to contact the server to function, they are often significantly faster to navigate.

–From the Adobe Photoshop 5.5 User Guide Supplement, Chapter 6, "Web Design Features." A similar topic can be found in ImageReady 2.0 online Help.

In this part of the lesson, you'll create an image map from an existing image. You define hotspots by placing each area on a separate layer. To save you the trouble of creating this multilayer image yourself, you will use a version of the zoo map that has each geographic region on its own layer.

1 Choose File > Open, and open the 14Start3.psd file, located in the Lessons/Lesson14 folder.

While this image looks similar to the previous zoo map, it is actually composed of several different layers. You'll make this map image into a graphical table of contents linking to different areas of the zoo's Web site. In order to define an image map, you must work in an optimized version of the image.

2 In the Optimize palette, choose GIF 64 Dithered from the Settings pop-up menu.

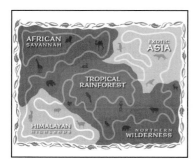 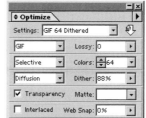

3 If the Layers palette is not already showing, choose Window > Show Layers.

Notice that the map pieces representing different sections of the zoo reside on separate layers.

4 In the Layers palette, double-click the African Savannah layer.

The Layer Options dialog box appears, letting you specify various settings for this layer.

5 In the Layer Options dialog box, select Use Layer as Image Map. For Shape, choose Polygon with the default tolerance settings.

The Shape option determines the boundary of the hotspot area.

The URL option lets you specify the target file for the hotspot link. You can link to another file in your Web site, or to a different location on the Web. For the purposes of this lesson, you'll link your hotspots to fictitious URLs for the zoo.

6 For URL, enter **http://www.zoo.com/african_savannah.html**, and click OK.

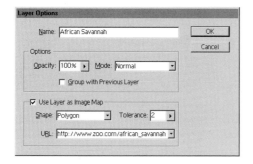

The URL you entered appears below the Africa layer name in the Layers palette.

7 Repeat steps 5 through 7 for the Exotic Asia, Tropical Rainforest, Himalayan Highlands, and Northern Wilderness layers, using the same settings but changing the URL so that the last word matches the name of the layer you are working with.

8 Choose File > Save.

Previewing and adjusting the cross-platform gamma range

Now you'll check to see if the brightness of your image is compatible across monitors on different platforms. Windows systems generally display a darker midtone brightness, or *gamma,* than do Mac OS systems. Be sure to preview and, if necessary, adjust the cross-platform brightness of your image before publishing it on the Web.

1 Choose View > Preview > Standard Macintosh Color or View > Preview > Standard Windows Color to preview the image as it will appear on the designated platform.

An image created on a Windows system will appear lighter on a Mac OS system. An image created on a Mac OS system will appear darker on a Windows system.

2 Choose Image > Adjust > Gamma.

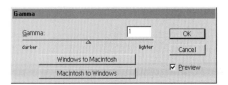

The Gamma dialog box appears, letting you automatically correct the image's gamma for cross-platform viewing.

3 Click the Windows to Macintosh button (if you are working on the Windows platform and want to preview how the image would appear on the Mac OS platform) or the Macintosh to Windows button (to preview the change from the Mac OS platform to Windows), and click OK.

4 Choose File > Save Optimized As, name the image **14Start3.gif**, and click Save.

Now you'll preview your image map in a Web browser.

5 Choose File > Preview In, and choose a browser from the submenu. Move the pointer over the different zoo regions, and notice that these elements contain hypertext links. If you had a modem and an Internet connection and if these were legitimate URLs, you could click the hotspots to jump to the specified page of the zoo site.

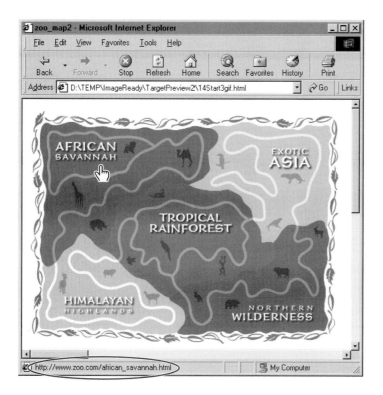

6 Exit your browser to return to Adobe ImageReady.

Creating the HTML file

When you save an image as an HTML file, the basic HTML tags needed to display your image on a Web page are automatically generated. The easiest way to do this is simply to select the Save HTML File option when you save the optimized image.

Once you have created the HTML file, it can be easily updated to reflect any changes, such as new or modified slices or new URLs. For more information on slices, see Lesson 16, "ImageReady Web Techniques."

1 If necessary, click the optimized panel to activate it, and choose File > Save Optimized As.

Note: In Photoshop, you create an HTML file in the Save Optimized As dialog box, which appears after optimizing the image and clicking OK in the Save for Web window.

2 Select the Save HTML File option, if it is not already selected.

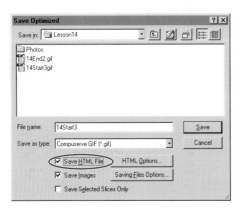

By selecting this option, an HTML version of the image will be saved automatically, in addition to the graphic file. This HTML file will have the same name as the image, but with the .html extension.

3 Name the file **14Start3.gif**, and click Save.

4 At the Confirm Image Replace dialog box, click Yes All.

Note: You could have bypassed this confirmation by deselecting the Save Images option in the Save Optimized As dialog box, in which case only the HTML version of the image would have been saved.

5 Double-click the African Savannah layer in the Layers palette.

6 Change the URL to **http://www.zoo.com/newafrica.html** and click OK.

7 Choose File > Update HTML.

8 In the dialog box, select the 14Start3.html file, and click Open.

9 At the Confirm Image Replace dialog box, click Yes All.

10 Click OK to dismiss the update message.

11 Choose File > Close to close the image. Don't save changes, if prompted.

If desired, you can use your Web browser to open and view 14Start3.html. You can also open the file in a word-processing or HTML editing program to make your own revisions to the HTML code.

> ### *For the Web: HTML File Naming Conventions*
>
> *Use the UNIX file-naming convention, because many network programs truncate (shorten) long filenames. This convention requires a filename of up to eight characters, followed by an extension. Use the .html or .htm extension. In Windows, InDesign automatically adds .html to the filename.*
>
> *Do not use special characters such as question marks (?) or asterisks (*), or spaces between the letters in your filename—some browsers may not recognize the pathname. If you must use special characters or spaces in the filename, check with an HTML editing guide for the correct code to use. For example, to create spaces between letters you will need to replace the space with "%20".*

Batch-processing file optimization

ImageReady supports batch-processing through the use of droplets—icons that contain actions for ImageReady to perform on one or more files. Droplets are extremely easy to create and use. To create a droplet, you drag the droplet icon out of the Optimization palette and onto the desktop. To use a droplet, you drag a file or folder over the droplet icon on the desktop.

1 Choose File > Open, and open any file in the Lessons/Lesson14/Photos folder.

2 Experiment with different file formats and other settings in the Optimize palette as desired until you are happy with the result.

3 Drag the droplet icon ( ) out of the Optimization palette and drop it anywhere on your desktop. (If you are using Windows, you may have to resize the ImageReady window to make your desktop visible.)

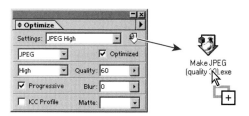

4 Close the file (without saving), and exit ImageReady.

5 From your desktop, drag the Photos folder (in Lessons/Lesson14) onto the droplet to batch-process the photographic images within the folder.

6 Open any of the files in the Photos folder. You will see that they have all been optimized according to the settings specified when the droplet was created.

7 Exit ImageReady when you are done.

Review questions

1 For image optimization, what are the advantages of using ImageReady rather than Photoshop?

2 What is a color table?

3 When does browser dither occur, and how can you minimize the amount of browser dither in an image?

4 What is the purpose of assigning matte color to a GIF image?

5 Summarize the procedure for creating an image map.

Review answers

1 There aren't really any advantages to using one application over the other for optimization. Both Photoshop and ImageReady can perform a wide range of image optimization tasks. ImageReady has many Web-specific features that you won't find in Photoshop, but image optimization is not one of them.

2 A color table is a table that contains the colors used in an 8-bit image. You can select a color table for GIF and PNG-8 images, and add, delete, and modify colors in the color table.

3 Browser dither occurs when a Web browser simulates colors that appear in the image's color palette but not in the browser's display system. To protect a color from browser dither, you can select the color in the Color Table palette, and then click the Web Shift button at the bottom of the palette to shift the color to its closest equivalent in the Web palette. Alternatively, you can protect your entire image from browser dither by choosing the Web palette option in the Optimize palette.

4 By specifying a matte color, you can blend partially transparent pixels in an image with the background color of your Web page. Matting lets you create GIF images with feathered or anti-aliased edges that blend smoothly into the background color of your Web page.

5 To create an image map, you first place the hotspot areas of the image on separate layers. Double-click each hotspot layer in the Layers palette to open the Layer Options dialog box; then select Use Layer As Image Map, specify the shape and target URL for the hotspot, and click OK. Finally, save the optimized image, and create an HTML file that references the optimized image.

Lesson 15

15 Creating Animated Images for the Web

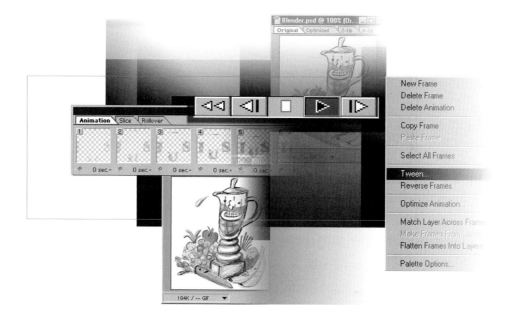

To add dynamic content to your Web page, use Adobe ImageReady to create animated GIF images from a single image. Compact in file size, animated GIFs display and play in most Web browsers. Adobe ImageReady provides an easy and convenient way to create imaginative animations.

In this lesson, you'll learn how to do the following:

• Open a multilayered image to use as the basis for the animation.

• Use the Layers palette in conjunction with the Animation palette to create animation sequences.

• Make changes to single frames, multiple frames, and an entire animation.

• Use the Tween command to automatically vary layer opacity and position across frames.

• Preview animations in ImageReady and in a Web browser.

• Open and edit an existing animated GIF image.

• Optimize the animation using the Optimize palette.

This lesson will take about 90 minutes to complete. You must do this lesson in Adobe ImageReady.

If needed, remove the previous lesson folder from your hard drive, and copy the Lesson15 folder onto it.

Creating animations in Adobe ImageReady

In Adobe ImageReady, you create animation from a single image using animated GIF files. An *animated GIF* is a sequence of images, or frames. Each frame varies slightly from the preceding frame, creating the illusion of movement when the frames are viewed in quick succession. You can create animation several ways:

• Using the New Frame button in the Animation palette to create animation frames and the Layers palette to define the image state associated with each frame.

• Using the Tween feature to quickly create new frames that vary a layer's opacity, position, or layer effects, to create the illusion of a single element in a frame moving or fading in and out.

• Opening a multilayer Adobe Photoshop or Adobe Illustrator file for an animation, with each layer becoming a frame.

When creating an animation sequence, it's best to remain in Original image view—this saves ImageReady from having to reoptimize the image as you edit the frame contents. Animation files are output only as GIF files. You cannot create a JPEG or PNG animation.

> ### For the Web: About layer-based animation
>
> *ImageReady treats layers as individual elements in an animation. You make changes to layer attributes to create animation effects. Changes you make to an image using Layers palette commands and options (including layer visibility, position, opacity, blending mode, and layer effects) affect selected frames only. These changes can be varied across frames to create animation effects. You can apply changes to a layer's opacity, position, or effects to a series of new frames using the Tween function. You can specify changes made in the Layers palette to be applied to all frames, using the Match Layer Across Frames command.*
>
> *Changes you make to a layer that affect actual pixel values (such as painting and editing, adjusting color and tone, applying transform commands, using type, and other image-editing changes) affect all frames in an animation in which the layer is visible. If you want to vary image-editing changes across frames, you can hide or show the layer with the image-editing changes in each frame separately. Applying a layer mask to a layer affects all frames in which the layer is present. However, you can vary the mask's position across frames.*
>
> *Using layer attributes to create animation effects is very simple and allows you to save an animation file in Photoshop format for later re-editing. When creating an animation in ImageReady, make sure that elements that are to be animated are placed on separate layers. Link layers that you want to animate together as a group.*
>
> –From the Adobe Photoshop 5.5 User Guide Supplement, Chapter 5, "Animation." A similar topic can be found in ImageReady 2.0 online Help.

Getting started

Before beginning this lesson, restore the default application settings for Adobe ImageReady. See "Restoring default preferences" on page 4.

In this lesson, you'll work with a set of images designed to appear on the Web page of a fresh juice company. If you have a browser application installed on your computer, you can preview the finished animations.

1 Start your browser application.

2 From your browser, choose File > Open, and open the Jus.html file, located in the Lessons/Lesson15/Jus folder.

3 When you have finished viewing the file, exit the browser.

Creating simple motion

You'll start by animating the construction of a text logo, using a multilayered Photoshop image.

Using layers to create animation frames

In this part of the lesson, you'll adjust the position and opacity of layers in an image to create the starting and ending frames of an animation sequence.

1 Choose File > Open, and open the Logo1.psd file, located in the Lessons/Lesson15 folder on your hard drive.

The logo consists of four different components that reside on separate layers. In the Layers palette, notice that all the layers are currently visible. Visible layers appear with eye icons (👁) in the palette.

To define an animation, you use the Layers palette in conjunction with the Animation palette. The Animation palette lets you add new frames, update existing frames, change the order of frames, and preview the animation.

2 If necessary, choose Window > Show Animation. (By default, Adobe ImageReady starts with the Animation palette open.)

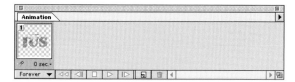

The Animation palette opens with a single default frame that reflects the current state of the image. The frame is selected (outlined with a border), indicating that you can change its content by editing the image.

You'll compose animation frames that show the letters of the logo appearing and moving into their final position from different areas. The current image state reflects how you want the logo to appear at the end of the animation.

3 At the bottom of the Animation palette, click the New Frame button (⬚) to create a new animation frame.

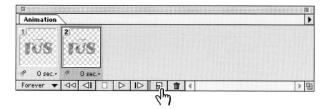

Each new frame you add starts as a duplicate of the preceding frame. Now you'll show the components of the logo text in different starting positions.

4 In the Layers palette, select the J layer.

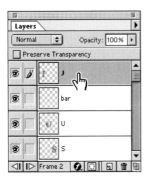

5 With frame 2 selected in the Animation palette, select the move tool ( ) in the toolbox. Hold down Shift to constrain the movement, and in the image, drag the J to the left, repositioning it at the left edge of the image. In the Layers palette, reduce the opacity of the J layer to 20%.

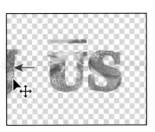

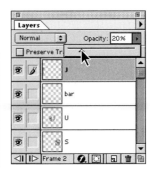

6 In the Layers palette, select the S layer. In the image, use the move tool, and press Shift as you drag the S to the right edge of the image. Then in the Layers palette, reduce the opacity of the S layer to 20%.

7 Repeat step 7 to select, move, and change the opacity of the bar layer and the U layer as follows:

• Move the bar to the top edge of the image, and reduce the opacity to 20%.

• Move the U to the bottom edge of the image, and reduce the opacity to 20%.

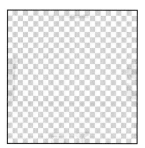

In the Animation palette, notice that frame 2 has updated to reflect the current image state. To make frame 2 the starting state of your animation, you'll switch the order of the two frames.

8 In the Animation palette, drag frame 2 to the left, releasing the mouse when the black bar appears to the left of frame 1.

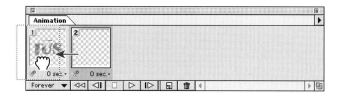

Tweening the position and opacity of layers

To finish the animation sequence, you'll add frames that represent transitional image states between the two existing frames. When you change the position, opacity, or effects of any layer between two animation frames, you can instruct ImageReady to *tween,* or automatically create intermediate frames.

1 In the Animation palette, make sure that frame 1 is selected; then choose Tween from the palette menu.

You can choose to vary only selected layers in the selected frame or frames, or you can vary all layers in the selection.

2 In the Tween dialog box, select All Layers, Position, and Opacity. (You can also select Effects to vary the settings of layer effects evenly between the beginning and ending frames. You won't choose this option here.)

3 Choose Tween With Next Frame to add frames between the selected frame and the following frame. Enter **4** for Frames to Add. Click OK.

ImageReady creates four new transitional frames based on the opacity and position settings of the layers in the original two frames.

4 At the bottom left of the Animation palette, position the pointer on the inverted triangle and press to display the Looping pop-up menu; choose Once.

At the bottom of the Animation palette, click the Play button (▷) to preview your animation in ImageReady.

For the Web: Tweening frames

You use the Tween function to automatically add or modify a series of frames between two existing frames, varying the layer attributes (position, opacity, or effect parameters) evenly between the new frames to create the appearance of movement. The term "tweening" is derived from "in betweening," the traditional animation term used to describe this process.

Tweening lets you easily create or modify a sequence of frames without having to set layer opacity, position, or effects in each frame individually. Tweening significantly reduces the time required to create animation effects such as fading in or fading out, or moving an element across a frame. You can edit tweened frames individually after you create them, to further modify the animation.

If you select a single frame when tweening, you choose whether to tween the frame with the previous frame or the next frame. If you select two contiguous frames, new frames are added between the frames. If you select more than two frames, existing frames between the first and last selected frames are altered by the tweening operation. If you select the first and last frames in the animation, these frames are treated as contiguous, and tweened frames are added after the last frame. (This tweening method is useful when the animation is set to loop multiple times.)

–From the Adobe Photoshop 5.5 User Guide Supplement, Chapter 5, "Animation." A similar topic can be found in ImageReady 2.0 online Help.

Preserving transparency and optimizing animations

Next you'll optimize the image in GIF format with background transparency and preview your animation in a Web browser. Remember that only the GIF format supports animated images.

1 In the Optimize palette, choose GIF for the format, Perceptual for the palette, and then choose a number of colors.

2 Choose Show Options from the palette menu, or click the Show Options button on the Optimize tab to display all of the options.

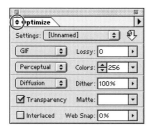

*Show Options button in
Optimize palette*

3 Select Transparency to preserve the background transparency of the original image, and set the matte color to White.

(An easy way to set the color to white is to click the Default Colors icon in the toolbox, and then choose Background Color from the Matte pop-up menu in the Optimize palette.)

4 From the Animation palette menu, choose Select All Frames. Then right-click (Windows) or Control-click (Mac OS) over one of the frames to display the Disposal Method context menu.

5 Make sure that the Automatic option is selected.

The disposal options (Restore to Background or Automatic) clear the selected frame before the next frame is played, eliminating the danger of displaying remnants. The Do Not Dispose option retains the frames. The Automatic option is suitable for most animations. This option selects a disposal method based on the presence or absence of transparency in the next frame and discards the selected frame if the next frame contains layer transparency.

Now you'll set options to optimize the animation.

6 Choose Optimize Animation from the Animation palette menu.

In addition to the optimization tasks applied to standard GIF files, several other tasks are performed for animated GIF files. If you optimize the animated GIF using an adaptive, perceptual, or selective palette, ImageReady generates a palette for the file based on all frames in the animation. A special dithering technique is applied to ensure that dither patterns are consistent across all frames, to prevent flickering during playback. Also, frames are optimized so that only areas that change from frame to frame are included, greatly reducing the file size of the animated GIF. To complete these tasks, ImageReady requires more time to optimize an animated GIF than to optimize a standard GIF.

7 Choose Optimize by Bounding Box to direct ImageReady to crop each frame to preserve only the area that has changed from the preceding frame. Animation files created using this option are smaller but are incompatible with GIF editors, which do not support the option. (This option is selected by default and is recommended.)

8 Choose Optimize by Redundant Pixel Removal to make all pixels in a frame which are unchanged from the preceding frame transparent. (This option is selected by default, and is recommended.) Click OK.

When you choose the Redundant Pixel Removal option, the Disposal Method must be set to Automatic, as in step 5.

9 In the image window, click the Optimized tab to build the optimized image. Then click the 2-Up tab to compare the original image on the left with the optimized image on the right.

Notice the Optimized file size at the bottom of the image window. Adding animation frames to an image also adds to the file size. To reduce the file size of your animated GIF images, experiment with different palette and color settings.

For complete information, see Chapter 4 in the Photoshop 5.5 User Guide Supplement or "Optimizing Images for the Web Publication" in Photoshop 5.5 online Help. A similar topic can be found in ImageReady 2.0 online Help.

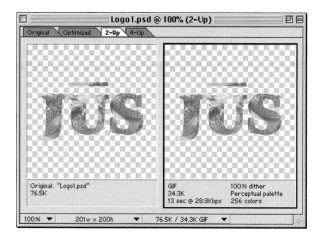

10 Choose File > Preview In, and choose a browser application from the submenu. This command plays back an animation accurately, according to the timing you've set

Note: To use the Preview In command, you must have a browser application installed on your system.

11 Return to the ImageReady application.

12 Choose File > Save Optimized As, name the image **Logo1.gif**, and click Save.

For the Web: Setting the frame disposal method

The frame disposal method specifies whether to discard the current frame before displaying the next frame. You select a disposal method when working with animations that include background transparency to specify whether the current frame will appear through the transparent areas of the next frame.

Choose the Restore to Background option to fully discard the current frame from the display before the next frame is displayed. Only a single frame is displayed at any time (and the current frame will not appear through the transparent areas of the next frame).

Choose the Do Not Dispose option to preserve the current frame while the next frame is added to the display. The current frame (and preceding frames) may show through transparent areas of the next frame with the Do Not Dispose option.

Choose the Automatic option (the default option) to have ImageReady automatically determine a disposal method for the current frame, discarding the current frame if the next frame contains layer transparency. For most animations, the Automatic option will yield the desired results. However, for special effects, you can control frame disposal manually.

–From the Adobe Photoshop 5.5 User Guide Supplement, Chapter 5, "Animation." A similar topic can be found in ImageReady 2.0 online Help.

Navigating animation frames

You can use a number of techniques to preview and scroll through your animation frames.

1 Use the following navigation controls to practice moving through the frames of the logo text animation.

• You can select a frame by clicking its thumbnail in the Animation palette. The image and the Layers palette update to reflect the state of the selected frame.

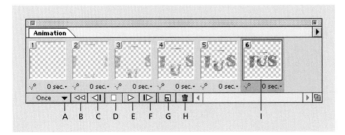

*A. Looping pop-up menu **B.** First Frame button **C.** Backward button*
*D. Stop button **E.** Play button **F.** Forward button **G.** New Frame button*
*H. Trash **I.** Selected frame*

• At the bottom of the Animation palette, the Forward and Backward buttons let you move forward and backward through the frame sequence. The First Frame button lets you select the first frame in the sequence.

• At the bottom of the Layers palette, the Forward and Backward buttons let you move forward and backward through the frame sequence. (These buttons are especially convenient when you want to quickly edit the layers for a succession of frames.)

A. Backward button
B. Forward button

2 When you have finished practicing, choose File > Close, and close the original image without saving changes.

Creating a transition between image states

Now you'll animate layer opacity to create the illusion of an image fading gradually into a different state.

1 Choose File > Open, and open the Logo2.psd file, located in the Lessons/Lesson15 folder.

The logo image contains two layers that represent different background styles. A photographic background of an orange tree currently appears in the image.

2 In the Layers palette, click in the eye icon(☻) column next to the Photo layer to hide the layer. The Illustration layer is now visible in the image and shows a version of the background tree that looks more hand-drawn.

You'll create an animation that shows the background changing from the photo style into the illustration style.

3 In the Layers palette, click in the eye icon column to make the Photo layer visible. Eye icons should appear next to both the Photo and Illustration layers.

The photo background appears in the image, defining the starting state of the animation. Notice that the first frame in the Animation palette appears with the photo visible. Now you'll define the ending state of the animation.

4 At the bottom of the Animation palette, click the New Frame button (▣).

5 In the Layers palette, click in the eye icon (☻) column to hide the Photo layer.

Photo layer visible   Photo layer hidden   Result in Animation palette

6 Choose Tween from the Animation palette menu. In the Tween dialog box, select All Layers. Deselect Position and Effects; select Opacity; for Tween With, choose Previous Frame; and for Frames to Add, enter **4**. Click OK.

ImageReady adds four transitional frames with intermediate opacities. When tweening the frames, ImageReady treats the hidden photo layer as a 1% opaque layer.

7 At the bottom of the Animation palette, choose Once from the Looping pop-up menu.

8 Click the Play button (▷) to play the animation sequence.

Although you can preview animations in ImageReady, the timing of this preview may not be accurate. This is because ImageReady takes a moment to build the composition of each frame during playback. For a more accurate preview, play your animation in a Web browser.

9 Choose File > Preview In, and choose a browser application from the submenu.

10 When you have finished previewing the animation, exit the browser and return to ImageReady.

11 Choose File > Save Optimized As, name the image **Logo2.gif**, and click Save. ImageReady saves the animation as a GIF using the settings in the Optimize palette.

Remember that you can change the palette and color settings in the Optimize palette to reduce file size.

12 Choose File > Close to close the original image without saving changes.

Creating a two-step animation

You can create a simple two-step animation by toggling the visibility of two layers. For example, you can make an animated character alternate between different expressions or make an object move back and forth in a simple pattern. In this part of the lesson, you'll animate the shaking of a cartoon juice blender.

1 Choose File > Open, and open the Blender.psd file, located in the Lessons/Lesson15 folder.

The blender image consists of several layers. You'll create animation frames that alternate between hiding and showing two layers representing different positions of the blender pitcher.

In the Layers palette, an eye icon (👁) appears next to Layer 1, indicating that this is the only visible layer in the image.

2 At the bottom of the Animation palette, click the New Frame button (🔲) to create frame 2.

3 In the Layers palette, click in the eye icon column next to Layer 2 to display this layer in the image. Because Layer 2 sits above Layer 1 in the stacking order, it's not necessary to hide Layer 1.

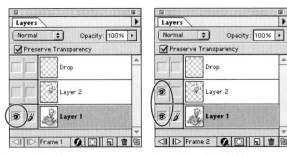

Layer 1 visible   Layers 1 and 2 visible

4 At the bottom of the Animation palette, choose Forever (the default) from the Looping pop-up menu.

5 Click the Play button (▷) at the bottom of the palette to preview the animation. Click the Stop button (□) to stop the animation.

Now you'll preview the animation in a Web browser.

6 Choose File > Preview In, and choose a browser application from the submenu. (You can also press Ctrl+Alt+P (Windows) or Command+Option+P (Mac OS) to launch a browser preview quickly.)

When you have finished previewing the animation, exit the browser window, and return to Adobe ImageReady.

7 Choose File > Save Optimized As, name the image **Blender.gif**, and click Save. Click Yes to confirm replacing the existing image.

Rotating and moving an object

Now you'll animate a different element in the blender image, adding to the existing animation. By successively copying and transforming a layer, you can make an object move or fall in a realistic trajectory.

Creating transformed layers

You'll start by creating layers that simulate the path of a juice drop falling from the top of the blender as the blender shakes.

Before adding layers to an image that already contains an animation, it's a good idea to create a new frame. This step helps protect your existing frames from unwanted changes.

1 In the Animation palette, select frame 2. Then click the New Frame button ( ) to create a new frame (frame 3) after frame 2.

2 In the Layers palette, make the Drop layer visible.

Notice the small juice drop that appears at the top left edge of the blender in the image.

3 In the Layers palette, select the Drop layer. Drag the layer name to the New Layer button ( ) to duplicate the layer.

4 With the Drop Copy layer selected, choose Edit > Free Transform.

The transformation bounding box appears around the Drop Copy layer.

5 Position the pointer outside the bounding box (the pointer becomes a curved double arrow (↰)), and drag to rotate the drop counterclockwise. Then position the pointer inside the bounding box (the pointer becomes an arrowhead (▶)), and drag to reposition the drop as shown in the illustration. (You may need to zoom in on the drop to see the pointer change to an arrow.) Press Enter (Windows) or Return (Mac OS) to apply the transformation.

Drop Copy selected

Rotating Drop Copy layer

Dragging Drop Copy layer

6 Now drag the Drop Copy layer to the New Layer button (▣) to duplicate the layer.

7 With the Drop Copy 2 layer selected, choose Edit > Free Transform. Rotate and reposition the layer as shown in the illustration. Press Enter or Return to apply the transformation.

You should now have two copied and transformed Drop layers.

8 Choose File > Save to save a copy of the original image with the layers you've just created. In ImageReady, the Save command saves the layered Photoshop file, including all of the animation and optimization information.

9 Click Yes to confirm replacing the image.

Creating simultaneous animations

Now you'll define the falling drop animation by successively hiding and showing the layers you've just created. You'll also build in the shaking blender animation as the drop falls.

1 In the Animation palette, make sure that frame 3 is selected. In the Layers palette, select Layer 1 and make the Drop layer visible; then hide all other layers.

When you hide or show a layer in a frame, the visibility of the layer changes for that frame only.

Now you'll add a frame that continues the shaking of the blender while the drop falls.

2 Click the New Frame button ( ) at the bottom of the Animation palette to create frame 4.

3 In the Layers palette, make Layer 2 visible, along with Drop Copy and Layer 1.

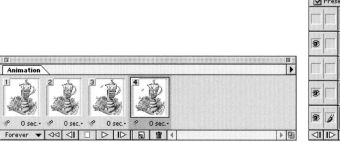

4 Continue to click the New Frame button at the bottom of the Animation palette to create new frames, and then use the Layers palette to change the layer visibility as follows:

- For frame 5, make Drop Copy and Layer 1 the visible layers.

- For frame 6, make Drop Copy, Layer 2, and Layer 1 the visible layers.

- For frame 7, make Drop Copy 2 and Layer 1 the visible layers.

- For frame 8, make Drop Copy 2, Layer 2, and Layer 1 the visible layers.

Now you'll set a delay for playing each frame in the animation.

5 From the Animation palette menu, choose Select All Frames. In the palette, position the pointer on the time beneath frame 1, and press the mouse button to display the Frame Delay pop-up menu. Choose Other. In the Set Frame Delay dialog box, enter **0.05** for the delay (0 seconds is the default). Click OK.

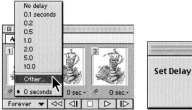
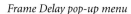

Frame Delay pop-up menu   Set Frame Delay dialog box

The value appears below each frame thumbnail, indicating that the time delay applies to all the frames in the palette. You can also vary the time delay for individual frames.

6 Click the Play button (▷) at the bottom of the Animation palette to view your animation.

The juice drop should fall as the blender shakes.

7 Click the Stop button (□) to stop the animation.

8 Choose File > Preview In, choose a browser application from the submenu to play the animation with accurate timing.

9 Choose File > Save Optimized As. Make sure that the image is named **Blender.gif**, click Save, and replace the existing file.

The Save Optimized As command saves a file in the GIF, JPEG, or PNG format, for use in you Web pages.

10 Choose File > Close to close your original image without saving changes.

Creating a montage sequence

In this part of the lesson, you'll create a quickly changing sequence, or *montage,* of fruit images. You create montage effects by hiding and showing layers in succession.

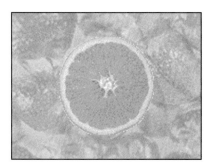

Setting the montage order

You'll work with an image that contains a number of layers showing different fruit images.

1 Choose File > Open, and open the Fruit.psd file, located in the Lessons/Lesson15 folder.

2 In the Animation palette, choose Make Frames From Layers from the palette menu.

The layers in the image appear as six individual frames in the Animation palette and six layers in the Layers palette.

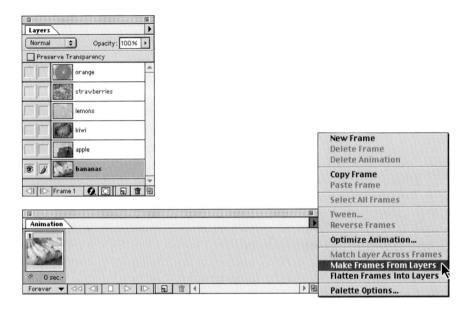

3 In the Animation palette, Shift-click to select all frames, or choose Select All Frames from the Animation palette menu. In the palette, position the pointer on the time beneath frame 1, and press the mouse button to display the Frame Delay pop-up menu. Choose Other. In the Set Frame Delay dialog box, enter **0.25** for the delay, and click OK.

Note: To select discontiguous multiple frames, Ctrl-click (Windows) or Command-click (Mac OS) additional frames to add those frames to the selection.

4 At the bottom of the Animation palette, choose Once from the Looping pop-up menu. Then click the Play button (▷) to view the sequence of images. (To repeat the loop, click Play again.)

Now you'll reorder the animation frames so that the lemons appear first in the sequence.

5 In the Animation palette, click to select the frame containing the lemons. Then drag the selected frame to the left until a heavy line appears before frame 1, and release the mouse.

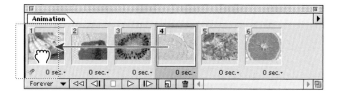

The lemons frame is now the first frame in the sequence.

6 Click the Play button (▷) to view the revised montage.

7 Choose File > Save Optimized As. Name the image **Fruit1.gif**, and click Save.

Smoothing the transition between frames

Now you'll enhance your newly assembled montage by adding intermediate frames that smooth the transition between the strawberries and the orange.

1 In the Animation palette, select the frame containing the strawberries. The image window and the Layers palette update to reflect the contents of the frame.

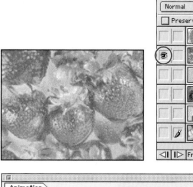

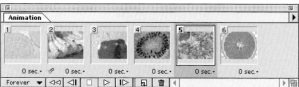

2 Click the New Frame button (⊡) at the bottom of the Animation palette to create a new frame after the strawberries frame.

3 In the Layers palette, select the Strawberries layer, and either drag the slider or enter **1** to set the Opacity to 1%.

4 Choose Tween from the Animation palette menu. In the Tween dialog box, choose All Layers; deselect Position and Effects, and select Opacity; for Frames to Add, enter **4**; and for Tween With, choose Previous Frame. Click OK.

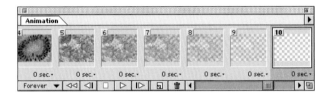

5 At the bottom of the Animation palette, choose Forever from the Looping pop-up menu. Then click the Play button (▷) to view the sequence of images. Click the Stop button (☐) to stop the animation.

If desired, you can add transitional opacities between the other fruit images in the sequence.

Making an object grow in size

For the grand conclusion to the fruit montage, you'll animate the orange swelling from a small to a large size.

First you'll copy and resize the orange layer several times.

1 In the Animation palette, select the frame containing the orange.

2 In the Layers palette, drag the Orange layer to the New Layer button (⊡) to create a duplicate layer. Repeat this step to create three more duplicates of the Orange layer.

When you create a new layer in a frame, the layer is added to all frames in the animation but is visible only in the current frame.

3 Double-click the Orange Copy layer to display the Layer Options dialog box. For name, enter **Orange 20%**. Then click OK.

4 Repeat step 3 for the other duplicate layers, renaming the layers **Orange 40%**, **Orange 60%**, and **Orange 80%**.

5 In the Layers palette, select and make visible the Orange 20% layer. Hide the other Orange layers.

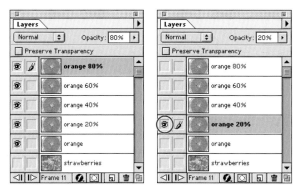

Renaming layers   *Making Orange 20% layer visible*

Now you'll create gradually larger copies of the orange.

6 Choose Edit > Transform > Numeric. For Scale Percent, enter **20**. Make sure that Constrain Proportions is selected, and click OK.

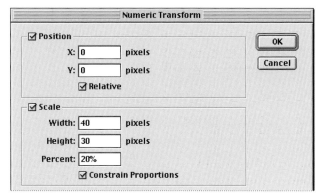

Scale the Orange 20% layer   *Result*

When you work with layers in a frame, you can create or copy selections in the layer; adjust color and tone; change the layer's opacity, blending mode, or position; add layer effects; and perform editing tasks as you would with layers in any image.

7 Do the following for the next frame:

• In the Animation palette with the orange frame selected, click the New Frame button (▣) to create a new frame.

• In the Layers palette, hide the Orange 20% frame. Select and make visible the Orange 40% layer.

• Choose Edit > Transform > Numeric, and resize the layer to 40%.

8 Repeat step 7 to create frames containing the Orange 40%, Orange 60%, and Orange 80% layers resized to their respective percentages, hiding the previous layer with each step.

9 Click the Play button (▷) to play your animation. Click the Stop button (□) to stop the animation.

10 Choose File > Save Optimized. ImageReady saves the animation as a GIF using the current settings in the Optimize palette.

11 Choose File > Close to close the original image without saving changes.

For the Web: Making layer changes in frames

Changes you make to a layer using Layers palette commands and options affect only the current frame in which the changes are made (except for layer masks, which affect all frames in which the layer is present). Layers palette commands and options include a layer's opacity, blending mode, visibility, position, stacking order, and layer effects. You can apply changes to a layer's opacity, position, or effects to a series of new frames using the Tween function.

Changes you make to a layer which change the layer's pixel values, using painting and editing tools, color and tone adjustment commands, filters, type, and other image-editing commands, affect every frame in which the layer is included.

You can specify changes made in the Layers palette to be applied to all frames in an animation, using the Match Layer Across Frames command. For example, if you add type to an animation and want to change the opacity and position of the type in all frames, you modify the type in the current frame and then choose Match Layer Across Frames from the Animation palette menu. The changes you made in the current frame are applied to all frames in the animation. (Alternatively, you can select all frames in an animation and then apply changes to layer attributes. Changes will be applied to all frames in the animation.)

–From the Adobe Photoshop 5.5 User Guide Supplement, Chapter 5, "Animation." A similar topic can be found in ImageReady 2.0 online Help.

Using advanced layer features to create animations

In this part of the lesson, you'll learn some animation tricks that can be created through the use of advanced layer features, such as layer masks and clipping groups.

You'll work with versions of the logo image that you saw at the beginning of the lesson.

Using layer masks to create animations

First you'll use a layer mask to create the illusion of juice filling slowly to the top of the "U" in the logo text.

1 Choose File > Open, and open the Logo3.psd file, located in the Lessons/Lesson15 folder.

2 In the Layers palette, hide the Photo layer, and leave the Text layer and the Juice layer visible.

The Juice layer contains a layer mask, as indicated by the grayscale thumbnail that appears to the right of the layer thumbnail in the palette. The layer mask is U-shaped, restricting the orange juice to appear only through the "U" in the logo text.

The orange juice currently fills to the brim of the "U." You'll move the Juice layer to define another frame that shows the "U" empty of juice.

3 At the bottom of the Animation palette, click the New Frame button ( ) to create a second frame. In the Layers palette, click to turn off the link icon ( ) between the layer and layer mask thumbnails.

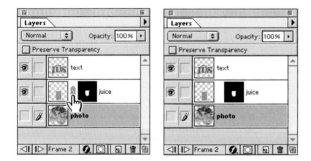

Turning off the link icon lets you move the layer independent of its layer mask.

4 Select the move tool ( ).

5 In the Layers palette, click the layer thumbnail for the juice layer to select the layer.

6 In the image, position the move tool over the orange color, and drag to reposition the orange color beneath the curve of the "U."

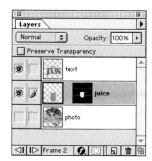 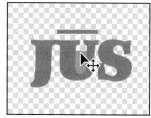 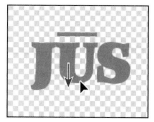

7 In the Animation palette, drag to reverse the order of frames 1 and 2.

Because you have defined the two frames by repositioning a single layer, you can generate intermediate frames automatically using the Tween command.

8 Choose Tween from the Animation palette menu. Select All Layers and Position; deselect Opacity and Effects; for Tween With, choose Next Frame; and for Frames to Add, enter **5**. Click OK.

9 In the Animation palette, select frame 1; in the Layers palette, select the Photo layer. From the Animation palette menu, choose Match Layer Across Frames to reveal the photo in all frames.

10 In the Animation palette, select frame 1. Then click the Play button (▷) to play the animation. Click the Stop button (□) to stop the animation.

11 Choose File > Preview In, and choose a browser application from the submenu to play the animation with accurate timing.

12 Choose File > Save Optimized As, name the file **Logo3.gif**, and click Save. Then choose File > Close to close the original file without saving changes.

Using clipping groups to create animations

Now you'll create the effect of strawberries shaking inside the logo text.

1 Choose File > Open, and open the Logo4.psd file, located in the Lessons/Lesson15 folder.

2 In the Layers palette, make sure that both the Strawberries and Text layers are visible.

To make the strawberries appear only through the shape of the logo text, you'll create a clipping group.

3 In the Layers palette, select the Strawberries layer. Hold down Alt (Windows) or Option (Mac OS), position the pointer over the solid line dividing two layers in the Layers palette (the pointer changes to two overlapping circles), and click the dividing line between the layers. You can also choose Layer > Group with Previous.

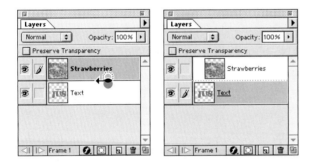

Notice that the strawberries now appear masked by the logo text. The thumbnail for the Strawberries layer is indented, indicating that the layer is grouped with the layer that precedes it.

4 At the bottom of the Animation palette, click the New Frame button.

For the second animation frame, you'll reposition the Strawberries layer slightly.

5 In the Layers palette, select the Strawberries layer. Then in the toolbox, select the move tool.

6 In the image, drag the Strawberries layer slightly to the right, or use the arrow keys to move the layer.

 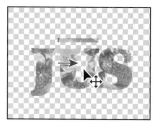

7 Click the Play button (▷) to play the animation. The strawberries shake from side to side inside the logo text.

8 Click the Stop button (□) to stop the animation.

9 Choose File > Preview In, and choose a browser application from the submenu to play the animation with accurate timing.

10 Choose File > Save Optimized As, name the file **Logo4.gif**, and click Save. ImageReady saves the animation as a GIF using the current settings in the Optimize palette.

11 Choose File > Close to close the original file without saving changes.

For the Web: Animating color changes

You can create an animation from a single-layer image using Photoshop adjustment layers and the ImageReady Animation palette. ImageReady allows you to quickly and easily create animations by varying layer attributes across animation frames. You can use adjustment layers to create an animation in which an object changes colors, posterizes, inverts colors, or displays some other color adjustment. Although you can apply adjustment layers in Photoshop only, adjustment layers applied in Photoshop are preserved when you open the image in ImageReady.

Now that you've used ImageReady to create a multilayered animation, try using Photoshop adjustment layers to create an animation in which an image changes color using the Hue/Saturation color adjustment command.

1 In Photoshop, position the image you want to animate in the center of a transparent background.

2 In the Layers palette, Ctrl-click (Windows) or Command-click (Mac OS) the New Layer button (⬚) at the bottom of the palette.

3 In the New Adjustment Layer dialog box, select Hue/Saturation from the Type menu and click OK. In the Hue/Saturation dialog box, make sure Preview is selected. Drag the Hue, Saturation, and Lightness sliders to change the color in the image, and click OK.

4 In the toolbox, click the Jump To button (⬚) to open the file in ImageReady. Click Save, name the file, and choose a location where it will be saved, and click Save again.

5 In the ImageReady Layers palette, select Layer 1 (the layer containing the image).

6 Select the move tool (⬚). In the image window, drag the layer to the left. Note that the image repositions in frame 1 in the Animation palette.

7 In the Animation palette, click the New Frame button (⬚).

8 With frame 2 selected in the Animation palette, select Layer 1 in the Layers palette.

9 In the image window, use the move tool to drag the layer to the right. Note that the image repositions in frame 2 in the Animation palette.

10 With frame 2 still selected, select the Hue/Saturation adjustment layer, and change the layer opacity to 1%.

11 In the Animation palette, select Tween from the palette menu. For Parameters, make sure Position and Opacity are selected. Enter a value for Frames to Add. (We entered 9.) Click OK.

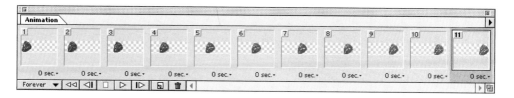

12 In the Animation palette, click the Play button (▷) to preview the animation. Click the Stop button (☐) to end the preview.

You can add, delete, or modify frames in the animation and set playback options as needed.

[?] For complete information on animation in ImageReady, see Chapter 5 of the Photoshop 5.5 User Guide Supplement or "Animation" in Photoshop 5.5 online Help. A similar topic can also be found in ImageReady 2.0 online Help.

13 Choose Optimize Animation from the Animation palette menu. In the Optimize Animation palette, select Bounding Box and Redundant Pixel Removal. Click OK.

14 In the Optimize palette, select GIF from the file format menu, and choose other options to optimize the file for display on the Web.

15 Choose File > Save Optimized to save the animation.

You can use adjustment layers to create animations with logos or text. Simply place the logo or text on a transparent background in step 1. When using text, render the text layer before applying the adjustment layer.

For an illustration of the artwork for this section, see the gallery at the end of the color section.

Review questions

1 Describe a simple way to create animation.

2 In what instances can you tween animation frames? When can't you tween frames?

3 How do you optimize an animation?

4 What does optimizing an animation accomplish?

5 What is frame disposal? Which frame disposal method should you generally use?

6 How do you edit an existing animation frame?

7 What file formats can you use for animations?

Review answers

1 A simple way to create animation is to start with a layered Photoshop file. Use the New Frame button in the Animation palette to create a new frame, and use the Layers palette to alter the position, opacity, or effects of one of the selected frames. Then create intermediate frames between the selection and the new frame either manually using the New Frame button or automatically using the Tween command.

2 You can instruct Adobe ImageReady to tween intermediate frames between any two frames, to change layer opacity or position between two frames, or to add new layers to a sequence of frames. You cannot tween discontiguous frames.

3 A frame disposal method specifies whether to discard the selected frame before displaying the next frame when an animation includes background transparency. This option determines whether the selected frame will appear through the transparent areas of the next frame. Generally, the Automatic option is suitable for most animations. This option selects a disposal method based on the presence or absence of transparency in the next frame, and discards the selected frame if the next frame contains layer transparency

4 Click the Show Options button in the Optimize palette, and then choose File > Save Optimized to optimize animations. Choose Optimize Animation from the Animation palette menu to perform optimization tasks specific to animation files, including removing redundant pixels and cropping frames according to the bounding box.

5 In addition to the optimization tasks applied to standard GIF files, ImageReady generates an adaptive, perceptual, or selective palette for the file based on all frames in the animation if you selected one of those palettes. ImageReady applies a special dithering technique to ensure that dither patterns are consistent across all frames, to prevent flickering during playback. The application also optimizes frames so that only areas that change from frame to frame are included, greatly reducing the file size of the animated GIF.

6 To edit an existing animation frame, you first select the frame, either by clicking the frame thumbnail in the Animation palette, or by navigating to the desired frame using the First Frame, Backward, or Forward buttons at the bottom of the Animation palette or Layers palette. Then edit the layers in the image to update the contents of the selected frame.

7 Files for animations must be saved in the GIF format. You cannot create animations as JPEG or PNG files.

Lesson 16

16 | ImageReady Web Techniques

In addition to animation and optimization, Adobe ImageReady allows you to create special design elements and effects, including image slices and rollovers. Slicing an image lets you define areas of an image, create buttons, and apply different optimization settings to different areas of an image. Rollovers display different states of an image based on mouse movement and actions, providing visual feedback to viewers.

In this lesson, you'll learn how to do the following:

• Understand and utilize effective Web development workflow techniques.

• Create and modify slices to define buttons and other elements of a Web page.

• Optimize individual slices using various settings and file formats to fully optimize Web graphics.

• Create rollovers for buttons and add secondary effects to display additional artwork.

This lesson will take about 60 minutes to complete. The lesson is designed to be done in Adobe ImageReady.

If needed, remove the previous lesson folder from your hard drive, and copy the Lesson16 folder onto it.

Understanding the Web workflow

Before starting any Web-related project, it is helpful to understand the process used to go from initial idea to finished Web site. While the steps you need to follow will vary greatly from one job to the next, the following steps are applicable to most Web-related work.

• First you need to create or acquire the artwork that you will use. This may mean purchasing or downloading clip art files, using stock photography, taking and scanning your own photos, creating your art from scratch using Adobe Illustrator, Adobe Photoshop, other graphics software, or a combination of several different methods.

• Once you have gathered all of the elements of your Web site or image, you will composite them in either Photoshop or ImageReady. In addition to compositing, subtle or dramatic image manipulation can be performed, ranging from minor adjustments in brightness or tone, to multiple applications of special effects filters that significantly alter the original elements. Organizing different elements on layers is necessary to create rollovers or animations in ImageReady.

• After you have prepared the image, you can bring it into ImageReady and divide it into slices. Dividing an image into slices creates an HTML table, with each slice corresponding to a cell in the table. Having buttons and other elements of a Web page in individual cells lets you create sophisticated links, rollovers, and animations.

• For these image slices, specify rollover states and animation frames, add and adjust layers to create the visuals for these rollovers and animations, and test the effects in one or more Internet browsers.

• Optimize the image for the fastest possible download times. You can apply optimization settings to the entire image, or to individual slices separately. As you optimize, it is a good idea to go back and preview your image and rollover and animation effects again.

• Finally, create your output files. ImageReady easily creates all of the necessary optimized image components, and HTML files (including JavaScript code) for buttons, button states, animations, and other effects.

About this lesson

Unlike most of the other lessons in this book, the topics discussed here are specific to Adobe ImageReady. If you have Adobe Photoshop open, you can leave it open, or you can close it to free up memory for ImageReady.

Getting started

Before beginning this lesson, restore the default application settings for Adobe ImageReady. See "Restoring default preferences" on page 4.

Laying out a Web page with slices

Slices are used primarily to define specific areas of an image. Once defined, these image areas can be used to initiate animations or other graphic effects, such as button rollovers. Typical areas that you might find on a Web page include navigation bars, button bars, and main information or image areas.

> ### For the Web: About slices
>
> *You can use slices in ImageReady to divide the document into smaller files. Each slice is an independent file, containing its own individual optimization settings, color palettes, URLs, rollover effects, and animation effects. You can use slices for faster download speeds and increased image quality when working with documents that contain mixed images, or text and images.*
>
> *Slices are assembled in an HTML table in the document's HTML file. By default, the document starts with one slice, comprising the entire document. You can then create more slices in the document—ImageReady will automatically make additional slices to complete the full table in the HTML file.*
>
> –From the Adobe Photoshop 5.5 User Guide Supplement, Chapter 1, "A Quick Tour of Adobe ImageReady." A similar topic can be found in ImageReady 2.0 online Help.

In the first part of the lesson, you will divide a single graphic into different logical components for an informative Web site for the World Zoo.

Slicing an image

You'll start by dividing an image into several slices. These slices will create logical sections for a logo, an advertising banner, an area for an index of the Web site, a navigation bar, and a main image area.

1 Restart ImageReady.

2 Choose File > Open, and open the 16Start.psd file, located in the Lessons/Lesson16 folder.

3 In the Layers palette, click in the eye icon column at the far left of the Slicing Layout layer to show the layer.

This layer contains labeled areas for use as guidelines while creating slices.

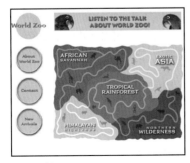

Original image

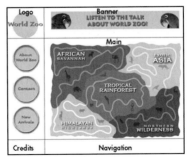

Slicing Layout layer with guides and labels

4 Click the slicing tool (✎).

5 Position the slicing cursor in the upper left corner of the image, and drag down and to the right to create a slice around the logo area. Try to match the guidelines in the Slicing Layout layer, but don't worry if you are a little off.

Note that the image has now been divided into three separate slices (the one you just created, one to the right of that, and a large slice that covers the rest of the image). Because slices are based on HTML tables, all space in the image must be accounted for. ImageReady creates additional slices (called *auto-slices*) as needed to fill any areas not covered by slices you create (called *user-slices*). When you add, delete, or rearrange user-slices, ImageReady creates or modifies auto-slices to fill any gaps in the table. User-slices and auto-slices are differentiated with different-colored slice labels and borders.

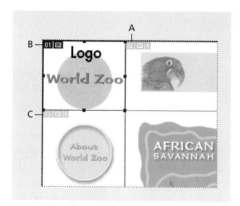

A. Auto-slice (02) *B. User-slice (01)*
C. Auto-slice (03)

If necessary, you can select, move, or resize a user-slice by selecting the slice selection tool (▸) and dragging the slice's selection handles.

6 Select the slicing tool.

7 Position the slicing tool cursor on the lower right corner of the slice you just created, and drag all the way up and to the right to create a slice around the entire banner area.

8 Repeat steps 5 through 7 to create and position slices around the remaining main elements of the Web page.

• Create one large slice around the main artwork area.

• Create a wide horizontal slice around the navigation area.

- Create a narrower horizontal slice around the credits area.

Don't create individual button slices yet or a slice around the button area. You will be creating button slices in the next step.

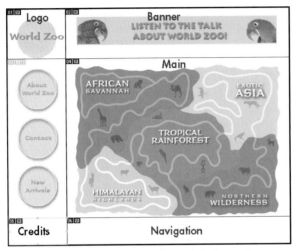

Five user-slices and one auto-slice (around the buttons)

Creating precise slices

Because slices determine exactly where an image is divided, it is sometimes important to specify the size and location of a slice precisely. You can do this by creating a slice from a selection or by specifying the location and dimensions of a slice using exact pixel values.

Creating slices from selections

The easiest way to create a slice for a small or unusually shaped graphic element is to first select the element, and then use that selection as the basis for the slice. This is also a useful technique for creating elements such as buttons, which are sometimes crowded together on a Web page.

1 Click the About World Zoo layer in the Layers palette to activate that layer.

2 Double-click the magic wand tool (✎) to select it and open the Magic Wand Options palette.

3 Enter **60** in the Tolerance field of the Magic Wand Options palette.

4 Click the yellow border of the About World Zoo button graphic.

Slices are created based on the outer boundary of the selection, so only the button's border needs to be selected.

5 Choose Slices > Create Slice from Selection.

6 Choose Select > Deselect.

No selection made   *A slice created from the selected button border*

7 Repeat this process to create precise slices for the Contact and New Arrivals buttons. Be sure to select the appropriate layer for each button.

8 Choose File > Save.

Resizing slices

User-slices can be manually resized using the selection handles around the perimeter of the selected slice. In addition, ImageReady offers precise sizing and positioning controls in the Slice palette.

1 Select the slice selection tool ( ), and click the banner slice.

A selected slice is highlighted by a selection border and handles.

2 If the Slice palette is not visible (in the lower left corner, docked with the Animation and Rollover palettes), choose Window > Show Slice, or click the Slice tab.

3 Click the Show Options button ( ) on the Slice tab in the Slice palette to expand the palette.

Clicking this button cycles you through three different palette sizes to display all, some, or none of the slice options.

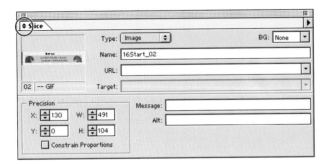

4 Under Precision, enter **130** for X and **0** for Y.

5 To ensure that the slice is the correct size (for a graphic that will be placed at a later date), enter **75** for H.

Naming and linking slices

ImageReady automatically names slices as they are created. The default naming scheme for slices consists of the filename, an underscore, and the slice number. To make it easier to work with the slices, you will give them more descriptive names.

Naming slices

1 With the slice selection tool (✋H), click the logo slice.

2 If necessary, click the Slice tab in the Animation/Slice/Rollover palette group to view the Slice palette.

3 In the Name field, select the current slice name and replace it with **Logo**.

4 Repeat this process to name the remaining slices.

• Name the banner slice **Banner.**

• Name the main image area slice **Main.**

• Name the navigation strip area slice **Navigation.**

• Name the credits area slice **Credits.**

• Name the button slices **About_Button, Contact_Button,** and **Arrivals_Button.**

Don't name the auto-slices surrounding the buttons.

5 In the Layers palette, hide the Slicing Layout layer by clicking the eye icon (👁) next to the Slicing Layout layer.

6 Choose File > Save.

Creating hyperlinks

One of the main reasons for dividing an image into slices is so that individual slices can link the user to specific files, other pages on the current Web site, or other Web sites.

1 With the slice selection tool (▸▥), click the About_Button slice.

2 Click in the URL field, and type **http://www.worldzoo.com/about.html**. This makes the entire Logo slice a hyperlink to the zoo's "About" page.

3 Repeat this process to create hyperlinks for the other two buttons.

- Enter the URL **http://www.worldzoo.com/contact.html** for the Contact_Button slice.
- Enter the URL **http://www.worldzoo.com/arrivals.html** for the Arrivals_Button slice.

These links refer to nonexistent pages, so that when you preview this file (later in this lesson), these links will not work. However, you can verify that the links exist by looking in your browser's status bar while the mouse is over any of the buttons. The URL will be shown in the status bar.

Creating No Image slices

In addition to specifying that a slice contains an image (called an Image slice), you can also specify that a slice is to contain no image. A No Image slice can contain a background color and can also contain HTML text. You can also leave a No Image slice empty to use as a placeholder for a file to be added later, but you have to be careful that the incoming file *exactly* matches the dimensions of the No Image slice.

Creating placeholder slices

Placeholder slices are No Image slices defined for the sole purpose of putting something in that table cell at some later point. For example, you would create a placeholder slice if a banner or other animation is being prepared by someone else and you need to allocate room for it. You can also use a placeholder slice to create an empty table cell for text.

1 With the slice selection tool (), click the Navigation slice.

2 In the Slice palette, choose No Image from the Type pop-up menu.

3 Select the Credits slice and repeat step 2.

Creating text slices

You can add HTML text to a No Image slice. The text will not appear in ImageReady, but will be displayed in the slice when the image is viewed with a Web browser. The primary advantage of using text slices for HTML text is that the text can be edited in any HTML editor. This saves you the trouble of having to go back to Photoshop or ImageReady to edit the text. The primary disadvantage of adding text to a No Image slice is that if the text grows too large for the slice, it will break the HTML table and introduce unwanted gaps.

1 Make sure that the Credits slice is still selected (click on it with the slice selection tool () if it is not), and make sure that the Slice palette is visible.

2 In the Text field, type **This Web site was created using Adobe Photoshop and Adobe ImageReady.**

Remember that this text won't appear in ImageReady. However, when you preview the image in a browser (which you will do shortly), you will see the text.

3 If you want, choose a different background color using the BG pop-up menu.

• Choose None for no background color.

• Choose Matte to use the image's current Matte (from the Optimize palette).

- Choose Foreground Color or Background Color to use the current ImageReady foreground or background color. (You can use the eyedropper tool to set the foreground color to match your Web page).

- Choose Other to select a color with the Color Picker.

- Choose one of the color swatches shown.

Creating rollovers

The simple definition of a rollover is any change to a Web page image that occurs when the mouse is moved over part of the image. The most common type of rollover is an effect that is applied to change the appearance of a button, such as changing its color or adding a drop shadow to it. ImageReady creates rollover effects by associating a different state of the image with a mouse location or action (such as moving over or clicking a particular image location). When the viewer performs the mouse action, the associated image state is displayed.

Creating simple button rollovers

One simple way to create a rollover effect is to create a multilayer image in which each layer contains a different version of the image and each rollover state shows a different layer.

For this exercise, you will use layers that already contain the rollover effects. For your own rollovers, you would need to create your own layers and effects.

1 Click the Rollover tab (in the Animation/Slice/Rollover palette group) to view the Rollover palette. The palette displays the current image as the Normal state.

2 Select the About_Button slice with the slice selection tool (⯑).

3 Click the New State button (⯑) at the bottom of the Rollover palette to create a new rollover state.

By default, the new state is the Over state, which is activated when the viewer moves the mouse over the slice containing the rollover. This is the most basic use of rollovers, and an important one for the end user because it helps to identify the graphic as a clickable button.

Later in this lesson you will be creating additional rollover states.

4 Make sure that the Over state is selected (it should have a dark border around it).

5 In the Layers palette, click in the eye icon column at the far left of the About-Rollover layer to show the layer.

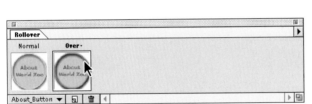

Select the Over state of the button slice

Reveal the layer that contains the desired effect

6 Repeat steps 3 through 5 to create rollovers for the Contact_Button and Arrivals_Button slices.

• For the Contact_Button slice, reveal the Contact-Rollover layer.

• For the Arrivals_Button slice, reveal the New-Rollovers layer.

7 Choose File > Save.

To view the effects you've just created, you'll preview the image in a Web browser.

8 Choose File > Preview In, and choose the desired browser application from the submenu.

Note: *To use the Preview In command, you must have a browser application installed on your system.*

If it is not already open, the browser application launches and displays the image in the top left corner of the page. In addition, the browser displays the pixel dimensions, file size, file format, and optimization settings for the image, along with the HTML code used to create the preview. You should also see the text that you specified for the Credits slice.

9 Test your new rollover effects by passing the mouse over each button.

Normal button　　　　　*With rollover effect*

10 Exit your browser to return to ImageReady.

Creating secondary rollover effects

A secondary rollover effect is an effect in which moving the mouse over a slice causes a change in the image state in one or more other slices.

Now you'll create a secondary effect so that when the user points to the New Arrivals button, the African Savannah graphic is replaced with a picture of Hathi, the zoo's new elephant.

1 Select the Arrivals_Button slice with the slice selection tool.

2 Select the Over state in the Rollover palette.

3 In the Layers palette, hide the African Savannah layer to reveal the image of Hathi the elephant.

4 Choose File > Save.

To view the effects you've just created, you'll preview the image in a Web browser.

5 Choose File > Preview In, and choose the desired browser application from the submenu.

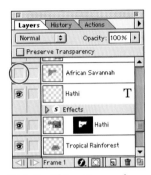

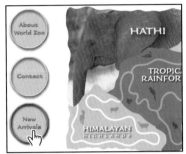

Hide the African Savannah layer for the Over state of the Arrivals_Button slice.

Preview the secondary rollover effect.

6 Test your new rollover effects by passing the mouse over the New Arrivals button.

7 Exit your browser to return to ImageReady.

Creating additional button states and effects

Simple rollovers are created using two states: Normal and Over. You can create additional states for any slice, allowing you to add graphic effects or animations that appear when the user clicks the mouse, moves out of a slice, and so on. You can even create your own custom states, which are useful if you want to program your buttons using Adobe GoLive™ or other JavaScript-capable Web applications.

Adding a down state

Additional states are added using the Rollover palette. New states are added easily using the New State button, in the same way as new layers are added to the Layers palette or new colors to the Swatches or Color Table palette.

You can change the action associated with a state by clicking the state label and selecting a new state from the pop-up menu.

Now you'll add a Down state to the Logo slice, so that the zoo's address and phone number appear while the user presses the mouse button on the Logo slice.

1 Select the Logo slice.

2 Click the New State button twice to create two new rollover states: Over and Down.

3 Click the Over state to select it.

4 Hide the Logo layer, and reveal the Logo-Rollover layer.

5 Select the Down state in the Rollover palette.

6 Hide the Logo layer, and reveal the Logo-Down layer.

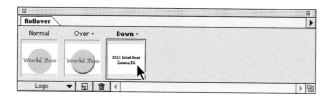

7 Choose File > Save.

To view the effects you've just created, you'll preview the image in a Web browser.

8 Choose File > Preview In, and choose the desired browser application from the submenu.

9 Test your new rollover states and effects by passing the mouse over the logo and pressing on the logo.

Normal state *Over state* *Down state*

10 Exit your browser to return to ImageReady.

Optimizing individual slices

One aspect of slicing images that may not be immediately obvious is that you can apply different optimization settings to individual slices. This allows you to select the ideal optimization settings for each area of the image.

Optimizing slices

The Web site graphic contains elements that could benefit from different optimization formats. Specifically, the banner area contains continuous-tone images that work better with JPEG optimization, while the index area and buttons are more appropriate for GIF optimization.

1 With the slice selection tool (➤ਮ), click the Main slice.

2 Click the Optimize palette tab in the Optimize/Info/Options palette group.

3 Expand the palette fully by clicking the Show Options button (♦) on the Optimize tab.

4 Choose GIF 64 No Dither from the Settings menu, and select the Transparency option if it is not already selected.

5 Select the Banner slice.

6 Change the format for this slice to JPEG and the quality to High.

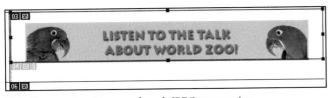

This slice contains pictures and needs JPEG compression.

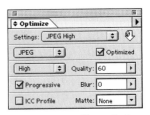

These settings affect only the selected slice.

7 Select the About_Button slice, and choose GIF 64 No Dither from the Settings pop-up menu in the Optimize palette. Repeat this procedure for the Contact_Button and Arrivals_Button slices.

8 Choose File > Save.

Thinking ahead

The Web site is now ready to go to the next step. From here you can create animations (see Lesson 15, "Creating Animated Images"), perform further optimization (see Lesson 14, "Optimizing Images for Web Publication"), or use Adobe GoLive to create even more sophisticated animations, rollovers, and interactive effects, or to publish and maintain these files as a finished Web site.

For the Web: Creating and viewing blended-tile backgrounds

The most efficient way to create a background for a Web page is with *tiling*, the repetition of a single, small image to fill a Web page. In a good tiled background, the edges of the tile are blended to get rid of the sharp edge between one tile and the next. It is very easy to create a perfectly blended tile with ImageReady using the Tile Maker filter. You can then preview how the tile looks when it is repeated to fill a background.

1 Open the image you want to work with in ImageReady.

2 Use the rectangular selection tool to select the area of the image you want to use as a tile.

3 Choose Filter > Other > Tile Maker.

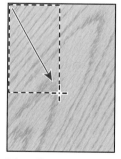
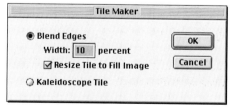

Select tile area.   *Create tile with Tile Maker.*

4 Make sure the Blend Edges option is selected, and enter a width percentage.

The percentage you use will depend on your image, but must be between 1 and 20. (We used 10.)

5 Make sure the Resize Tile to Fill Image option is selected, and click OK.

6 Choose Image > Crop.

7 Select the Deleted option, and click OK.

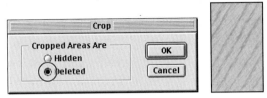

Crop the file with Deleted selected.   Result

8 Optimize the file using a GIF format, and save the optimized file. (We used 16 colors, no dither for this image.)

Note: Always create your tile before optimizing the image as a GIF, because resizing GIFs can create undesirable results.

That is all there is to creating the tile. Follow the remaining steps only if you want to see a preview of your tile repeated to fill a background.

9 If the entire image is not still selected, choose Select > All, and then choose Edit > Define Pattern.

10 Create a new blank document. (You can use any size, but 640 x 480 or 800 x 600 make the most sense.)

11 Choose Edit > Fill, select Pattern from the Contents pop-up menu, and click OK.

Resulting tiled web area.

For the Web: Creating a tiled border stripe

An interesting and useful variation of the tiled background is the creation of a vertical or horizontal border. Basically, you create a tile that is as wide or as high as your Web page, which forces each tile to appear directly below or to the right of the previous tile. You can use this technique for an amazing reduction in file size by creating a tile that is only one pixel high or wide. This miniscule tile can then be repeated to fill your entire Web page, creating a solid-color stripe.

The steps here are for a vertical border along the left side of the page, but a top border could be created just as easily by simply changing the orientation in a few of the following steps.

1 Create a new Photoshop or ImageReady file that is 1 pixel high and as wide as you want your border to be.

2 Change the foreground color to the color that you want to use as your stripe color.

3 Choose Edit > Fill.

4 Make sure that the Contents option is set to Foreground Color and click OK.

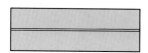

Fill the image with the color you want your striped border to be.

5 Choose Image > Canvas Size

6 Change the width of the canvas to 1000 pixels to ensure that the background easily fills the browser window for the most common display sizes (640 x 480 and 800 x 600).

7 Click the middle-left button in the Anchor section, and click OK.

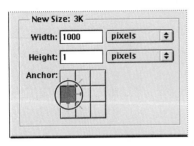

Changing the Canvas Size settings expands the tile to fill the width of a Web page.

8 Optimize the file using a GIF format, and save the optimized file.

That is all there is to creating the border tile. Follow the remaining steps only if you want to see a preview of your tile repeated to fill a background.

9 Choose Select > All, and then choose Edit > Define Pattern.

10 Create a new blank document. (You can use any size, but 640 by 480 or 800 by 600 makes the most sense.)

11 Choose Edit > Fill, select Pattern from the Contents pop-up menu, and click OK.

For an illustration of the artwork for this section, see the gallery at the end of the color section.

Review Questions

1 Describe the method for creating a slice whose boundaries exactly encompass a small or unusually shaped object.

2 How do you create a slice that contains no image? What purpose would such a slice serve?

3 Name two common rollover states and the mouse actions that trigger them. How many states can a slice have?

4 Describe a simple way to create rollover states for an image.

Review Answers

1 Using the most appropriate selection tools (usually the magic wand), select the object. Then choose Slices > Create Slice from Selection.

2 Select the slice with the slice selection tool. In the Slice Palette, choose No Image from the Type menu. No Image slices can contain a background color and HTML text, or they can serve as a placeholder for graphics to be added later.

3 Normal and Over. Normal is active in the absence of any mouse action, and Over is triggered by moving the mouse over the slice. Down is another state, which is triggered by pressing the mouse button while the mouse is within a slice. There are seven predefined states (including None), and you can create your own Custom states, so there is really no limit to the number of states a slice can have.

4 Using a multilayer image, hide and reveal layers to create different versions of the image for each rollover state.

Index

Production Notes

This book was created electronically using Adobe FrameMaker. Art was produced using Adobe Illustrator, Adobe ImageReady, and Adobe Photoshop. The Minion® and Myriad® families of typefaces are used throughout the book.

Photography

Photographic images intended for use with lessons only.

CMCD, Inc.: Lesson 11 (hammer)

EyeWire, Inc.: Lesson 8 (tulips, sunflower, winter, leaves); Lesson 11 (framing, woman on phone): Lesson 13 (duck): Lesson 14 (elephant, parrot, bear, leopard, orangutan); Lesson 15 (bananas, kiwi, lemons, apple, strawberries); Lesson 16 (parrots)
All EyeWire images: ©1999 EyeWire, Inc.

PhotoDisc, Inc.: Lesson 3 (keyboard, clock, bearing, gauge); Lesson 10 (box, cap, cup)
All PhotoDisc images: ©1997 PhotoDisc, Inc., 2013 Fourth Ave., Seattle, WA 98121, 1-800-528-3472, www.photodisc.com.

Leon Sobon: Lesson 6 (grapes)

Also from Adobe Press

For more information on Adobe Press books, visit the Adobe web site at www.adobe.com.

Classroom in a Book

Classroom in a Book, the world's best-selling series of hands-on software training workbooks, offers complete self-paced training based on real-world projects. Books include intermediate and advanced techniques for both Windows and Macintosh. Use the specially created files on the CD as you work through the lessons and special projects in the book.

Print Publishing Guide and Electronic Publishing Guide

An essential resource for publishing professionals and novices, these books provide succinct, expertly illustrated explanations of the basic concepts and issues involved in electronic and print production, along with Adobe's tried-and-true guidelines, tips, and checklists for ensuring high-quality output.

Productivity Kit

Adobe Productivity Kits, the latest workbooks in the Classroom in a Book series, include ready-made projects to help you get quick results with professionally-designed templates. Step-by-step instructions guide you through the design and development of publications for print and the Web.

Design Essentials, Third Edition

This is the completely revised third edition of the bestselling *Design Essentials*. This creative guide provides innovative and inspiring design techniques broken down into illustrated steps.

Web Sites That Work

By celebrated designer Roger Black, with Sean Elder, Web reviewer for the New Yorker, this book brings Black's extensive experience in design to the competitive arena of the Web. Aimed at site creators, graphic designers, corporate managers, and advertising agencies, this book combines a sophisticated aesthetic with a practical approach to understanding the Web.

Adobe Certified Expert Program

The Adobe Photoshop Certification Guide contains comprehensive study material as well as Practice Proficiency Exams to help better prepare users for the Adobe Photoshop Proficiency Examination!

What is an ACE?

An Adobe Certified Expert is an individual who has passed an Adobe Product Proficiency Exam for a specific Adobe software product. Adobe Certified Experts are eligible to promote themselves to clients or employers as highly skilled, expert-level users of Adobe software. ACE certification is a recognized worldwide standard for excellence in Adobe software knowledge.

An Adobe Certified Training Provider (ACTP) is a certified teacher or trainer who has passed an Adobe Product Proficiency Exam. Training organizations that use ACTPs can become certified as well. Adobe promotes ACTPs to customers who need training.

ACE Benefits

When you become an ACE, you enjoy these special benefits:
• Professional recognition
• An ACE program certificate
• Use of the Adobe Certified Expert program logo

Additional benefits for ACTPs:

• Listing on the Adobe Web site
• Access to beta software releases when available
• *Classroom in a Book* in PDF

For information on the ACE and ACTP programs, go to partners.adobe.com, and look for Certified Training Programs under the Support section.